Islamic Symbols and Sufi Rituals for Protection and Healing

Religion and Magic in the Writings of Ahmad ibn Ali al-Buni (d. 622/1225)

Edgar Francis IV

ABJAD Book Designers and Builders

Printed in the United States of America.
Library of Congress Cataloguing-in-Publication Data
Edgar Francis IV
Islamic Symbols and Sufi Rituals for Protection and Healing: Religion and Magic in the Writings of Ahmad ibn Ali al-Buni (d. 622/1225)
• 1. Magic. 2. Religion. I. Title II. Author

ISBN 10: 1-56744-615-9
ISBN 13: 978-1-56744-615-9

Cover Image: *Shams al-maᶜārif wa-laṭāʾif al-ᶜawārif al-kubrá* (Bibliotheque nationale de France, MS Arabe 2650), fol. 14v. For all translated items, read counterclockwise from the top of the circle:
Outer Circle: [1] *al-sharṭayn*-[2]. *buṭayn*-[3]. *thurayyā*-[4]*dabarān*-[5]. *haqᶜah*-[6]. *hanᶜah*-[7]. *dhirāᶜ*-[8].*nathra*-[9]. *ṭarf*-[10]. *jabha*-[11].*khirsān*-[12]. *ṣarfa*-[13]. *āwwaʾ*-[14]. *simāk*-[15]. *ghafr*-[16]. *zubānān*-[17]. *iklīl*-[18]. *qalb*-[19]. *shawla*-[20]. *naᶜāʾim*-[21]. *balda*-[22]. *saᶜd al-dhābiḥ*-[23]. *saᶜd bulaᶜ*-[24]. *saᶜd al-suᶜūd*-[25]. *saᶜd al-akhbiya*-[26]. *al-fargh al-muqaddam*-[27]. *al-fargh al-muʾakhkhar*-[28].*al-rishā*. [These are the twenty-eight stations of the moon in Arab astronomy.]
Second Circle In: *alif-bāʾ-jīm-dāl-hāʾ-wāw-zāʾ-ḥāʾ-ṭāʾ-lām-mīm-nūn-sīn-ᶜayn-fāʾ-ṣāḍ-qāf-rāʾ-ṣhīn-tāʾ-thāʾ-khāʾ-dhāl-ḍāḍ-ghayn*. [These are the twenty-eight letters of the Arabic alphabet, listed in *abjad* order for the eastern Arab world.]
Third Circle In: Aries-Taurus-Gemini-Cancer-Leo-Virgo-Libra-Scorpio-Saggitarius-Capricorn-Aquarius-Pisces
Fourth Circle In: *Tishrīn al-Awwal* (Fiery)- *Tishrīn al-Thānī* (Earthy)- *Kānūn al-Awwal* (Airy)-*Kānūn al-Thānī* (Watery)-*Shubāṭ* (Fiery)- *Ādhār* (Earthy)-*Nīsān* (Airy)-*Ayyār* (Watery)-*Ḥazīrān/Ḥuzayrān* (Fiery)-*Tammūz* (Earthy)-*Āb* (Airy)-*Aylūl* (Watery). [These are the twelve months of the Arabic solar calendar, beginning with October. In the circle, each month is also given a corresponding element.]
Inner Circle: The quarter of spring: hot and wet-The quarter of summer: hot and dry-The quarter of autumn: cold and dry-The quarter of winter: cold and wet

Published by ABJAD Book Designers and Builders
Distributed byKazi Publications
3023 W. Belmont Avenue
Chicago IL 60618
(T) 773-267-7001; (F) 773-267-7002
email: info@kazi.org www.kazi.org

Table of Contents

List of Figures

Foreword

In 1996, when the *New Encyclopaedia of Islam* finally reached the volume for "s," Toufic Fahd's article on "siḥr" (Arabic "magic," "witchcraft") proclaimed that the study of Islamic magic was a wide open field, with an abundance of primary sources for the study of magic in the Islamic world and relatively little secondary scholarship on the topic. This assessment was one of many factors that led me to search for a research topic in this area. This interest culminated in a doctorate in Islamic Studies at the University of California, Los Angeles. For my dissertation, I examined a selection of works attributed to one of the most famous magical authors in the Arabic language, Aḥmad al-Būnī.

This book reproduces that dissertation with very few changes. I have eliminated all the typographical errors I could find and I have edited a few passages for clarity, but the original evidence, analysis, and even wording have been retained for the present work. Therefore, this work represents my thoughts from 2005 regarding al-Būnī, the works attributed to him, and more generally magic in the Muslim world. I believe that my work from that time is still valuable to scholars, even as I have continued to grow as a scholar and as the field has continued to develop.

Since 2005, there has been a flowering of scholarship about magic in the premodern Middle East, and about al-Būnī in particular. Senior scholars like Jan Just Witkam and new scholars such as Noah Gardiner, Jaime Coullaut Cordero, and Jean-Charles Coulon have all added substantially to our understanding of how texts attributed to Aḥmad al-Būnī—the "Corpus Būnīanam"—emerged.

Indeed, it is thanks to Professor Witkam's work that we have the very term Corpus Būnīanam". In his 2007 essay "Gazing at the Sun: Remarks on the Egyptian Magician al-Būnī and His Work," Witkam presented the most thorough argument at that time that most works circulating under al-Būnī's name were written long after al-Būnī's death. Since then, Noah Gardiner and Jean-Charles Coulon have both added greater detail to this argument through their thorough analyses of numerous manuscripts from the Corpus Būnīanam. Both have used the manuscript evidence to more accurately date different texts in the Corpus Būnīanam" and, based on this dating, they have both presented new historical explanations of these works and their circulation.

Another significant change in recent years is that many more texts from the Corpus Būnīanam" are available to a wider audience in a variety of forms. In his doctoral dissertation, Jaime Coullaut Cordero has produced a scholarly edition of the first half of *Shams al-maʿārif al-kubrá*, along with a Spanish translation. In the future, we can hope that Dr. Coullaut will complete and publish a critical edition of the entire text. Similarly, in his own dissertation, Jean-Charles Coulon has edited large sections of the Corpus Būnīanam and translated them into French, in addition to providing his own masterful analysis. I must also mention that Kazi Publications is in the process of producing its own English translation of *Shams al-maʿārif al-kubrá*. Furthermore, digitization projects at various libraries around the world have made numerous manuscripts and printed texts of the Corpus Būnīanam available for viewing or download.

With all of these developments in mind, I have included a supplemental bibliography to call attention to selected scholarship and primary sources which were not available when I wrote my dissertation, but which will be of interest to contemporary scholars.

Since I first was inspired by Professor Fahd's article in 1996 and since I completed my own work in 2005, we have learned much more about al-Būnī, the Corpus Būnīanam, and the history of magic in the Muslim world more generally. Even so, I can still echo Professor Fahd's assessment of "Islamic magic" as a field of study, albeit in a modified form: a wealth of primary source material remains unexamined and, more importantly, developments of the last twelve years have brought to light new sources and new approaches to this material. It is still a fresh and exciting time to be a scholar in this field, and I look forward to what the next twenty years will bring.

Transliteration Tables

All Arabic transliterations utilize the American Library Association/Library of Congress romanization (transliteration) tables, summarized below. The only exceptions are the title and abstract (which utilize a simplified version of those tables) and direct quotations of sources using different transliteration systems (which preserve the original text).

ALA/Library of Congress Arabic Transliteration Tables (summary)

Letter	Romanization	Letter Name	*Abjad* value (Eastern Arab World)
ا	ā	*alif*	1
ب	b	*bāʾ*	2
ت	t	*tāʾ*	400
ث	th	*thāʾ*	500
ج	j	*jīm*	3
ح	ḥ	*ḥāʾ*	8
خ	kh	*khāʾ*	600
د	d	*dāl*	4
ذ	dh	*dhāl*	700
ر	r	*rāʾ*	200
ز	z	*zāy*	7
س	s	*sīn*	60
ش	sh	*shīn*	300
ص	ṣ	*ṣād*	90
ض	ḍ	*ḍād*	800
ط	ṭ	*ṭāʾ*	9
ظ	ẓ	*ẓāʾ*	900
ع	ʿ	*ʿayn*	70
غ	gh	*ghayn*	1,000
ف	f	*fāʾ*	80

Letter	Romanization	Letter Name	*Abjad* value (Eastern Arab World)
ق	q	*qāf*	100
ك	k	*kāf*	20
ل	l	*lām*	30
م	m	*mīm*	40
ن	n	*nūn*	50
ه	h	*hāʾ*	5
و	w (consonant) ū (vowel)	*wāw*	6
ي	y (consonant) ī (vowel)	yāʾ	10
ء	ʾ	hamzah	----
ة	h (normal) t (construct)	tāʾ marbūṭah	----
ى	á	alif maqṣūrah	----

For more information, see: Randall K. Barry. *ALA-LC Romanization Tables: Transliteration Schemes for Non-Roman Scripts*, pp. 10-19. Washington, DC: Library of Congress Cataloging Distribution Service, 1997. Available online at <http://www.loc. gov/catdir/cpso/romanization/arabic. pdf>. Last accessed May 25, 2017.

ACKNOWLEDGEMENTS

This work originated as a doctoral dissertation in Islamic Studies at the University of California, Los Angeles (UCLA). I wish to thank my graduate advisor, Michael Morony, and the rest of my doctoral committee: Ismail Poonawala, Irene Bierman, S. Scott Bartchy, and the late Hossein Ziai. I wish to thank them for their support and advice throughout the writing of this work. Ultimately, of course, this work is my own and I bear full responsibility for all errors contained therein.

I conducted research for this work in Tunisia with the assistance of a Fulbright Grant from the Institute of International Education (IIE) and a Small Grant from the American Institute for Maghrib Studies (AIMS). I am grateful to both organizations and their officers for their support.

I also wish to thank the staff of the institutions in Tunis where I conducted my research, namely the Bibliothèque nationale de Tunisie, the Centre d'études maghrébines à Tunis (CEMAT), and the Institut des belles lettres arabes (IBLA).

Finally, I want to thank those who helped this work reach final publication. Kazi Publications gave me the opportunity to bring this work to a wider audience with their interest and support, and I had the time to prepare this material for publication thanks to a sabbatical from the University of Wisconsin-Stevens Point (UWSP).

Introduction

> *And do you not see that the masters of these secrets, when they comprehend the secrets of intervention of the [Quranic] verses and other things, they are healthy amid a hundred chronic illnesses? And their journey in it does not cease to be useful to travelers, save by their lack of knowledge of humors and intervention.*[1]

This is the essence of the teachings attributed to Aḥmad ibn ʿAlī al-Būnī (d. 622/1220): knowledge is power, particularly knowledge that is connected to God, and that power can preserve the body as well as the soul. At the same time, to know God and His secrets is the best way to worship Him.[2]

The material purportedly written by al-Būnī includes the earliest surviving collections of "Islamic magic"—that is to say, efforts to influence the world through the manipulation of Islamic symbols. These texts are also of continuing relevance, since they influenced generations of authors and are published and used throughout the Islamic world to this day.[3]

To understand al-Būnī's work and its significance properly, one must situate the corpus both in terms of its historical context and more broadly in terms of the relationship between magic, religion, and science as understood (and debated) in Western scholarship. This issue will be addressed in greater detail in the following chapter. For the present, suffice it to say that "magic" signifies the use of rituals that manipulate either spirits or unseen, occult forces in order to control the world. In practicing "religion," on the other hand, spirits are propitiated rather than controlled. In an Islamic context, of course, this means obeying the will of God, as expressed in tradition and the Quran. "Science" refers to technical ability, based on observable forces understood to operate on their own, divorced from interference by spirits of any kind.

While al-Būnī's writings certainly represent a kind of magic, his use of Islamic—and particularly Sufi—symbols and practices influenced how they were understood and applied. The "secrets" mentioned above, for instance, are those of the

Names of God. Each verse of the Quran has letters and numbers which are essential to revealing these secrets as well as an image which will force spirits to respond and assist. Quranic authority is also invoked in the mention of prophets and observed in the understanding of the spirit world in the corpus. Because of the close connections to Sufi belief and practice, Sufis such as al-Rāzī and al-Ghazālī are cited throughout al-Būnī's corpus as supporters of his use of different occult practices.[4]

The use of Islamic symbols in al-Būnī's corpus also influenced the ends for which those symbols could be applied. Frequently (although not always) they were restricted to defensive purposes, rather than offensive ones. Because of this and other reasons addressed below, Islamic magic for health and healing in al-Būnī's corpus will be the primary topic of this study. It must be remembered, however, that many other needs were addressed in these works as well. These included social issues (e.g., how to influence rulers or free people from prison), wealth and well-being (e.g., how to find and retrieve buried treasure). In some instances, the texts even described how to foment strife or to kill. Other occult topics addressed in *Shams al-maʿārif* particularly include alchemy and divination by letters (*jafr*). In short, although it is impossible to give exact numbers, charms for protection and healing apparently make up a significant portion of al-Būnī's writings but not necessarily the majority.

Furthermore, none of these works separates out health and healing as a different kind of activity. The uses of Quranic verses, Names of God, and the like for protection and healing were not the basis for any broader medical system. Instead, these symbols were said to have special properties that made them useful for particular needs, and that was all that the reader (or author) needed to know. In fact, the organization of these texts suggests that the effect of particular Islamic symbols was not as important as the symbols themselves, since the texts are organized by the category of symbol rather than the effects they had.

The focus on magic for protection and healing will allow for the study of a smaller volume of material in greater detail.

It also makes it possible to situate the corpus with respect to "science" (represented by Graeco-Islamic medicine) as well as "magic" and "religion." As will be discussed in the following chapter, these three together are identified in Western scholarship as the major areas of human perception and endeavor.

The Secondary Literature

As will be seen, the scholarly understanding of magic, religion, and science is very contentious, though this debate has hardly touched studies of Muslim societies. Also lacking from any investigation of magic in al-Būnī's work in particular has been any attempt to place it in a historical context. There has been a great deal of scholarship done on the early history of magic in Arabic texts, and on contemporary practice, but much less on the particular history of the emergence of Islamic magic in al-Būnī's corpus.

The depth of the scholarship on earlier Arabic magical literature may well be a result of that literature's closer connection with Western European intellectual history. As will be discussed in greater detail in chapter three, those works trace their origins back to ancient magical literature, particularly from the Greeks. Also, this genre had a direct impact on occultism in the West, particularly through *Ghāyat al-ḥakīm*, translated into Latin as *Picatrix.* The specific history of these texts will be discussed in greater detail in chapter three. That chapter will also utilize much of the meticulously researched scholarship on early Neoplatonic magic written in Arabic.

With respect to the history of the scholarship as such, two scholarly editions of major texts are particularly worthy of note: Toufic Fahd's critical edition of *al-Filāḥah al-Nabaṭīyah* (Damascus, 1993-1998)—with extensive scholarly apparatus and appendices—and Hellmut Ritter's edition and translation of *Ghāyat al-ḥakīm* (edition: Berlin, 1933; translation: London, 1962). Fahd has also produced an impressively detailed work on another topic, namely his *Divination arabe* (Leiden, 1966). David Pingree has also contributed a number of fine, well-researched articles on this period of Islamic magic, particularly the relationship with Hellenistic Neoplatonism.

The subjects for all of this scholarship predate al-Būnī by several centuries, as will be discussed in greater detail later. Another large body of scholarship does deal with al-Būnī's writings and related texts in varying levels of detail as an aspect of contemporary magical practice, particularly in the Arabic-speaking world.

Two of the best-known and most comprehensive exemplars of this style are Edmond Doutté's *Magie et religion dans l'afrique du nord* (Algiers, 1908; repr. Paris, 1994) and Kriss and Kriss-Heinrich's *Volksglaube im Bereich des Islam* (Wiesbaden, 1960). More recent but lesser known works have also followed this pattern. Both Mohammed El-Ǧawhary's "Die Gottesnamen im magische Gebrauch in den al-Buni zugeschriebenen Werken"[5] and Dorothée Anna Maria Pielow's *Die Quellen der Weisheit* combine discussions of al-Būnī's corpus with discussions of modern practice. El-Ǧawhary included modern talismans (as well as photographs of modern fabricators of such talismans). Pielow extensively cited a modern author, ʿAbd al-Fattāḥ al-Sayyid al-Ṭūkhī, whose works are still popular. This is appropriate when considering the corpus in that context, since the texts (or many of them) are clearly still in use, but it confuses any attempt to look at the corpus in a historical context.

Doutté's work deserves special attention, not only for its comprehensiveness, but also for its relative theoretical sophistication. In the early 1900s, when the comparative scholarship on this question was in its infancy, Doutté wrote *Magie et religion dans l'afrique du nord* with the explicit purpose of giving a case study of Islamic phenomena, based on these anthropological and sociological studies.

Since then, however, scholars writing about Islamic phenomena have been notably lacking in any theoretical sophistication. If scholars make reference to any general theories or definitions of magic, any such references are usually restricted to a passing reference to the earliest scholars in the field—Frazer, or perhaps Hubert and Mauss[6]—with no regard for any criticisms or modifications of their theories that have appeared since.

Even with this limitation, such earlier scholarship on magic in Muslim societies remains useful. For example, while Toufic Fahd apparently assumes in his scholarship that his reader simply knows what "magic," "religion," and "divination" all are and how they relate to one another, he has provided a vast catalogue of magical and divinatory practices in medieval Islam, as well as the sources for their study.

The works of Emilie Savage-Smith are also worthy of note. Most recently, her introduction to the edited volume *Magic and Divination in Early Islam* (Aldershot, U.K., 2003) provides a solid historical framework for understanding the topic, even if the understanding of what "magic" consists of is never made explicit. Also, the chapters themselves represent a collection of useful (if limited) scholarship on various related topics. Similarly, her work on magical objects in *Science, Tools, and Magic* (London, 1997) provides useful historical analysis of the use of such objects in Muslims' daily lives.

Much of the earlier scholarship on magic and other "superstitions" in the Islamic world had an agenda of demonstrating that Islam was an inferior, "primitive" or "decadent" religion (or society) and that Muslims themselves were in need of the European colonial and missionary enterprise. Emile Mauchamp's *Sorcellerie au Maroc* (Paris, 1910), Samuel Zwemer's *Influence of Animism in Islam* (London, 1920) and Edward Westermarck's *Pagan Survivals in Mohammedan Civilization* (London, 1933) all exemplify this sort of scholarship.

This focus on the idea of decline associated with magic is found in some of the earliest articles to place al-Būnī's corpus in its historical context. In the mid-1950's, at a conference actually devoted to "Classicism and Cultural Decline in Islamic History," A. Abel observed that al-Būnī's major work, *Shams al-maʿārif*, marked the integration of magic into Islamic religion. Abel provided an excellent brief survey of medieval Arabic magic, and recognized the importance of al-Būnī's writings.

However, his conclusion that the writings signified, or perhaps even caused, a general religious, cultural, and political decline of Islam cannot be sustained.

In fact, most treatments of al-Būnī and his works in any historical context have been fairly short and generally restricted to articles. In particular, Fahd's "Magie comme 'source de la sagesse' dans l'oeuvre d'al-Būnī" (2002) gives an excellent overview of the corpus, and in particular provides a fine guide to *Shams al-maʿārif*. Pierre Lory, in a number of articles about *sīmīyāʾ* in general and the works of al-Būnī in particular, has taken a more sympathetic approach than many earlier scholars. According to him, magic and Sufism are integrated in a single world-view in al-Būnī's work. The quest for such power goes hand in hand with the quest for divine union: if one is united with God, there is no reason why he should not have access to divine levels of power. Lory has broadly sketched this idea out with regard to al-Būnī in particular and Sufis in general, but his articles lack specific references to al-Būnī or to the works of any of his contemporaries.

Vocabulary

Before continuing, it is appropriate to define briefly a few words which will be used frequently. First among these terms must be "magic." For now, it will suffice to discuss "magic" as ritual action directed towards practical ends. The full history of the debate over how—or whether—to define "magic," particularly as distinct from "religion" or "science" in other societies, will be discussed in detail in the following chapter.

The "occult" literally means that which is hidden. It encompasses all of the arts and sciences discussed here. Magic, as a technique for influencing the world, is distinct from divination (including, but not limited to necromancy, astrology, and geomancy) in that divination is concerned with simply gathering information about the world—particularly predicting the future. Divination does not seek to influence the world in any way, merely to learn about it.

"Sorcery" (and its cognates) will be used here in its original sense of the word, that is to say, as a synonym for "witchcraft;" to describe harmful or aggressive magic directed against another. As such, it will be used to translate the Arabic word *siḥr* and its cognates.

"Talismans" and "amulets" will refer to objects usually worn or carried and supposed to have magical properties to aid and protect. "Spells" and "incantations" will refer to rituals which are meant to bring about some effect and are usually (but not necessarily) verbal rituals. The word "charm" is ambiguous in English, and that ambiguity will be used intentionally here to encompass both objects and rituals, whether in cases where the source material is itself ambiguous or when it is desirable to refer to a wide range of practices.

Topics to Be Addressed

These questions of definitions and interpretations will be addressed in much more detail in the first two chapters to follow. Chapter one will summarize and evaluate the debates among Western scholars about how to discuss "magic," particularly in relation to "religion" and "science," and also whether it is even wise to do so. Chapter two will take up the different ways that Muslims up through al-Būnī's lifetime discussed occult phenomena, including the existence of such phenomena and the permissibility of manipulating them.

The next two chapters will provide additional background information relevant to the study of al-Būnī's writings. Chapter three addresses the magical and occult literature written in Arabic up until the seventh/thirteenth century. Chapter four introduces al-Būnī himself through a survey of what is known about his life and works, and the unresolved questions which still hover around both. This chapter will conclude with a discussion of the primary sources consulted.

The last four chapters search these sources for discussions of how to use Islamic symbols for protection and for healing (both broadly defined). Chapter five introduces various forms and methods used throughout al-Būnī's corpus for manipulating these symbols, including both written forms (e.g., magic squares) and the picture of the spirit world which emerges in the corpus. This chapter discusses how these different elements represented both innovations and continuity with previous magical literature. This will be followed by discussions of al-Būnī's application of different Islamic symbols for protection and healing in the last three chapters, namely: Arabic letters, the Names of God, and verses of the Quran.

Significance

The earliest scholarship on magic—not just in Islamic societies, but across the world—was the ethnographic or anthropological study of "primitive" peoples. In the past thirty years, however, there has been a growing interest in magical practices and beliefs in literate, complex societies, such as sixteenth and seventeenth-century Europe and the Greek, Roman, and Byzantine classical world. However, historical studies of such practices in Islamic cultures remain rare, and what scholarship does exist is largely divorced from debates about the nature of magic, religion, and science.

Any historical study of Islamic magic would be a significant contribution to our knowledge of Islamic societies and to the study of magic in general. The texts attributed to Aḥmad ibn ʿAlī al-Būnī prescribing the use of Islamic symbols for practical ends are particularly valuable for two major reasons. Firstly, these texts have been influential throughout the Islamic world over the last eight centuries, both in terms of the creation of a literature, and in terms of how Muslims have used this literature in their daily lives. Secondly, these writings—especially when addressing questions of health—touch on not only magic and religion, but science as well.

Chapter One: Theories of Magic, Religion, and Science

Introduction

Traditionally magic has been highly concerned with power that comes from words and names, so it is ironic that the name and category "magic" has itself resisted attempts at definition and control so strongly over the years. It is unlikely that this issue will be settled in the foreseeable future, and perhaps that is for the best. While not all approaches are equally valid, scholarship with differing views on the general issue of magic can produce fascinatingly diverse and useful interpretations of the same data. So, for the time being, it appears that every discussion of magic will have to begin with a footnote, paragraph, or chapter such as this one explaining what is meant by the term.

This chapter lays out the most significant discussions of the category magic and its relationship to religion and science (particularly the former). These come primarily from anthropology, sociology, history, and the study of religion. The goal is to critique this material in order to come to an informed and conscious decision as to the most useful methods for discussing the various Islamic practices addressed in this dissertation.

It should be noted, however, that neither in this chapter nor elsewhere in this dissertation are any claims made to produce a definition of magic which will work for all societies and all times. One should not presume to define magic for another complex, literate society (e.g., ancient China), let alone preliterate tribes in Malaysia or Borneo, based solely on the study of medieval Arabic texts.

Three major schools of thought on the role and definition of magic, particularly in comparison with religion and science, will be considered here. The intellectualist school, originated by English anthropologists, concentrates on the practical role of magic and contrasts it primarily with science. Theories of magic's social role (sometimes referred to as structural functionalism) have predominated among French sociologists, and have focused on the contrast between magic and religion. While earlier scholars, such as Frazer and Durkheim, quoted each other with a mix of agreement and respectful difference, in later years their disciples developed more rigid and mutually antagonistic schools of thought which only quote scholarly "enemies" to attack them. A third school of thought holds magic to be so prejudicial or imprecise a term that it must be abandoned for emic terms, various neologisms, or specific subcategories.

Intellectualist Approaches

"Intellectualism" is a term grouping together a variety of theories concerning magic, religion, and science, as well as relationships among the three. Intellectualist scholarship is distinguished by the assertion that the primary purpose of all three is to explain and influence natural events. The earliest intellectualists included nineteenth-century English anthropologists such as Edward B. Tylor, and Sir James George Frazer. Defenders of intellectualism in the last half century have included Jack Goody, John Skorupski, and C. A. Hoffman.

Tylor

In *Primitive Culture*, Edward Tylor argued that both magic and religion came out of fallacious reasoning, though of two different kinds. Tylor described magic as "a false or occult science," based on the fallacious assumption that associations in thought correspond to associations in reality.[7] Since Tylor focused on differences between primitive societies and modern ones, he was more concerned with how magic and religion differed from science than how they differed from each other. Therefore, he never explicitly laid out a minimal distinction between magic and religion. He defined religion as the belief in spiritual beings[8]—a definition that included some kinds of sorcery, protection from demons (and diseases associated with them), and various kinds of divination.[9] This and his discussion of oneiromancy (dream-interpretation) suggest that he considered magic a relevant term only when it dealt with mechanical procedures but not any occult aspect related to spirits in any way.

Seven of *Primitive Culture*'s nineteen chapters (and most of the book's second volume) are occupied with the study of primitive animism, the "general belief in spiritual beings." This includes "fetishism," namely beliefs in the presence of spirits in objects or exercising influence through those objects.[10] He even compared certain Catholic practices to primitive animism (e.g., exorcism, the cult of saints, or "hagiolatry.")[11] Tylor's definition of religion as "belief in spiritual beings" is the definition of religion most used in anthropology[12] and is at the heart of intellectualist definitions of religion and magic. As alluded to earlier, there are also indications that his conception of animism and of primitive survivals influenced Orientalist scholarship not only on Islamic magic, but on many areas of Islamic practice (e.g., the veneration of saints).

Frazer and The Golden Bough

After Tylor's ideas concerning the minimal definition of religion and the evolution of magic, religion, and science emerged, Sir James George Frazer developed and documented these more fully in the various editions of *The Golden Bough* from 1890 through 1922.[13] Frazer's scholarship on the topic includes a number of separate assertions. While he brought them together to present a uniform picture, each can be judged independently as useful or not. If one falls it will not affect the others. These cover the following areas: the relationship between magic and science, the causal laws of magic, the relationship of magic and science (particularly the former) to religion, and the evolution of these different modes of thought.

Frazer asserted that magic and science were qualitatively different from religion in that they both assume sets of universally applicable laws. The difference is that science is based on "correct" laws of causality—i.e., those which have currently been proven to be true. Frazer states as a tautology that magic is, necessarily, false; if it were true, it would be science.[14]

Frazer specifically attributed two particular laws of "false causality" which are unique and necessary to magic (that is, all magic involves one or the other): "The Law of Similarity" and "The Law of Contact or Contagion." The former essentially means that like produces like; magicians imitate the end result they desire (like the famous example of seeking to harm an enemy stuffing pins into a wax voodoo doll in their likeness). The second law declares that two objects once in contact will retain an influence over one another even when separated. To return to our theoretical voodoo doll, many such curses require a bit of the victim's hair or nails, or something owned by the victim. Similarly, on a less destructive note, the "weapon salve" of Early Modern Europe could supposedly heal a sword wound by its application to the sword rather than to the wound.[15] Frazer defined taboo as the negative (i.e., non-performative) application of magical principles of causation: while magic or "sorcery" were actions undertaken to take advantage of sympathy and contagion so as to achieve positive outcomes, taboos were actions *avoided* so as to avoid negative outcomes.[16] In reviewing the impressive array of secondary ethnography which Frazer cited in support of his theories, one is given the impression of him forcing the data on "sympathetic" and "contagious" magic to fit his theories rather than altering theories to fit the data.

While, according to Frazer, both magic and science propose universal laws (be they false or true) governing the operation of the natural world, religion proposes that the world is governed by spiritual entities, and that furthermore people may conciliate or propitiate these entities. Frazer freely admitted that his definition of religion was a construct[17]—something he did not say of his definitions of magic and science. Frazer acknowledged that at the same time that a great deal of the magic he described involved spirits and the like. However, he said that the difference between that and religion was that while religious acts make requests of spirits, magic compels them. When so compelled, such spirits are reduced to another mechanical element in a spell, rather than entities with wills of their own.[18] On a practical level, he admitted that in many cases magic and religion were intertwined and gave several concrete examples of such intermingling, including aspects of the Roman Catholic cult of saints.[19] In the end, he acknowledged that the difference was entirely a matter of internal attitude: two people could be performing the exact same actions, with one performing a religious act and the other not.[20]

Goody

As mentioned earlier, proponents of intellectualism and of structural-functionalism have become more and more mutually antagonistic over time. Jack Goody, writing in 1961, compared intellectualist and structural-functionalist conceptions of magic to demonstrate the superiority of the former.[21] First of all, he claimed, Durkheim's spheres of the "sacred" and the "profane" are so indistinct and poorly defined that in practical terms they are usually intermingled. Also, despite Durkheim's claims that the distinction between the sacred and profane is intrinsic to any society under study, Goody asserted that these are characteristics determined and imposed by outside observers (i.e., Western scholars) just as much as Taylor and Frazer's definitions of magic and "religion."[22] Furthermore, while Durkheim and the structural-functionalists claimed that the distinction between magic and religion was its social aspect, Goody made the counter-claim that magic, witchcraft, and sorcery are social. To the extent that they work, it is through common agreement within the society that such things do work. (He did not, however, mention that Mauss had already stated something very similar.)[23]

For Goody, the key category is ritual, and the key distinction which sets that apart from other behavior is whether or not the relationship between the means and the ends is "intrinsic."[24] Any acts which do not have this "intrinsic" relationship, including both religion and magic, are "ritual." Magic is specifically irrational ritual "since it has a pragmatic end which its procedures fail to achieve, or achieve for other reasons than the patient, and possibly the practitioner, supposes."[25] Religion can be either irrational or "non-rational"/ "transcendental." That is to say, it can have the same ends-based operation as magic or its operations may have no function other than their own performance. Therefore, there's no way to evaluate whether or not an action has achieved or failed to achieve its ends.[26] However, he maintained the intellectualist position that religion is distinguished by the belief in and supplication of supernatural or spiritual beings.

Skorupski

In *Symbol and Theory*, John Skorupski used tools from philosophy to craft a qualified defense of the intellectualist position, including the relationship between magic and "religion." In this area, he concentrated on magical beliefs and actions, deliberately avoiding consideration of social effects of magic or belief in it.[27] In developing criteria for magic and religion his guiding principle was the normative English use of the terms.

At the same time, he stated that any definition of the terms has to come after the fact, after the analysis of the evidence.[28] This is problematic and contradictory. Any researcher's definition of magic, be it explicit or implicit, will influence the questions asked and evidence presented in their work. The purpose of any universal definition of magic, then, is to state from the beginning the scholar's assumptions so that the remainder of the material can be properly understood.

With regard to religion, Skorupski essentially accepted Frazer's definition of it as a belief in spirits and the means to propitiate them. However, he did qualify this as a "sufficient but not necessary" trait of religion—allowing the inclusion of world religions which have little to do with spiritual beings as such (e.g., some forms of Buddhism). One of Skorupski's major criticisms of Frazer is his rejection of "homeopathic" and "sympathetic" magic (using Skorupski's terms, "contagious transfer" and "symbolic identification"). Skorupski definitively demonstrated that, in fact, they are not necessarily an operative principle in magic (nor in religion).[29] Otherwise, he supported Frazer's distinctions between religion and magic as being one of supplication or control of spiritual beings.

Skorupski specifically rejected Durkheim and Mauss' definition of magic as rites outside the official cult, claiming that there are many magical beliefs and actions present in what would normally be called "religious" rituals. For instance, baptism in the Roman Catholic Church is supposed to automatically and mechanically cleanse the baptized of original sin.[30] Skorupski did, however, acknowledge that in practice it is difficult to draw a precise demarcation "between the religious and the magical unless 'magical action' is to become a catch-all category which sucks in any action in the class which does not fall into the category of a religious rite"[31] (i.e., unless the researcher uses the structural-functionalists' categories, which Skorupski rejected as unhelpful).

Hoffman: an Intellectualist Historian

In recent years, the greatest challenge to intellectualism has not been any rival definition of "magic," but rather a full-scale revolt against using such external definitions (see below). Some classical historians have argued for employing traditional methods for distinguishing magic from religion as universal categories, in opposition to calls for the abandonment of the terms in favor of emic categories.

There is, of course, a problem with attempting to derive universal definitions of magic from classical history. Such examples are not selected at random, but rather are part of the whole tradition which has built up the whole allegedly tendentious concept of magic in Western Europe, extending into Protestant arguments against Roman Catholic ritual. Of course, since Islam is as much the inheritor of these traditions as Protestant Christianity is, their arguments may still be valid and useful for the present study.

In particular, C. A. Hoffman has presented some convincing positive arguments based on classical examples. First, he argues that even those who oppose or eschew the term magic are using it as an organizational category in their choices of what to study (and around what to organize conferences, books, etc.) Second, any sign (including the terms magic and religion) is an arbitrary mark. It does not especially matter what we define magic as, so long as we are clear about the referent and use the term consistently.[32]

The difficulty with this relativist approach is that no matter how clearly scholars may precede their works with discussions of what they mean when they mention "magic," the audience will always bring their own preconceptions to their readings of the text. Contrary to some of Hoffman's arguments,[33] not every word in our scholarly vocabulary is as vague and imprecise as "magic" and "religion."

It is, of course, interesting to see Hoffman defending Frazer on relativistic grounds when Frazer, with his evolutionary scheme of magic—religion—science was far from relativist himself in his own scholarship. It is also interesting to see this relativist defense, along with a relativist accommodation of those who have criticized the terms magic and "religion," and the intellectualist school in particular, at the end of an article which harshly criticizes those arguments opposing the use of magic and religion as scholarly categories.

A critique of the intellectualists

While critiques of certain intellectualist authors have already been mentioned, some general remarks on the school of thought as a whole are appropriate. One critique of Tylor and subsequent intellectualists has been that reducing religion to the belief in spiritual beings is too restrictive in that it excludes well-known and accepted "world religions" which, in fact, have little to do with spirits or gods (e.g., certain forms of Buddhism)—to say nothing of religious studies scholarship on sports, American "civic religion," and the like. Even though Goody acknowledged early in his article that this many had criticized this as excluding world religions such as Buddhism from consideration, he offered no explanation for how to get around this dilemma.

Be that as it may, such considerations are irrelevant in the specific case under consideration here, namely the role of certain practices in medieval Islamic societies. This is because, as mentioned earlier, Islam and its spiritual life are sufficiently well-understood and not a point of contention.

Some intellectualist discussions of science are more worthy of comment and critique. Frazer in particular apparently uses the term in two different ways indiscriminately: sometimes as a stand-in for any practical knowledge, and at other times he speaks of science as the self-conscious intellectual enterprise which emerged after the Scientific Revolution. More generally, the intellectualist conception of magic as "false science" (or, in Frazer's words, "science's bastard sister") at least implicitly leaves open the door to interpreting it both ways: not only is all magic false science, but all false science is magic. It is hard to dismiss theories and techniques which have been falsified (e.g., Newtonianism, the ether, relativity, the health benefits of smoking) as merely magic when they have been developed within the rigors of the scientific method.

The intellectualists' reliance on practitioners' attitude as the distinction between magic and religion raises the difficulty of how an outside observer (particularly a historian dealing with practitioners centuries dead) can make such distinctions.[34]

Structural-Functionalism: Social Functions of Religion and Magic

Durkheim

In *Elementary Forms of the Religious Life* Émile Durkheim criticized Frazer and the intellectualist definition of religion, specifically citing the aforementioned case of Buddhism as a religion which does not necessarily have anything to do with gods or spirits. He proposed a different distinction, namely that it is the difference between the sacred and the profane, which distinguishes magic, and religion) from other aspects of life. The simplest definition of the "sacred" is that which is forbidden and set apart, while the profane is that which is not—i.e., those things which are part of normal, everyday life.[35]

Both magic and religion deal with the "sacred" according to Durkheim. Religion, however, binds its adherents together while magic does not.[36] The three functions of religion are:

1. It symbolizes the social structure. In essence, the totem does not just represent the clan; it is identified with the clan.
2. Religion is a classification system for the society.
3. Religion integrates the society by reaffirming social identity.

Durkheim concentrated on the religious aspect of the sacred in his writings, but it may be assumed that magic does none of these things. By way of concrete example, he asserted that magic and religion can be distinguished by beliefs surrounding their prohibitions and transgressions. Religious prohibitions imply respect and awe—that is to say, sacredness. Magical prohibitions, on the other hand, are purely territorial or related to preserving the magician's property. Religious transgressions are punished both by misfortune and condemnation, while magical transgressions bring misfortune only.[37]

Mauss

Durkheim's nephew, Marcel Mauss, expanded on Durkheim's categories and principles, supplementing the scholarship with more concrete examples. Mauss' work is particularly important for the study of magic in Islamic societies since his concepts of magic were explicitly used as the basis for Doutté's *Magie et religion dans l'afrique du nord*.

He rejected Frazer's critera for distinguishing between magic and religion. According to him, "sympathy" does not distinguish magic from religion (*contra* Frazer), since many religious rites are sympathetic. Nor can one say that the idea of compulsion distinguishes magic, since many religious rites can be seen to compel gods; by the same token, the spiritual beings invoked in magical acts do not necessarily obey the magician automatically.[38]

For him, the key difference is the social roles of magic and religion. A rite is any act considered efficacious in and of itself.[39] Both magical and religious acts are rites, but of different kinds. Magical rites play no part in the organized cult, as seen in differences of who performs the rite, when where, and how. The magician and the priest are two different people (or two very different roles for the same person), magic ceremonies usually do not take place in the cult worship center, nor at the usual times, etc. Religion (best exemplified by acts like public sacrifice) is public, involving the entire community. Magic (best exemplified by curses or black magic) is furtive and private, perhaps even illegal.[40] Even so, magical acts are real social acts, supported by the society's belief in them, even if this is a society of two (the practitioner and the client or other believer).[41] Mauss readily acknowledged that there is a great deal of indistinguishable "gray area" between these two poles: some religious acts are private rather than public, while there are certainly licit magical acts.[42]

With regard to science, Mauss posited similarities and synergistic relationships between the two. Magic, like technical skill, is a practical art of doing things. Furthermore, by focusing and expressing desires, magic can lead to practical techniques and results.[43] Magic is different from science, though, since practitioners do not really believe that the gestures themselves bring about results.[44]

In the end, sociological and other theories of magic which emphasize its social or psychological function do not really believe in magic. The presence of magic in societies is a social fact. Where people practice magic they spend good money to have other people prepare it for them; where witch persecutions occur it is a very real presence for those who are prosecuting and burning the witches. Kathleen O'Connor, in her dissertation on Islamic alchemy, points out the very real presence which magic (and alchemy and all aspects of the occult) had for premodern Muslims, Christians, and Jews.[45]

Combinations and Compromises

Malinowski and Functionalism

Like Spencer and Tylor, Branislaw Malinowski proposed that a society worked as an integrated whole of multiple parts, but held that this served to fulfill the biological and emotional needs of individuals rather than some amorphous goal of the society as a whole. For this reason, his theoretical school is called "functionalism."

Malinowski agreed with the intellectualists' (especially Frazer's) assessment of magic as a pseudo-science and with Durkheim's division of social knowledge into the sacred and the profane.[46] In his synthesis, he was able to create distinctions between magic and science on the one hand, and between magic and religion on the other. In both cases, magic lost out.

Malinowski claimed that science existed in even the most primitive societies. He was able to make this broad assertion partly by broadly defining it as any kind of technical knowledge, even without the theoretical foundations of the scientific method. Thus, the agricultural, shipbuilding, and sailing skills of Trobriand Islanders were all a part of science. Magic was a means to achieve that end when technical methods fell short (or might very well fall short). For example, among Trobriand Islanders, safe, easy lagoon fishing involved no magic whatsoever, but fishing in the open sea, which was fraught with uncertainty and peril, abounded in magic.[47] So, science is based on observation and practical knowledge according to Malinowski and magic is nothing more than a projection of wishful thinking. Using these definitions, he saw it perfectly reasonable to call magic a "pseudo-science" and furthermore to assert that the distinction is made by its practitioners as well.[48]

Malinowski also used Durkheim's distinctions between the "sacred" and the "profane." The latter is the realm of science, of prosaic, practical activity; while the former is the realm of magic and religion. The main distinction between the two is that magic is a ritual directed toward a practical end, while religion (including religious acts) is directed toward much more nebulous ends, generally expressing communal emotion of some kind. An exemplary contrast he uses is that between fertility magic and post-natal religious ceremonies. According to him, the former have a clear, practical goal (and are therefore magic) but the latter acts are ends in and of themselves, and are therefore religious.[49] As a result of this distinction between the practical goals of magic and the more esoteric goals of religion, Malinowski claimed that the mythological and spiritual world of magic is much simpler than that of religion.[50]

Daniel O'Keefe: Magic, Religion, and the Individual

In *Stolen Lightning*, Daniel O'Keefe combined structural-functional sociological approaches with Freudian theory to develop thirteen premises with respect to magic and its relationship to the individual, the society, and religion. Some of these bear directly on the question at hand, some relate to issues which will come up later, and others are completely irrelevant to this work.

O'Keefe's first postulate addresses the question of just how real magic is in society. He asserted that magic does exist as a sort of social action. It is action in that something happens, and social in that it is based on an interaction between people—even if one of them is only symbolically present.[51] There is, however, a continuum, including "all the varieties of crippled magic that has little effect on others because the individual uses it on itself [sic], to turn himself off and to accommodate society."[52] This leads directly to O'Keefe's distinction between magic "in the strong sense" and "in the weak sense." The former includes any institutionalized magic, specifically:

> well-known sacred institutions...which are widely designated as magical in many societies, which are derived from religion, associated with religion or respond to religion, which are often of a secret or illicit or peripheral nature, or tend at least to organize themselves separately from (or within) religion, more often on a professional-client

> rather than community relationship, and which tend to serve fractional rather than fully collective ends, especially those of individuals and of subgroups in any collectivity.[53]

This could mean an African anti-sorcery society, a zār cult, or the Roman Catholic cult of relics or of saints. It is clear from this that he considers many aspects of institutionalized religion—including Christianity—to be magical. He even goes so far to suggest a magical dimension to salvation, immortality, prayer, rituals, and many other aspects of "ethical religions."[54]

Magic "in the weak sense" is a much broader category, including a variety of applications of the sympathetic effects of language, religion, and social symbolism—up to and including many actions that might be considered mere wishful thinking. This includes "certain actions of the human self," and "*defective* metaphors of magic."[55]

Much of *Stolen Lightning* concerns the relationship between magic and religion. O'Keefe's Postulates 4 and 5 directly address the relationship in the following manner:

4. Magical scripts achieve their social effects largely by pre-existing or prefigured agreements
5. Magic borrows symbolism from religion and uses it to argue with religion in a dialectic that renews religion.

That is to say, magic works because the forms are generally agreed to work. This agreement emerges because the forms come from religious practice, which leads to the dialectic O'Keefe describes in postulate 5 and later postulates. Magic takes its symbols and its framework from religion, since these are the most deeply accepted symbols and framework of a society. At the same time, religion continually seeks to suppress magic, but this only results in more magic, which in turn reinvigorates religion.

This is reinforced in postulate 8, where O'Keefe claims that "religion is the institution that creates or models magic for society."[56] Here he mentioned "religious magic," and illustrated the different ways that magic and religion can interact:[57]

1. Magic "in the strict sense" can encompass institutions separate from religion

2. Religious magic such as exorcism, the cult of saints, etc. has its existence within the religion
3. Core religious rites such as sacrifice, initiation, etc. These are magic "in the weak sense" in that they model sympathetic effects.
4. "Pure" religion without any magical "coloration" such as organization or views of the cosmos.

Interestingly, in his discussion of postulate 13, "Magical symbolism travels easily and accumulates a history," O'Keefe establishes that while there are certain constant elements in the relationship between magic and religion, there is no determinate relationship between magic and science.[58] Certainly, the presumption in earlier histories of science was that magic in Islamic societies "depressed" science and scientific development. One can see this in A. Abel's discussion of the "decadence" which emerged in Islam after al-Būnī introduced his "Islamic magic."

O'Keefe argued that magic and religion are separate entities with an ongoing dialectic relationship, reflecting the continuing battle between the individual and society as a whole. Following the structural-functionalists, he asserted that the distinction between magic and religion is manifested in the relationships of the practitioners. The magician deals with individual clients, while a priest has an entire congregation of parishioners. Contrary to the intellectualists' view of magic as "irrational thought" or "science's bastard sister," O'Keefe argued that magic does produce real results on a social level: it "organizes action," "'inspires confidence' in practical action," and produces "psychological healing." Going even further, he claimed that some techniques are condemned as "magical" under the intellectualists' criteria because "they use forces we do not yet understand, others because they contribute nothing to the result and we just have not found that out yet."[59]

Following Tambiah and others, O'Keefe argued that magic is a kind of performative utterance[60]. However, the speech of magic is not necessarily the speech of communication. Furthermore, he argues that the symbolic language of magic comes out of religion, since it is religion that provides the symbolic framework for magic to work. Therefore, he asserted that magic develops out of religion, taking the exact opposite view of the intellectualists.

The Death of "Magic"

The idea of magic as a term designating those on the "outside" has been carried a step further since the middle of the last century. This new approach has called into question the whole idea of magic as a useful category for research. Their assertion is that in Western scholarship, the term magic has been used to identify practices of other peoples and label them "primitive" or "backward." Instead of speaking of magic and religion as universal categories, these scholars assert that it is more useful to consider rituals and practices within the context of a given culture to see how that culture categorizes such actions.

Pettersson

Writing in the late 1950's, Olaf Pettersson also asserted that both religion and magic included elements of submission and command, of thought and of action. At the same time, he pointed out that it is impossible to distinguish the state of mind of a practitioner, as was attempted by so many other previous scholars. This makes drawing any dividing line between magic and religion completely arbitrary.[61] Furthermore, Pettersson rightly pointed out that many of the distinctions laid out between magic and religion presupposed that religion was supposed to be just like Christianity—particularly Protestant Christianity.[62]

Douglas

In *Purity and Danger* Mary Douglas was mostly concerned with ideas about pollution and taboo. She concluded that religious constructs organize knowledge and represent the society. Those things which are taboo are considered so not out of fear of negative effects but because they do not fit the system. As for pollution, it offends the idea of order, in effect threatening the social order. In the course of her argument she fiercely criticized the distinctions between religion and magic as laid out by previous scholars, particularly Taylor, Frazer, Malinowski, Lévy-Bruhl, and Durkheim.[63] Besides the "instrumental efficacy" (or inefficacy) of magic emphasized by the intellectualists, she drew attention to the efficacy of magic for enforcing the social order, "achieved in the action itself, in the assertions it makes and the experience which bears its imprint."[64] In *Natural Symbols* her continuing interest in the relationship between symbolic systems and the social structure—including the symbolism of the body itself—led to proposals for new categories. Instead of distinguishing between magic and "religion," she recommended distinguishing between "low ritualism" and "high ritualism," where "ritualism" has to do with the amount of concern over the proper manipulation of the correct efficacious symbols in the right order.

Tambiah

In *Magic, Science, Religion and the Scope of Rationality* S. J. Tambiah argued that the intellectualists' distinctions between magic and religion came out of doctrinal disputes in their own historical background. According to him, the Old Testament condemnation of witches and worshippers of other gods as essentially false and ineffective was one source. The tradition of English Protestantism was another. It portrayed magic as an attempt to coerce divine or demonic forces (which made it necessarily ineffective), while religion could only request intercession. He also asserted that "magical acts are ritual acts and ritual acts are in turn performative acts."[65] Performative acts are a linguistic category: to pronounce the thing is to do the act (e.g., declaration of war, marriage, or divorce).

Smart

Phenomenology—the study of religious phenomena as observed rather than the religious experience itself—has fallen out of favor with anthropologists, but it is still valued by historians of religion. In *Dimensions of the Sacred*, Ninian Smart explored the different social dimensions present to one degree or another in all religions (emotional, ritual, doctrinal, ethical, institutional, political, mythical/ narrative, and material). By laying these out, he provided an alternative to evaluating religions solely on the basis of a single dimension of their experience (e.g., the mythic dimension of Hinduism). Presumably as an aspect of this, he opposes restricting the definition of religion solely to a belief in spirits.

Throughout the book, Smart attempted to resolve or clarify old problems and debates with new terms. This also applies to his approach to magic and its contrast with religion. This is a fairly minor part of his work, mostly in his discussion of "the ritual dimension" of religion. His glossary does not even include an entry for magic, though several related terms are present (e.g., alchemy, animism, apotropaic rituals, devic causation exorcism, mantric causation, paranormal, superstition). Because of the controversial nature of the terms, Smart preferred "mantric causation" to describe magic and "devic causation" for animism (as used by earlier scholars). Mantric causation is the belief that formulae are effective in and of themselves.[66] Devic causation is the belief that effects can be caused by communication with "devas"—i.e., spiritual beings of various levels, from the lowliest demons to the highest gods.[67] Although not stated specifically, there is presumably a wide range of "communication" possible with devas in various religions. Smart explicitly contrasted "pure" devotional worship (worship of divinities simply for being divine) with other kinds of ritual and worship centered on deities in hopes of obtaining some favor.[68] The only explicit examples he gave relate to worship rather than compulsion, but it is not difficult to imagine ways in which "devic causation" and less "pure" forms of worship could, effectively, be considered to be ways of compelling devas to do one's will.

Even though Smart's new terms allow a certain level of specificity and they avoid prejudicial connotations, they add nothing new to the debate. Smart's ideas about mantric causation and devic causation have been expressed by others before, only phrased in terms of "magic" and "animism," contrasted with real "religion." What is perhaps even more telling is that nobody else has seen fit to apply any of these terms in further studies, and few have seen fit to even acknowledge their development.

Thomas

Keith Thomas' *Religion and the Decline of Magic* provides a wealth of information on magical, religious, and scientific practices and institutions in sixteenth- and seventeenth-century England. However, the book was criticized in reviews for not including a theoretical approach to the study of magic.[69] In his responses to these criticisms, Thomas expressed some wish that he had included such a discussion, but also explained that his goal in the book was to describe practices which would have been identified by practitioners or observers as magic (or some cognate term).[70] In effect, he was using emic terms for his study, even if he did not explain his work quite that way. As Thomas explained in more detail later, this was connected to his use of more specific terms (e.g., "healing," "divination," etc.). Quite simply, a single term as wide-ranging as the current English usage of "magic" simply was not widespread until the end of his period of study. In effect, there was no broad term for magic in general use until the magic itself had fallen out of use. *Religion and the Decline of Magic* also demonstrated the possibility of discussing "Christian magic"; religion and magic did not necessarily have to be separate and opposite (at least for the society Thomas was studying and describing).

Smith

Many useful theoretical discussions about the usefulness of magic as a scholarly category (both pro and con) have come out of the series *Religions in the Graeco-Roman World*. This series contains collections taken from various conferences on magic in the ancient world. Not only has this gathered some fine scholars in the field of the history of the classical world and comparative religion to discuss issues related to magic in general and to such practices in the ancient world in particular, but the ancient world has a number of relevant connections for this work. Firstly, scholarship on the ancient world focuses on historical studies of magic in complex, literate societies which therefore are much more similar to the medieval Islamic societies examined here. Secondly, as has been pointed out frequently in these collections (cf. Smith, Ritner), Western European thought on magic owes a significant debt to the ancient Greeks and Romans, and it is worth noting that the same influences worked on Islam.

Jonathan Smith's most concise discussion of magic is a chapter, in "Trading Places," in one such volume in the series (vol. 129, *Ancient Magic and Ritual Power*). Here he recommended abandoning the term altogether in favor of more specific "mid-range" terminologies (e.g., divination, healing, exorcism, cursing, etc.). These would avoid the twin dilemmas of magic as an overly broad and pejorative term, and of using solely native terminologies (or glosses).[71] With respect to the former, Smith pointed out that in most of the scholarship to date, magic has been used as a "contrast term...known only by looking at the reflection of its opposite ('religion,' 'science') in a distorting fun-house mirror."[72] That is to say, magic has consistently been defined as a pseudo-science or corrupt religion. However, restricting oneself solely to native categories (for instance, in an Islamic context, only referring to practices as *siḥr*) makes it difficult if not impossible to for scholars to compare or explain similar phenomena, which is perhaps the most useful aspect of the enterprise.[73] As Hoffman has pointed out, however, it is unclear just how much more useful it is to define the various sub-categories instead of the broad category magic itself. One will encounter many of the same problems in constructing such universal definitions.

Ritner

In his scholarship on ancient Egyptian religion, medicine, and "magic," Robert Ritner has provided some of the most eloquent arguments against the adoption of a universal definition of "magic," suggesting that such definitions tell us far more about the society producing the scholar and the scholarship than they do about the magic in the society under study.[74] These have been put most succinctly in his contribution to the collection *Ancient Magic and Ritual Power*. Here he suggests that it is just as inappropriate for outsiders to establish a universal definition for magic as for them to produce a single, universal definition of what religious doctrines are heretical.[75] In his introduction to the chapter, he lays out the cause and the nature of the problem not just in social science scholarship, but in Western European language and theology generally:

> The Romans prosecuted the early Christians for practicing magic. In turn, the politically secure Catholic Church prosecuted pagan Romans for magic, only to be charged again with magic by schismatic Protestant critics during the Reformation.[76]

Ironically, Protestants accused the Catholic Church for promulgating magic because they sponsored the worship of idols and believed in a mechanistic model of spiritual causation in this worship (*ex opere ex operato*), while the ancient Romans would have seen just this kind of worship as good and proper religion.[77] This history demonstrates the problems involved in developing a universal definition of magic, since even though all of these different groups were accused of practicing "magic," they certainly did not all do or believe similar things to be so accused. In essence, each religious group labeled what its rivals did as "magic." This indicates that magic (and its cognates) is an irredeemably pejorative term with no meaning of its own other than the denigration of practices of outside groups.[78] This argument is eloquent, but since it centers on the different groups' accusations against each other rather than what they were actually doing, it is of limited usefulness.

Conclusions

This mass of erudite scholarship has not been not collected and analyzed for its own merits here, although that would be a worthwhile task in and of itself, but rather in order to develop tools for analyzing and discussing certain rites, beliefs, and procedures in medieval Muslim societies.

Firstly, magic is a useful category for a historical study such as this one. Not only does the term have a life of its own in the English language but it also corresponds to an organizing principle which has been implicit in my own selection of materials and which appears to govern the organization of materials in the writings attributed to al-Būnī.

Secondly, after examining numerous approaches, it is clear that the modified intellectualism of the last half-century provides the most useful model for understanding the materials under study here. The one modification that needs to be made is in the relationship between magic and science. Rather than rejecting as magic any techniques or theories which do not conform to contemporary scientific principles, as with the relationship between magic and religion, the relationship between magic and science is in the eye of the practitioner. The essential question is whether or not practitioners believe a technique to be effective because it follows their particular understanding of the natural world (e.g., germ theory or humoral theory) or because it is an effective rite.

Without embracing O'Keefe's definition of magic, his analyses are still useful, particularly his understanding of the importance of religious symbolism in magic. For reasons which should be clearly apparent from the nature of the materials under study, the relationship between magic and religion will be a primary concern in the examination of al-Būnī's writings.

As stated earlier, in studying medieval Islam, the question of religion is largely self-evident and needs little external definition.

It will be possible to speak of "religious magic" or, specifically, "Islamic magic" when the symbols of that faith are manipulated in rites for magical ends. A rite, in and of itself, can influence anything beyond the participants in a rite, and one does not necessarily have to be physically present to be a "participant." Those who know they're being cursed or that friends are enacting a healing ritual for them are participating in their own ways.

This is not to ignore the criticism, particularly as elucidated by Pettersson, that it can be difficult to know if a participant's attitude toward the spirit world is one of supplication or command. Fortunately, in the material under study we will see explicit explanations of rites as well as implicit suggestions of their function, as seen in their address to God and His angels.

In conclusion, then, magic is not necessarily antisocial, benefiting the individual at the expense of the community or other individuals; it is not necessarily opposed to the official cult; it is not necessarily primitive. It is, instead, an attempt to gain control of the world through the manipulation of symbols.

Both magic and religion posit that unseen or spiritual entities can affect the world around us. The practitioner of magic seeks to control these entities for his own ends, while the practitioner of religion believes this cannot or should not be done. All one can do is attempt to propitiate the residents of the spirit world. In the Abrahamic religions in particular, the emphasis is not so much on how to propitiate God so as to get what one wants out of the world, but rather how to behave in the world the way God wants one to.

It must be noted that this establishes something of a dichotomy between "religion" as an ideal type and the actual social practice of a religious identity—in this case, particularly, Islam. It is quite possible to speak of "Islamic" history, art, or society to describe things not directly connected to Islam as a religion. As will be demonstrated, however, al-Būnī's corpus is not "Islamic" simply because it was produced by a Muslim writing in an Islamic society. On the contrary, the forms and rituals in the corpus are explicitly drawn from Islamic religious belief and practice, even while they are applied for magical purposes.

Chapter Two: Islamic Perspectives on Magic

Introduction

Having addressed the discussions and definitions of magic in Western scholarship over the last century, it is at least as important to consider Islamic definitions and evaluations of such phenomena from the first/seventh centuries through the early appearance and spread of al-Būnī's corpus. This chapter will cover the treatment of those phenomena in legal and theological writings, as well as in sources such as the Quran[79] and the *Sunnah* of the Prophet. Following a brief discussion of the relevant Arabic vocabulary, various perspectives will be addressed in turn: magic as illusion or falsehood, magic as blasphemous witchcraft, magic as an ambiguous power—able to heal or harm, and magic as something good or even holy.

With respect to the Arabic vocabulary, *siḥr* is the word most often used for the English "magic" and its cognates. As discussed below, the term carried many of the same negative connotations in the medieval Islamic world as "magic" does in the West: It was something unreal, harmful, or offensive to God. Here the term will sometimes be translated as "magic," sometimes as "sorcery" or "bewitchment," depending on the context, in order to give a truer sense of the intended meaning of the Arabic source material.

In addition to *siḥr*, however, many other specific practices (e.g., *tamāʾim*—"amulets") also fall under the broad category of "magic" outlined in the previous chapter. Whereas *siḥr* was almost universally condemned, these other magical practices were sometimes accepted under certain circumstances, as discussed below.

Unreal Illusion

Almost every mention of *siḥr* and its cognates in the Quran implies that it is an illusion, a bewitchment, or some other unreal deception. Usually this is in the context of a disbelieving people claiming that God's prophets are *sāḥir*s or that the signs they have brought are *siḥr* rather than any real sign or miracle.[80] More rarely, the people accuse the prophets of being *masḥūr* ("bewitched," "deluded").[81]

Not surprisingly, most of these mentions of *siḥr* come from the various versions of Moses' story, particularly in connection with his confrontations with Pharaoh's magicians. Not only do the accusations that Moses is merely a magician provoke the contest with Pharaoh's own magicians (see above for Quranic references), but usually whenever the Quran mentions the incident, it describes the *siḥr* of Pharaoh's magicians as something unreal, as opposed to the very real signs and miracles practiced by Moses.[82]

However, as discussed below, very few Muslim scholars appear to have seized on this understanding of *siḥr* as something unreal. The *Rasāʾil Ikhwān al-Ṣafāʾ* ("Epistles of the Brethren of Purity") were a notable exception. As discussed below, they defined *siḥr* at least as broadly as the English "magic," and held the "true magic" of the enlightened elite in high regard. However, the Brethren also asserted that at least some *siḥr* was false and useless. Specifically, they complained that when the ignorant (particularly women) dabbled in *siḥr*—including illusion, trickery, and deception (e.g., prestidigitation and stage magic)—such practices were useless and gave magic a bad name among people of quality and intelligence.[83]

The Ikhwān al-Ṣafāʾ believed some uses of this magic were evil in and of themselves. In particular, they wrote that the magic of the ignorant was that used by the enemies of prophets and philosophers. These opponents hoped thereby to distract the people—as well as the prophets and philosophers themselves—from true faith and the path to God.[84] What's more, those ignorant people who tried to practice magic endangered both their bodies and souls by dabbling in something they did not truly understand. *Siḥr* was not a science for them. Also, this false and forbidden magic could be used for poison as well as other corruption of bodies through manipulation of their special physical properties.[85]

However, the Brethren ultimately held that the worst thing about such magic was that it was *bāṭil* ("false"), not that it was harmful. According to them, it was forbidden not because it was evil in and of itself or because it was used for evil ends, but rather because it had no evidence, proof, or support.

Forbidden Sorcery

Even though most Quranic discussions of *siḥr* assume it is unreal or illusory, there are instances where it does mention real and harmful sorcery which defies God himself. *Siḥr* is described this way in the mention of King Solomon and the angels Hārūt and Mārūt in II:101-102. The passage begins by declaring that Solomon had never practiced it, nor did he ever disbelieve, indicating that if Solomon had practiced sorcery that would have been a sign of disbelief. It may well be that this vociferous denial of any association of Solomon with *siḥr* is intended to make a distinction between it and the wisdom, knowledge and control of the world and spirits attributed to Solomon in the Quran.

The verse goes on to explain that instead it was the renegade angels Hārūt and Mārūt who practiced sorcery, and further that they taught this profane art to humanity in Babylon. The Quran describes three characteristics of their sorcery. First, it had real power, but apparently only to harm—specifically, to cause conflict between husbands and wives. Second, it was damning disbelief. Not only did the angels say so to any who wanted to learn their secrets, but the verse also described the damnation of such sorcerers. This account of Hārūt and Mārūt's education of witches and sorcerers is further embellished in the tradition of a woman who confessed to ʿĀʾishah that she had learned witchcraft from them but repented.[86] Thirdly and finally, this sorcery only operates because God allows it to.

Usually Hārūt and Mārūt are identified with the *shayṭān*s who listen for secrets at the gate of heaven and are driven away.[87] It must be noted that there is no explicit connection between the two passages. There is no mention of how Hārūt and Mārūt learned their sorcery in II:102, and XV:16-18 doesn't mention the names of any of the *shayṭāns* driven away, nor does it mention *siḥr* or anything else about the heavenly secrets they are trying to discover.

Although the *muʿawwidhatān* ("the two verses of refuge": CXIII [*al-Falaq*, "The Dawn"] and CXIV [*al-Nās*, "The People"]) don't refer to *siḥr* as such, they do mention harmful magical practices: "the women who blow on knots" and "every envier when he envies" (i.e., the evil eye). According to tradition, these were revealed to Muḥammad when he himself was bewitched.

Unlike the Quran, the *ḥadīth* literature never treats *siḥr* as anything unreal or nonexistent. It is very real in the tradition, with the capacity to harm. In fact, many traditions explicitly quote Muḥammad as stating that both *siḥr* and the evil eye were real.[88] All the traditions which address *siḥr*, however, are extremely hostile. It is generally condemned[89] and furthermore declared *shirk*[90] ("idolatry") and a capital crime.[91]

In various traditions, many other magical practices are also condemned. In the jahiliyah a *tamīmah* was a speckled stone suspended on a string as an amulet. In addition to the defensive, apotropaic functions typical of such amulets, they could also be used to influence people, specifically to arouse love, hatred, enmity, or sexual passion. They could even curse or kill others.[92] The wearing of such amulets is said to be one of ten things detested by Muḥammad.[93] They, along with *rūqayāt* (charms) and *tiwalah* (charms by which a woman seeks to gain a man's love) were condemned as *shirk* (idolatry).[94]

In general, while all Islamic legal authorities agreed that *siḥr* was a bad thing, they were not at all in agreement on what its actual nature was or why it should be condemned. According to one set of definitions, *siḥr* by its very nature must involve idolatrous words or acts, such as prayers addressed to the stars.[95] Since such acts would merit the death penalty in and of themselves, there were consequent legal arguments as to whether the death penalty for *siḥr* was due to the sorcery itself or the idolatrous actions which it necessitated. This would be a moot point except insofar as it raised the legal question of whether or not non-Islamic sorcerers might be put to death. Such a definition was also liberal towards sorcerers in another way: if, by its nature, *siḥr* involved idolatrous words or actions, any magical acts which did not include such things must be something other than *siḥr*, and therefore not liable for capital punishment.[96]

In his discussion of the sciences, al-Ghazālī (d. 1111) claimed that *siḥr* and the manufacture of talismans were blameworthy because they necessarily harmed either the practitioner or somebody else. At the same time, his description of the sorcerer's work indicates that he was more disturbed with how they accomplished their goals than with what those goals were. Specifically, he claimed that sorcerers used invocations which involved evil and idolatry.[97]

His description of the elements necessary for *siḥr* correspond well with those used in the "natural magic" outlined here in later chapters: a figure must be constructed at the moment when the astrological influences are just right, and must be made with materials which have the appropriate special properties.

Presumably it was the assumption that magic necessarily involved idolatry that led some jurists to declare a whole range of occult activities forbidden. Wider legal definitions of *siḥr* asserted that it encompassed anything which affected or modified any body or spirit regardless of whether or not it did any harm.[98] For instance, Hanbalī jurists ruled that even if a person who healed with incantations was guilty of sorcery.[99] The Shāfi'ī jurist Sufyān al-Thawrī (d. 161/778) further stated that divination was prohibited. Another Shāfi'ī, Muḥyī al-Dīn al-Nawawī (d. 676/1277) concurred, and furthermore asserted that prestidigitation was prohibited as a form of *siḥr*. Three of the four Sunni law schools declared that even studying sorcery was *shirk*, with the Shāfi'īs being the only exception.

Writing some time after al-Būnī's death, Ibn Khaldūn differentiated between the "science of sorcery and talismans" on the one hand and *sīmīyā'* on the other. According to him, the distinction was that "sorcery and talismans" operated by calling on divine powers other than God, specifically the stars and the jinn. Authors such as al-Būnī, Ibn Khaldūn claimed, worked instead with words, letters, the Names of God, etc. In this way they achieved their goals through spiritual exertion and "removal of the veil," which forced nature to obey them. Even this, in Ibn Khaldūn's opinion, was blameworthy sorcery. Even though the forms appeared to involve actions which were allowed, they were still a front for idolatrous magical practices which called on powers other than God for their operation.

Occasionally Acceptable Magic

While some legal definitions of *siḥr* assumed that it was prohibited because it necessarily involved idolatry, others said it was prohibited because it was harmful (e.g., injuring or killing them, making them ill, or sowing discord).[100] This was supported by several traditions that Muḥammad gave his approval to spells and charms as long as they did no harm and did not rely on non-Islamic powers.[101]

Thus, some jurists accepted certain magical practices, as long as they did not involve any crimes in and of themselves (i.e., their forms were not idolatrous and their ends were not harmful). Saʿīd ibn al-Musayyab (d. 94/712-13), one of the "seven jurists of Medinah," is cited as saying anyone who cures another with incantations shouldn't be condemned as a sorcerer, since God only forbids what is harmful and not what is useful.[102] Similarly, Aḥmad ibn Ḥanbal suspended judgement on whether or not somebody who healed by incantations should be considered a sorcerer.[103] According to the Ḥanafīs, magic was permitted as a prophylactic, but was not allowed to take action.[104] Such attitudes allowed supernatural cures a place in the *ṭibb al-Nabī*, as discussed in the following chapter.

It is telling that even though al-Ghazālī denounced *siḥr*, he accepted other practices here defined as "magical." He even cited the special properties of a particular magic square as an example of things beyond the understanding of philosophers, and therefore a proof of prophecy and prophetic knowledge.[105] Some key elements, found in other acceptable magic forms are worth noting. Since the magic square utilized Arabic letters (representing numbers), it didn't involve any invocation of beings other than God. At the same time it was clearly used to help rather than to harm.

Holy, Praiseworthy Magic

While others were ambiguous or openly hostile to *siḥr*, the Ikhwān al-Ṣafāʾ (Brethren of Purity) redefined it for themselves and embraced it enthusiastically. To start with, they defined *siḥr* more broadly than any of their contemporaries, at least as broadly as the English conception of "magic" or "occult arts."

By their definition, *siḥr* included any influence of one soul upon another. By extension, this could also affect the subject's body.[106] Thus, *siḥr* encompassed transmutation, interactions with spirits, divination, astrology, eloquence, trickery, and fumigation (i.e., producing illusions or hallucinations by burning foul-smelling substances).[107] The Brethren also considered medicine a magical art, since it was concerned with the interaction of the four qualities and the influence of the stars.[108] They even described the miracles of Muḥammad and other prophets as a kind of *siḥr*.[109]

According to the Ikhwān al-Ṣafāʾ this magic was a way of understanding the universe as opposed to a purely practical technique used by the ignorant.[110] The Brethren explained that prophets and philosophers received their power and guidance from divine sources. Prophets received theirs directly from the Universal Intellect and philosophers received theirs from a slightly lower level, the Universal Soul.[111] Another distinction between the prophets and philosophers was that the latter got their power and knowledge through their own efforts while the former received divine inspiration and power directly, and furthermore were responsible for bringing a divinely inspired and ordained law.[112] Even Muḥammad's mission (and that of other prophets) were aspects of prophetic *siḥr*, as were their miracles and those of the saints (*awlīyāʾ*).[113]

Naturally, the Brethren supported all their arguments with references to the Quran and the *Sunnah* of the Prophet.

They also referred to other religious traditions, such as those in the Torah, haggadah, apocalyptic Christian texts, and various ancient Greek authorities (e.g., Plato, Socrates, etc.).[114]

While they could not avoid the fact that, as discussed above, most examples of *siḥr* in Islamic sources involved defying God or harming other people, the Brethren reinterpreted such accounts to give *siḥr* a positive value. For instance, they accepted the accusations against Muḥammad, as well as those against other prophets, that they were *sāḥir*s, but reinterpreted that so that calling them *sāḥir*s was not an accusation of fraud, but an acknowledgement of their power.[115] Similarly, in recounting the Quranic description of Hārūt and Mārūt, they de-emphasized the charge that these angels disobeyed God and worked against faith, while emphasizing the power which magic could wield.

Conclusions

Thus we see several competing views in the medieval Islamic world with regard to "magic," as defined earlier—including *siḥr* and a variety of other practices. A literal reading of the Quran would suggest most *siḥr* was unreal, or deceptive at best. Other Quranic verses and many traditions of Muḥammad, however, suggested that it was possible at least to do real harm by occult means, though such means involved idolatry.

It seems likely that such attitudes were related to the extra-Islamic sources of such magic, either practices of the pre-Islamic Arabs or the different kinds of magic found among the populations of the newly conquered Byzantine and Sasanian empires. The literary magical tradition found in the two latter cultures, and as adapted by Muslim authors, will be addressed in the next chapter.

Some traditions, however, suggested that occult action was not necessarily idolatrous or harmful, that it was possible to aid others through occult means not offensive to God. The Ikhwān al-Ṣafā' took a very different approach, radically reinterpreting the Quran and *Sunnah* to hold up occult knowledge and power as exemplary charactersitics of the holy and the wise. While it is difficult to adduce any direct influence of the Brethren of Purity on al-Būnī or other authors, this perception of occult knowledge and power as not just permissible but actually praiseworthy best characterizes the attitude expressed towards the subject in al-Būnī's corpus.

Chapter Three:
Magic in the Islamic World before al-Būnī

Introduction

Both the archaeological record and historical accounts provide abundant evidence that the practice of magic had a long history throughout the Mediterranean long before the birth of Muḥammad and that this continued into the Islamic era with some gradual changes. In the interest of conciseness, and in view of the fact that the main purpose of this dissertation is a study of the magical literature which emerged under al-Būnī's name, the primary reference point for context must be the magical literature (broadly defined, as discussed in the first chapter) which flourished in the Islamic age, rather than taking in the broad sweep of historical and archaeological evidence for daily use and practice.

Neoplatonic Magic: Ancient Wisdom or Forbidden Sorcery?

The key elements in most magical literature of the Islamic world before the seventh/thirteenth century were the power of the heavens and the special properties of materials (*khawāṣṣ*). The two were, in fact, linked; most *khawāṣṣ* of materials were related to pre-Islamic notions of the materials' affinity with celestial divinities.

At the same time, this conception of occult powers residing in the stars and in the properties of materials was not exclusive to such magical texts. Celestial powers could also play an important role in Graeco-Islamic medicine. A doctor might take a patient's horoscope to determine the right time for treatment—or, indeed, to determine whether the patient would live.[116] Similarly, *khawāṣṣ* were also discussed in works of Graeco-Islamic medicine, particularly in translations of Alexander of Tralles.[117]

Underlying these works was a Neoplatonic conception of magical power: that power was believed to originate with the One (i.e., the Primal Cause) and the power was believed to be diffused to earth through the celestial spheres. Differences in the details of these operations will be addressed below.

David Pingree has suggested that these Neoplatonic connections had their origins in a need to justify magic as such against critics who claimed that the sources of such power were necessarily evil. He went on to point out that this perfectly describes the situation when the Ḥarrārians were confronted by the caliph al-Maʾmūn in 215/830.[118] Faced with the accusation of being pagans (and therefore liable to be wiped out by the Muslims), the Ḥarrārians called themselves Sabians (*Ṣābiʾūn*), so as to identify themselves with the Sabians mentioned in the Quran.[119] As such, they claimed they were monotheists (*ḥanīfs*) and that they followed a prophet, namely Hermes Trismegistus, and that therefore they merited protection as "people of the book."[120]

There was an abundant medieval Arabic literature on the *khawāṣṣ* of materials. No attempt will be made here to cover the entire scope of this rich literature. Instead, the focus will be on a few highly influential men credited with writing important magical texts. Those authors (or supposed authors) will include: Hermes, Arīyūs, Apollonius of Tyana, Muḥammad ibn Zakarīyāʾ al-Rāzī, Ibn Waḥshīyāʾ, Abū Maslamah al-Majrīṭī, Fakhr al-Dīn al-Rāzī, and the Ikhwān al-Ṣafāʾ. This literature will be discussed based on secondary scholarship about those texts which exist in manuscript and on descriptions of magical texts and their authors found in the *Fihrist* of Ibn al-Nadīm.

Introduction: Ibn al-Nadīm's evaluation

Ibn al-Nadīm's *Fihrist*, probably the best source for a survey of the fourth/tenth-century Arabic literary world, devotes a chapter to various occult arts.[121] In this chapter the author explained the difference between *saḥarah* (sing. *sāḥir*, "sorcerers") and *muʿazzimūn* (those who cast spells). He called the former system "blameworthy" (*madhmūmah*) and the latter "praiseworthy" (*maḥmūdah*). He also described a variety of occult practices particular to the ancients, to the Turks, and to

Indians without attaching any value judgment to any of them. Naturally, he also listed what books he knew in each category.

Even though Ibn al-Nadīm made these distinctions and used different words for these various magical systems and practices, the fact that he grouped all of them together indicates he did see common characteristics which connected them. Some of these similarities were purely material. Ibn al-Nadīm explained that practitioners of both the licit and the illicit systems claimed to employ *khawātim* (seals); *ʿazāʾim* (incantations), *rūqá* (charms), *ḥizāb* (spells, incantations); *ṣanādil* (sandalwood), *dakhan* (fumigation), and *fuṣūṣ* (stones set in rings).[122] It is worth noting, too, that all of these materials were also found in the works ascribed to al-Būnī.

As discussed below, Ibn al-Nadīm grouped some books of Neoplatonic magic with the forbidden system and some with a magical miscellany of illusions, talismans, and charms. This latter group was apparently neither blameworthy nor praiseworthy in his opinion. It may well be that he considered these practices and the books describing them to be morally neutral because he understood them to be mechanistic rather than animistic. That is to say, they operated not by attempting to cajole or bully spirits into action, but rather by taking advantage of the interaction of elements of the natural world. Such an assessment must remain speculative, since Ibn al-Nadīm did not explicitly make this distinction anywhere in the *Fihrist*.

With regard to sorcery (*siḥr*), or "the blameworthy system," he explained that *saḥarah* enticed spirits by offerings and evil deeds, since these were pleasing to the spirits. This continued the long-standing association of *siḥr* with sin and unbelief in Islamic thought, as discussed previously. According to Ibn al-Nadīm the particular sins used to cajole the spirits could be sins of omission (i.e., neglecting prayers or fasting). They could also be various sins of commission. Ibn al-Nadīm specifically mentioned spilling blood and marrying unsuitable women (i.e., women too closely related).[123]

Ibn al-Nadīm (himself writing in Baghdad) called Egypt "the Babylon of sorcery." He reported that there and in the adjoining countries, *siḥr* and talismans were openly used by both men and women, and there were many books about them.[124] He gave no further details on such sorcerous books from Egypt and only mentioned a few Arabic books and authors in this genre.[125] Unfortunately most of them are unknown apart from Ibn al-Nadīm's mention of their works, though one prominent exception will be addressed below.

As discussed below, Neoplatonic magic as promulgated by both neutral and "blameworthy" authors influenced thinking about magic in Islamic societies up through the development of the "Islamic magic" discussed later. This is clear not only from the way in which Ibn al-Nadīm described their works and their practices, but also from the authors he mentioned.[126]

Hermes

In medieval Arabic literature, Hermes Trismegistus ("Thrice-Great Hermes") was transformed from the Egyptian god Thoth into a wise man or prophet. Most early Arabic authors spoke of Hermes as three different individuals. The first Hermes was identified with the prophet Akhnūkh and Idrīs. He lived before the Flood and built the Pyramids and other sanctuaries. The second Hermes, "al-Bābilī," lived in Babylon after the Flood, and there restored the study of the sciences. The third Hermes wrote about various sciences In Egypt after the Flood.[127] Ibn al-Nadīm's account of Hermes describes him as a single man who once ruled Babylon, but later emigrated to Egypt, thus merging elements of the first and second Hermes.

As for his bibliography, Ibn al-Nadīm gave an extensive list of books attributed to Hermes Trismegistus in his discussion of illusion, talismans and charms—that is to say, magic which was neither blameworthy nor praiseworthy. In his chapter on alchemy, Ibn al-Nadīm also gave a highly detailed biography of Hermes as he was understood in the Islamic world at that time.

According to Ibn al-Nadīm, Hermes wrote about how to utilize the spirits of the planets, just as other Neoplatonic authors did. For instance, Ibn al-Nadīm wrote that Hermes' *Kitāb al-isṭamāṭīs* dealt with the spirits of the planets and the rituals associated with them, as well as instructions for protection against *nīranjāt*.[128] Therefore it is unclear why Ibn al-Nadīm grouped his texts with the more neutral magic, rather than the "blameworthy system." One possibility may be that since some identified Hermes with a Quranic prophet (even if Ibn al-Nadīm did not), Ibn al-Nadīm was reluctant to suggest that any of his writings could deal with forbidden or evil subjects.

Based solely on a direct comparison of titles, there appears to be little overlap between Ibn al-Nadīm's list of Hermetic literature and those works that actually exist in manuscript. Only one of those mentioned in the *Fihrist* actually exists; conversely, of the existing manuscripts, several of the texts are mentioned by Ḥajjī Khalīfah or by the Ikhwān al-Ṣafā', but not by Ibn al-Nadīm.[129] For instance, Hermes' *Kitāb kanz al-asrār wa-dhakhā'ir al-abrār* (Book of the Treasure of Secrets and Treasury of Good Works), on letters and magic squares, was mentioned by Teukros the Babylonian (AKA Tankalūsh al-Bābilī, ca. 1st century CE), Thābit ibn Qurra (d. 288/901), and Ḥunayn ibn Isḥāq al-Ibādī (d. 260/873); furthermore, it does exist in manuscript.[130] Ullmann suggested that this was identical with *Frīqūyūs*,[131] a book mentioned by Ibn al-Nadīm who said this book included talismans based on the letters of the sun, moon, planets, and the names of the philosophers.[132]

Apollonius

Ibn al-Nadīm also mentioned the works of "Bulīnās al-Ḥakīm" from Ṭūnah in Byzantium—in all likelihood, Apollonius of Tyana. Little is known about this author, to the point that some Arabic authors confused him with Apollonius of Perge (ca. 200 BCE) "the geometer." As for Apollonius of Tyana, we do know (as did some Arabic biographers) that he lived in the first century CE and wrote a number of magical texts. Arabic authors frequently referred to him as *Ṣāḥib al-ṭalismāt* ("master of talismans") or simply, as Ibn al-Nadīm called him, *Bulīnās al-ḥakīm* ("Apollonius the wise").[133]

Like other authors of Hermetic magic, Apollonius of Tyana devoted books to the *khawāṣṣ* of materials.[134] He also described the influence of the planets, including their application for talismans and medical uses.[135] His *Risālah fī ta'thīr al-rūḥānīyāt fī al-murakkabāt wa-a'māl al-ṣuwar wa-daf' al-amrāḍ wa-ḥulūlihā* (Treatise on the Influence of Charms on Compounds, [on] Statues' Actions, and [on] Healing the Sick and What Is Necessary for Them) described how to manufacture talismans with magical inscriptions and figures of the stars.[136] Ibn al-Nadīm only ascribed one book to him, an account of the talismans which he erected in different cities to protect them.[137]

Arīyūs

Most mysterious of all, perhaps, are Ibn al-Nadīm's references to Arūs Rūmī and Arīyūs al-Rūmī. Ibn al-Nadīm mentioned Arūs in his discussion of (presumably) morally neutral natural magic and talismans, but listed the works of Arīyūs among the books of licit magic.[138] Fuat Sezgin believed these two authors were identical.[139] Flügel, on the other hand, believed that this "Arūs" referred to the Egyptian god Horus, the son of Isis, and furthermore that he might have been identical to the alchemist "Ārūs al-Qaṣṣ."[140] It is unclear whether Ibn al-Nadīm thought they were not the same man, or whether he categorized different books by this author in different sections depending on their contents. In any case, Ibn al-Nadīm only credited each man with one book: Arīyūs wrote a work describing the children of Iblīs and Arūs wrote one on *nīranjāt*.[141]

Muḥammad ibn Zakarīyā' al-Rāzī (d. 313/925)

Although the *Fihrist* only mentions Muḥammad ibn Zakarīyā' al-Rāzī in the chapters on alchemy and medicine, many later magical authors cited his magic works and his writings on the special properties of materials. His *Kitāb khawāṣṣ al-ashyā'* lists more than a hundred materials and their special properties, particularly for medical uses. This work cites some authors from the Muslim era (e.g., 'Alī b. Rabbān al-Ṭabarī, Ḥunayn al-

Kindī), but also numerous ancient ones (e.g., Aetios, Alexander of Tralles, Aristotle, Hermes, Galen).[142] His *Kitāb al-Ḥāwī* mentions magical protections as well. However, works such as these represent a relatively small fraction of his total output, as listed in the *Fihrist* and in *GAS*, so it is perhaps unfair for Ullmann to have said that he had a "strong predilection" for magic.[143]

Ibn Waḥshīyah (d. ca. 340/951)

Abū Bakr Aḥmad ibn ʿAlī ibn Qays Ibn Waḥshīyah (d. ca. 340/951) was one of the most important and prolific magical authors of the Islamic era mentioned in the *Fihrist*. According to Ibn al-Nadīm, he translated some thirteen works dealing with the occult and special properties of materials, and wrote two of his own. However, since the mid-nineteenth century the authenticity of Ibn al-Waḥshīyah's translations—particularly *al-Filāḥah al-Nabaṭīyah*—and even his very existence have been subject to widely divergent opinions. At one extreme, David Chwolson dated *al-Filāḥah al-Nabaṭīyah* to the fourteenth century BCE. At the other, Alfred von Gutschmid and Theodor Nöldeke asserted that the text was a forgery from the Islamic era, dating from no earlier than 700 CE and perhaps as late as the fourth/tenth century.[144] Scholarship in the last seventy years, most recently by Toufic Fahd, has sought to re-establish the text as an authentic compilation of ancient agronomy and occult science and Ibn Waḥshīyah's place as its translator into Arabic.[145]

Such considerations regarding the authenticity of Ibn Waḥshīyah and his writings are less important here than the question of how these works were received and used by medieval Arabs and Muslims. There is every indication that Ibn Waḥshīyah was accepted by medieval Arabic readers as the translator of ancient works, and a number of works on the occult in particular.

The best-known of his works is *al-Filāḥah al-Nabaṭīyah* (Nabataen Agriculture). It is true that this text is less concerned with occult subjects than many of Ibn Waḥshīyah's other works, which address topics such as alchemy, astrology, talismans, and magic alphabets.[146] However, *al-Filāḥah al-Nabaṭīyah* acquired a tremendous reputation as an occult text as soon as it was translated into Arabic.[147]

Furthermore, even though its main subject is agronomy, this topic is broadly conceived, encompassing not only descriptions of what different plants were and how to grow them, but also the usefulness of different plants. This encompassed not only their material uses but also their affinities with particular deities, religious uses, and special properties, as well as myths concerning their origins.[148] In more general discussions in the book, *al-Filāḥah al-Nabaṭīyah* also explained the effects of the sun, moon, planets, and stars on the sublunar world, from changes in weather to the diseases of plants.[149] Given these considerations, it is therefore appropriate to discuss *al-Filāḥah al-Nabaṭīyah* as representative of Ibn Waḥshīyah's occult writings and translations.

Abū Maslamah al-Majrīṭī (d. 395/1005)

One of the best-known Neoplatonic magical texts from the medieval Islamic world post-dates Ibn al-Nadīm's *Fihrist* by approximately one hundred years. *Ghāyat al-ḥakīm* (The Goal of the Wise), also known by the title of its Latin translation, *Picatrix*, was written by Abū Maslamah Muḥammad al-Majrīṭī (d. 395/1005)[150] between 443/1052 and 448/1056.[151]

Al-Majrīṭī proudly asserted that he had drawn on some two hundred and twenty-four books in compiling *Ghāyat al-ḥakīm*, and this debt to ancient authors is clearly demonstrated in the book's contents. Furthermore, in various places al-Majrīṭī explicitly attributed his knowledge and rituals to ancient authorities such as Plato and Aristotle. David Pingree confirmed *Ghāyat al-ḥakīm*'s debt to the ancients, illustrating traces of Mesopotamian, Egyptian, Iranian, Indian, Syrian, Hellenistic, and Roman magic in the text's treatment of the occult.[152]

Without describing all of these constituent elements in detail, it is sufficient to state that it is a work of Neoplatonic magic. That is to say, it asserts that the magical power which it draws on is the One, that is to say, the primal cause of the universe.[153] Al-Majrīṭī described how the user could gain access to this power through the One's intermediaries, the angels and other spirits associated with the celestial spheres. In order to perform this "celestial magic," the magician would utilize various rituals to place him in close connection with the appropriate celestial body. This would include wearing clothes, eating food, making sacrifices, and using inks with terrestrial substances associated with the celestial bodies through their own special properties. Naturally, this also included performing the appropriate rituals at a proper astrological time, when the correct body's rays would be unobstructed by those of any other planet. Very often, the form this would take was infusing the star's power into a talisman (which had the benefit that the magician could continually utilize its power, even though the magician had performed the ceremony only once).[154]

Even though the ultimate source for all this power was the One (that is to say, the Divine), it is fair to say that the ends of *Ghāyat al-ḥakīm*'s magic were completely base and amoral (if not immoral). A quick survey of the text reveals that al-Majrīṭī gave instructions for how to perform numerous curses. Pingree explicitly bemoaned the fact that by the time of *Ghāyat al-ḥakīm* Neoplatonic ideas "intended to facilitate the communication between the divine and the human and the eventual ascent of the human soul"[155] had been perverted to a variety of "base aims, such as the acquisition of health, wealth, and women, and the destruction of [the magician's] enemies."[156]

One should not think that these were the only ends which could be achieved by the methods outlined in *Ghāyat al-ḥakīm*. Al-Majrīṭī described how a magician following his methods could also have spiritual visions and reach divine states and knowledge of the earliest philosophers.[157]

Fakhr al-Dīn al-Rāzī (d.606/1209)

The work of Fakhr al-Dīn al-Rāzī (d.606/1209) represents something of a bridge in the magical literature. On the one hand, it is primarily a Neoplatonic magic text, but on the other, it clearly contains elements recognizable in al-Būnī's work. Specifically, most of al-Rāzī's *Sirr al-maktūm fī mukhāṭabāt al-nujūm* (Hidden Secret Concerning Those Who Address the Stars) is occupied with celestial magic and talismans. Furthermore, most of his sources were authors writing about celestial and natural Neoplatonic magic in Greek or Arabic.[158] However, the text also includes the "seven Solomonic signs" for the Greatest Name of God, which is clearly a part of the "Islamic magic" to be discussed later in al-Būnī's oeuvre.

The Ikhwān al-Ṣafā' (Brethren of Purity)

Even though their writings were never evaluated or even mentioned by Ibn al-Nadīm, it would be fair to say that the fifty-second treatise by the Ikhwān al-Ṣafāʾ "On the reality of magic and incantations and the evil eye" (*fī māhīyat al-siḥr wa-al-ʿazāʾim wa-al-ʿayn*)[159] stands somewhere between Ibn al-Nadīm's conception of the "praiseworthy" and "blameworthy" systems of magic.

On the one hand, their conception of magic was clearly Neoplatonic. According to the Ikhwān al-Ṣafāʾ astrology was the foundation of the occult arts and should be studied first. Their description of the angels fit in well with their Neoplatonic ideology. According to the Ikhwān the stars were actually angels and as such occupied an intermediate position between God and the world, both physically and spiritually. That is to say, as God's angels, the stars were responsible for mediating the relationship between God and the world, and for enforcing God's will.[160]

On the other hand, the Brethren tried to identify the One as discussed in Neoplatonic writings with the Islamic conception of Allah, which led to certain contradictions. Most notably, they portrayed Him as providing guidance to humanity and peoples in general, and to individuals in particular, which was a far cry from the unknowable Primal Cause of Neoplatonism.[161]

On a practical level, when they spoke of the influence of one soul upon another, they particularly emphasized the influence of celestial souls upon terrestrial ones.[162] Astrology was also one of the important arts for divination, and the Brethren even devoted most of the fifty-second treatise to prediction through practical astrology.[163]

Medicine was another magical art, according to the Ikhwān al-Ṣafā', since it was concerned with the interaction of the four qualities and also with the influence of the stars.[164]

Ibn al-Nadīm's "Praiseworthy" or "Permitted" System

Ibn al-Nadīm contrasted the "blameworthy system" with the licit or praiseworthy system—that of the *muʿazzimūn*. According to Ibn al-Nadīm they claimed they obeyed Islamic law scrupulously and could compel spirits by performing actions pleasing to God. These included abandoning fleshly lusts, devoting themselves to religious observances, and adjuring the spirits by God and His Names. The spirits would obey out of fear of God or observance of oaths sworn to Him or because of the special properties (*khāṣṣīyah*) of the Names of God.[165]

Although Ibn al-Nadīm mentioned both ancients and Muslims who wrote books about "licit magic,"[166] none of their works survive. This means that almost all that we know of them are the scanty details of these men and their works mentioned in the *Fihrist*.

The one exception is Solomon, whose reputation for magical ability is well known both in the *Midrash* and in Islamic scholarship and legend.[167] Though the *Fihrist* does not mention any books written by Solomon, it does name seventy *ʿafārīt* compelled into covenants by him through the Names of God, as well as seven offspring of those *ʿafārīt*.[168]

As for those authors whose books the *Fihrist* does mention, it states that Abū Naṣr Aḥmad ibn Hilāl al-Bakīl was the first to use "licit magic" in Islam and that "Ibn al-Imām" specifically worked with the Names of God in the time of the caliph Muʿtaḍid (279-289/892-902).[169] Ibn al-Nadīm also described his own encounter with another author who worked with "licit magic," Abū ʿUthmān Ibn Abī Rasṣāṣah, who was around eighty at the time. When Ibn al-Nadīm expressed his surprise and consternation that such a distinguished man should waste his time with such nonsense, Ibn Abī Rasṣāṣah replied that he thoroughly believed in the efficacy of his techniques, otherwise he would not waste his time with it.

Ṭibb al-Nabī

Although none of these early texts in the permitted magical system survive, the *ṭibb al-Nabī* (medicine of the Prophet) does include elements which would fit Ibn al-Nadīm's definition of "licit magic" very well. Comments on this literature must be prefaced with a few caveats, however.

First of all, even though such magical elements of the Prophet's medicine have attracted the most attention in Western scholarship and are of most relevance for this study, they did not represent the sum total of its content. Particularly in its later stages of development, the medicine of the Prophet explicitly accepted the humoral system and other aspects of Graeco-Islamic medicine, and applied their etiologies and treatments.[170]

Furthermore, as mentioned earlier, various *aḥādīth* are hostile to magic (by various names). Nonetheless, others mention the Prophet's approval or use of incantations and talismans, particularly for protection and healing. As with most *aḥādīth*, these were not seen only as value judgements or as theoretical standpoints, but as practical examples for daily life.

The earliest known compilations under the title *Ṭibb al-Nabī* date from shortly before the *Fihrist* was written,[171] but Ibn al-Nadīm did not mention any of these in his discussions of medicine nor in his chapter on *ḥadīth*. Nonetheless, it is fair to say that those elements of the medicine of the Prophet which touch on the occult definitely could be placed with the "licit" system.

The Prophet's words and actions relating to health and healing were set aside in separate chapters in the earliest *ḥadīth* collections. Soon, they were also organized in separate books. The earliest known text under the title *al-Ṭibb al-Nabawī* was written by ʿAbd al-Mālik ibn Ḥabīb al-Sulamī al-Qurṭubī (d. 238/853).[172] Though this treatise is lost to us, the oldest surviving book on the subject is *al-Ṭibb al-Nabawī* by Aḥmad ibn Muḥammad ibn al-Sunnī al-Dīnawarī (d. 364/974).[173] The earliest texts of the Prophet's medicine were collected by *ḥadīth* scholars and contained no medical theory of their own nor did they analyze any of the *aḥādīth* according to contemporary Graeco-Islamic medicine. By the seventh /thirteenth century, practicing doctors with an interest in *ḥadīth* studies were compiling their own books of the *ṭibb al-Nabī*, along with their own medical analyses of the remedies recommended and integrating the *aḥādīth* into a comprehensive medical system.[174]

In comparison with Graeco-Islamic medicine (the "scientific" medicine of the time), the medicine of the Prophet placed a greater emphasis on the spiritual aspects of disease and treatment—both figuratively and literally. Authors in the genre claimed that these considerations made their medicine superior to the Graeco-Islamic system.

On the one hand, patients' souls, being eternal, were considered more important than their ephemeral bodies. Therefore, treatments which might contradict Islam or endanger the soul (for example, medicines using pork or wine) were prohibited. Furthermore, in an interesting acknowledgement of the placebo effect, authors and practitioners of the *ṭibb al-Nabī* argued that a good Muslim would not trust such treatments and therefore they would be ineffective.

With respect to the literally "spiritual" aspect of the Prophet's medicine, many *aḥādīth* cited in the literature asserted that illnesses could have supernatural or occult causes, such as witchcraft, jinn, or the evil eye. Therefore to combat diseases with supernatural cures, supernatural remedies—both magical and strictly religious—were recommended. Examples of the latter might include fasting, prayer, giving alms or simply bearing the illness patiently. The former category, the magical, advocated *duʿā*, *rūqá*, and *ṭilismāt*—invocations, charms, and talismans—based on Quranic verses.

Conclusions

As will be seen in succeeding chapters, al-Būnī's corpus owes a great debt to the Neoplatonic magic which preceded it. Ibn al-Nadīm's mention of a "licit" magical system in the fourth/tenth century is tantalizing, but until texts in this tradition from that period have been identified it will remain impossible to say to what extent al-Būnī drew on this literature. The idea that Islamic symbols and rituals could have automatically efficacious power was articulated in the *ṭibb al-Nabī* and in the "licit" system. For some reason, however, from the thirteenth century on, al-Būnī became the dominant name in this field.

Chapter Four: The Biography and Bibliography of Aḥmad ibn ʿAlī al-Būnī

Al-Būnī's Biography

Since it is his writings which are under study, it is appropriate to consider the life and works of Abū al-ʿAbbās Aḥmad ibn ʿAlī ibn Yūsuf al-Qurashī al-Ṣūfī Muḥyī al-Dīn al-Būnī.[175] Sadly, there is little certain knowledge about the man and his life. It is agreed that his *nisbah* refers to the city of Būnah (Fr. Bône; present-day ʿAnnābah in northeastern Algeria), that he spent the latter part of his life in Cairo, and that he died there in 622/1225. At least one source also records that he was buried in the Qarafah Cemetery.[176] It is also clear that he was a Sufi during his lifetime, as indicated in one of his *nisbahs*, explicit biographical references,[177] and the content of some of his writings (as will be discussed in later chapters).

Many Sufi biographical dictionaries mention al-Būnī, but due to their hagiographical nature they provide few details about his life. *Karāmāt al-awliyāʾ* by al-Nabhānī (1849/50-1932), for instance, reports that among al-Būnī's miracles was that his prayers were answered and that he is known for an account in which he claimed that Muḥammad told him [God's] "Names of Retreat" (*Asmāʾ al-khalwah*).[178] Similarly Muḥammad b. al-Ṭayyib al-Qādirī (d. 1773 CE) gave al-Būnī long and flowery praise as an illuminator, revealer of secrets, and as a worker of miracles. As eloquent as this praise is, it tells us nothing about al-Būnī's life.

Where did "The Man from Būnah" Come from?

In fact, no biographical dictionaries provide any solid information on al-Būnī's life before he came to Cairo. They cannot tell when he was born, with whom he studied, or even when he came to Cairo. Even so, many have emphasized his connections to the Magrhib, taking his *nisbah* to indicate that he was actually born in Būnah. As a result the most detailed scholarship on his biography has come out of twentieth-century biographical dictionaries of Maghribi and particularly Algerian scholars. These works assert that al-Būnī was born in the Maghrib despite a lack of evidence one way or the other. For example, ʿĀdil Nuwayhiḍ's *Aʿlām al-Jazāʾir* uses the ambiguous phrase *min ahl Būnah* (from the people of Būnah) to describe al-Būnī and goes on to say that he "emigrated" (*raḥala*) to the Mashriq.[179] Abdelwahab Benmansour also wrote that al-Būnī "emigrated" to Egypt and mentioned that nothing was known of his life in "his native land" (i.e., in Algeria).[180] Contrariwise, working on the assumption that al-Būnī's work in Cairo was the most important aspect of his life, more recent Western scholars have spoken of al-Būnī as an Egyptian Sufi and author.[181]

Biographical dictionaries are not the only source for information on al-Būnī's life, however. His writings also include occasional clues about his life and background. For instance, in his doctoral dissertation, Mohammed El-Ğawhary noted that the long recension of *Shams al-maʿārif* mentions al-Būnī's travels to Jerusalem, Damascus and Aleppo, and a sojourn in Akhmīm.[182] This last is particularly interesting because of that town's reputation. Akhmīm is a town some 312 miles south of Cairo, best known in the Arabic geographical literature for its ancient temple, which was associated with Hermes Trismegistus. The town was also the birthplace of Dhū al-Nūn al-Miṣrī in the second/eighth century.[183] It can be no mere coincidence that al-Būnī's visit to this town is mentioned in *Shams al-maʿārif*. Clearly, whether the incident actually took place or not, the intent is to link al-Būnī with Hermes, and quite possibly with Dhū al-Nūn as well.

Although there is no specific reason to doubt this account of al-Būnī's travels, almost all of the other clues to his life found in his writings are unhelpful or contradictory in learning anything about the author's life. Others are so plainly impossible that they support the thesis that some of the texts ascribed to him actually were written by various later authors over the centuries (regarding which, see more below).

For example, El-Ǧawhary has also noted that colloquial Egyptian Arabic is found throughout the long recension of *Shams al-maʿārif.* If this analysis is accepted, it does demonstrate that it is an Egyptian text, but it tells us nothing further about al-Būnī's national origins. It is unclear whether this is because al-Būnī himself was born in Egypt or adopted the Egyptian idiom as his own, or because the text itself was supplemented by later Egyptian authors.

Also, the long recension of *Shams al-maʿārif* concludes with a list of the shaykhs with whom al-Būnī studied, including some *silsilahs* (chains of spiritual authority) going all the way back to the Prophet. El-Ǧawhary concluded from this list of shaykhs that al-Būnī was a Shiite, a contention supported by mention of his works in *al-Dhariʿā fī taṣānīf al-Shīʿah.*[184] However, such an argument cannot be taken at face value. Firstly, the simple fact that Aga Buzurg Tehrani claimed him as a Shiite means nothing; as has already been seen, Maghribi scholars have claimed that he was Maghribi, though the evidence for such a contention is far from certain. Secondly, at least some of al-Būnī's writings have strong connections to the Shādhilīyah Sufi order. Both al-Shādhilī himself and the order were staunchly Sunni, so it is inappropriate to use some isolated mentions to suggest that either al-Būnī's or his works were Shii.

Not only is it dangerous to draw these particular conclusions from the list of shaykhs, but also the list turns out to be very unreliable in general. To start with, virtually none of the shaykhs named can be found in the biographical literature. Other teachers on whom information can be found either died too early or were born too late to have taught al-Būnī. For instance, Benmansour has pointed out that one of these purported shaykhs, Abū al-ʿAbbās al-Mursī, died sixty-four years after al-Būnī's purported death date.[185]

Eliminating all the scholars who cannot be found or who lived at the wrong time leaves two men about whom information can be located who could have conceivably taught al-Būnī. However these two lived long enough apart that it is virtually impossible that they both could have taught al-Būnī.

One of these was Abū Ḥasan ibn ʿAlī ibn Muḥammad ibn Ibrāhīm ibn Muḥammad al-Ḥūrānī. His mention in *Shams al-maʿārif* gives his death date as 538 AH/1143-44.[186] Assuming that al-Būnī studied with him as an adolescent just before al-Ḥūrānī's death, that would place al-Būnī's birth date around 522/1128—meaning that he was about one hundred years old when he died. Muḥammad Balghrad clearly had his own doubts about this possibility, as he concluded his mention of this teacher and al-Būnī's calculated birth date with the phrase *Allāhu aʿlam* (God knows best [whether or not this is true]).[187]

At the same time, another of al-Būnī's purported teachers, Muḥammad ibn Aḥmad Abū ʿAbd Allāh al-Qurashī, died in 599/1202-1203 at the age of fifty-five. If al-Būnī were born around 522/1128, that would put him well into his forties before he studied with al-Qurashī—an unlikely scenario at best. With no way to judge whether al-Būnī is more likely to have studied with one or the other of these men, the mutually contradictory information about these two shaykhs means that they cancel each other out and are totally useless for determining anything about al-Būnī's life.

Given the current state of research, it is impossible to state with exact confidence much about al-Būnī's life. We do not know where he was born; we do not know much about where he studied or with whom. It is certainly plausible (if not certain) that, as has been generally assumed, al-Būnī was born in Būnah and emigrated to Cairo early in his career. In this period, talented and respected men such as he could easily travel from one part of the Islamic world to the other, seeking patronage and/or greater security. Many certainly did, including Maimonides, Ibn al-ʿArabī, and most of the other authors discussed below. In particular, many were emigrating to the central Islamic lands in Egypt and Syria, especially Cairo and Damascus.

Al-Būnī's Bibliography

With as little known about the man's life, it would appear that the most solid information available about al-Būnī is his bibliography. Al-Būnī is, of course, best known as an author of texts about the Arabic alphabet, the Beautiful Names of God, and the Quran and its verses—and particularly how to use the special properties of these Islamic symbols.[188] The list of works attributed to al-Būnī cannot be taken at face value, however. An initial survey of texts and the manuscript tradition suggests that others may have tried to credit some of their own works to al-Būnī to give them greater credibility and circulation. This is certainly not unknown in medieval Arabic literature, and it may be a particular problem in occult writings.

The arguments over the exact provenance of the Jābirian alchemical corpus are well-known and well-established; similarly any number of occult texts ascribed to otherwise "legitimate" or "orthodox" authors have been dismissed as erroneous attributions. For instance, "many occult writings" were falsely attributed to Abū Ḥāmid al-Ghazālī (d. 1111).[189] With particular reference to al-Būnī's writings, a treatise on *jafr* excerpted from *Shams al-maʿārif* was attributed to Ibn al-ʿArabī.[190]

With respect to al-Būnī's corpus, Julius Ruska illuminated how some of the discussions of alchemy in *Shams al-maʿārif* consist largely of quotes from Abū Bakr Muḥammad al-Rāzī's (d. 925 CE) *Kitāb al-asrār.*[191] It is unclear at this point just when the addition was made. It is equally possible that al-Būnī himself quoted al-Rāzī, or the selection might have been added by a later copyist. Even Ruska was uncertain of the passage's wider significance for al-Būnī's original text.

Taking a more radical approach, Mohammed El-Ğawhary proposed that *Shams al-maʿārif* was not written by al-Būnī, but in fact by his pupil (or a succession of pupils). First, he noted the text is not mentioned in Shihāb al-Dīn Aḥmad ibn ʿAbd al-Wahhāb ibn Muḥammad al-Nuwayrī's (d. 732/1332) grand encyclopedia *Nihāyat al-ʿArab*, though it is mentioned in Qalqashandī's (d. 821/1418) *Ṣubḥ al-aʿshā.*[192] El-Ğawhary also cited several features of the style and language of *Shams al-maʿārif* that suggest that it was written after al-Būnī's lifetime.[193] In addition, El-Ğawhary pointed out that the text includes various anachronistic references such as the mention of Abū al-Ḥasan al-Shādhilī (d. 656/1258) as a teacher, even though he died after al-Būnī.[194] Finally, between chapters thirty-four and thirty-eight of *Shams al-maʿārif* El-Ğawhary found responses which were specifically in response to arguments against magic promulgated in the eighth and ninth centuries Hijri (fourteenth and fifteenth centuries CE).[195]

More recently, Pierre Lory and Toufic Fahd have pointed out further anachronisms regarding al-Būnī's supposed sources. Even though they died after 622/1225, Muḥyī al-Dīn Ibn al-ʿArabī (d. 638/1241) and Tāj al-Dīn Ibn ʿAṭāʾ Allāh al-Mālikī al-Shādhilī (d. 709/1309) appear in the middle of al-Būnī's *silisilahs* in the conclusion to *Shams al-maʿārif.*[196] Other similar anachronisms include an anecdote about al-Būnī's master, al-Khwārizmī, in Mecca in 670/1272, as well as references to a text by Ibn Sabʿīn (d. 669/1271).[197]

It is also worth noting that in a discussion of *jafr* (divination by letters) attributed to the sixth Imam Jaʿfar al-Ṣādiq (d. 148/765), *Shams al-maʿārif* describes events in 627—after al-Būnī's death. These include the defeat of Jalāl al-Dīn Khwārzim Shāh (d. 628/1231) in 627/1230, and the arrival of crusaders in the Maghrib.[198] Mention of these events supports the contention that *Shams al-maʿārif* (at least in its long recension) was an ongoing project added to by many after al-Būnī's death.

There are also clues to the history of *Shams al-maʿārif* in the manuscript history. Toufic Fahd has observed that the oldest manuscripts of *Shams al-maʿārif* in the collections he researched were the shortest, whereas longer manuscripts were more recent.[199] The same pattern may be seen in the manuscripts held by the Tunisian Bibliothèque Nationale. The earliest dated manuscript attributed to al-Būnī in that library is a short recension of *Shams al-maʿārif* (BN Tunis 8784, 989 AH/1581-82 CE, 153 folios). The latest such manuscript is the "long recension" (BN Tunis 4920, 4921; 1308 AH/1890-91 CE, 334 folios total).

It is also worth noting that the oldest manuscripts are not labeled *ṣughrá* (short), *kubrá* (long), or *wusṭá* (medium). That division does not appear until 1055/1645-46. Furthermore, this distinction is not made in the earlier bibliographies (e.g., Ḥajjī Khalīfah).

Nonetheless, at least one manuscript of *Shams al-maʿārif* dates from al-Būnī's lifetime.[200] This manuscript, *Manisa Genel Küt* 1445, was copied in 618/1221 (assuming the colophon is authentic) and consists of 60 folios. Although undated, the manuscript "Arabe 2647" in the Bibliothèque nationale de France is also thought to come from the seventh/thirteenth century. It is also fairly short, consisting of 148 folios.[201]

Based on the manuscript evidence, then, it seems reasonable to conclude that al-Būnī wrote some version of *Shams al-maʿārif* and that this text was progressively added to over the years and centuries. It may well be that the distinction between the short, medium, and long recensions emerged to reflect different stages of the text's development, recognized by Arabic bibliographers as different versions of the same text. A definitive answer must await a more thorough examination and comparison of the available manuscripts.

However, such an ambitious undertaking is beyond the scope of the present project. For the time being, it seems most reasonable to accept that *Shams al-maʿārif* is, at least in part, the work of later authors and not solely that of al-Būnī.

In some ways, this makes the task of analysis easier. It has long been recognized that *Shams al-maʿārif* combines a variety of different materials and approaches.[202] The various contradictions which emerge with respect to different treatments of various elements (e.g., the Names of God) may now be understood not so much as the internal contradictions of an author who was unable to make up his mind, but rather discussions (and even debates) among mystics and occultists of diverse opinions.

Although most of the limited scholarship dealing with al-Būnī has focused on the long recension of *Shams al-maʿārif*, it is reasonable to suspect that other works may have been falsely attributed to al-Būnī, or at least supplemented by later authors. In fact, El-Ǧawhary asserted that the only text which may be reliably attributed to al-Būnī is *al-lamʿa al-nūrānīyah.*[203] However, no reason was given why this text in particular, out of the dozens attributed to al-Būnī, should be regarded as his sole authentic work.

A more thorough survey of catalogues containing manuscripts of al-Būnī's works could yield more definitive information concerning the spread of these works—how quickly they spread, and where. Naturally, this would be even better accomplished if it were possible to examine the manuscripts (and their colophons) themselves.

In any case, al-Būnī was widely known throughout the Arabic-speaking world within a short time after his death as an author of occult texts. While al-Nuwayrī may not refer to *Shams al-maʿārif* by name, he does mention a book by al-Būnī entitled *Kitāb laṭāʾif al-ishārāt fī asrār al-ḥurūf al-ʿulwīyāt* (The Delicacies of Signs in the Greatest Letters).[204] The Tunisian Bibliothèque Nationale holds an eleventh/seventeenth century manuscript with a synonymous title (*Kitāb laṭāʾif al-ishārāt fī asrār al-ḥurūf al-ʿālīyāt*), also attributed to al-Būnī. This text is particularly significant, since it frequently refers to al-Būnī's other writings—especially *Shams al-maʿārif.* While not conclusive, this does support manuscript evidence that some version of *Shams al-maʿārif* was in circulation in the seventh/thirteenth century. *Kitāb laṭāʾif al-ishārāt* itself is probably a relatively late text, as evidenced by its reference to al-Būnī's earlier works and its mention of an event in 621/1224—a year before al-Būnī's purported death date.

Even more significantly, by the eighth/fourteenth century al-Būnī had the dubious distinction of being denounced by name by Ibn Khaldūn (d. 784/1382) in the *Muqaddimah.*[205] Ibn Khaldūn mentioned only one text by name, *Kitāb al-anmāṭ.*[206] Though there is no reference to this book in *GAL*, *Kashf al-ẓunūn*, or *Hadīyyat al-ʿĀrifīn*, Rosenthal pointed out that chapters twenty-one through thirty of the long recension of *Shams al-ma'ārif* consist of *anmāṭ* (sing. *nimṭ*: "sorts, species").[207] However these chapters deal with the Beautiful Names of God, and not with Arabic letters, as *sīmīyā'* proper would.

Even so, the *Muqaddimah* describes key features of al-Būnī's corpus which are still seen in the modern printed editions of *Shams al-ma'ārif* and other texts. Specifically, Ibn Khaldūn observed that al-Būnī prescribed the use of Islamic symbols for practical ends, but with assistance from the influence of heavenly bodies and the special properties of earthly substances.

In addition to this denunciation, to the extent that many of the texts attributed to al-Būnī are the work of later authors, this would suggest that al-Būnī's name carried great authority in the occult. (After all, impersonation, like imitation, is the sincerest form of flattery.)

Texts under study

As desirable as it might be to study all of the texts attributed to al-Būnī, limitations of time and availability make this impossible. Therefore this dissertation considers a selection of texts attributed to al-Būnī, including manuscripts available in the Tunisian Bibliothèque Nationale and printed texts. The titles examined are: *Shams al-ma'ārif wa-laṭā'if al-'awārif* (The Sun of Gnosis and Delicacies of Knowledge), *al-Uṣūl wa-al-ḍawābiṭ* (The Foundations and Rules), *Bughyat al-mushtāq fī ma'rifat waḍ' al-awfāq* (What is Desirable in Making Magic Squares), *Sharḥ al-Barhatīyah al-ma'rūf bi-sharḥ al-'ahd al-qadīm* (Explanation of the famous *Barhatīyah*, According to the Ancient Commentary), *Sharḥ al-Juljulūtīyah al-kubrá* (The Long Commentary on the *Juljulūtīyah*), *Tartīb al-da'wāt* (The Arrangement of Invocations), and *Kitāb laṭā'if al-ishārāt fī al-ḥurūf al-'ālīyāt* (The Delicacies of Signs in the Greatest Letters).

As discussed above, *Shams al-ma'ārif* is the most popular and influential text in al-Būnī's corpus; it is arguably the most influential text by anybody dealing with "Islamic magic." Analysis in this dissertation is based primarily on the Beirut edition of *Shams al-ma'ārif al-kubrá* published in1420/2000. This is the most recent printed edition available, and the text is the most legible of all such editions. The only difficulty is that many figures—virtually anything more complex or unusual than simple tables—are much less legible. These were probably reproduced from poor copies, or even copies of copies. Therefore it has been useful to check these tables, as well as the text itself, against several other printed editions, as well as a selection of manuscripts. Two of the other printed editions are also from Beirut: one was published in 1405/1985 but the other is undated. The latter, referred to here as the "saffron-paged" edition, appears to have been published later and is notable for its identification of *sūrah* and verse citations for Quranic quotes in the text. The other two printed editions are two different printings of an identical text. Both were published in Cairo and are undated. The UCLA Library Catalog suggests a date of 1905 CE for the older of the two, and sometime in the 1920's for the later printing. All of these different printed editions appear to come from a single copy edited by ʿAbd al-Qādir al-Adhamī al-Ḥusaynī (fl. 1306/1889). All five include an additional four treatises on astrology and divination by al-Ḥusaynī after the text of *Shams al-maʿārif*. Furthermore, some (but not all) of the editions credit him as editor.

MSS 4920 and 4921 from the Tunisian Bibliothèque Nationale also comprise a full copy of *Shams al-maʿārif al-kubrá*. This manuscript was produced in 1308 AH/1890-91 CE by Muḥammad b. Sulaymān al-Ṭawīl, and is written in a "Maghribi" hand. The text is essentially the same as the printed editions, though without the additional treatises at the end. There are also slight discrepancies in the table of contents. This does not indicate a major difference in content, only in the determination where a particular *faṣl* indicates the start of a new chapter or sub-heading. Like the printed edition, the Tunisian manuscript contains forty chapters, and these are listed at the start of the text.

Printed editions of the medium or short recensions of *Shams al-maʿārif* are nearly non-existent, but the Tunisian Bibliothèque Nationale holds complete manuscripts of both. *Shams al-maʿārif al-wusṭá*, BN Tunis 7401, was produced in

1137/1724-25, but no name is given for the copyist. The handwriting is "Eastern." The text is approximately one-fifth as long as the long recension. *Shams al-maʿārif al-ṣughrá*, BN Tunis 6711, was produced by Muḥammad ibn Aḥmad b. Muḥammad al-Kātib, and is written in a "Mashriqī" hand. No date is given. At 210 folios, it is still several times longer than the oldest copy of *Shams al-maʿārif*, which contains only sixty folios. An initial comparison, based on the number of pages, lines per page, and average number of words per line indicates that the text is approximately one-seventh as long as the long recension. These latter two manuscripts will provide an excellent basis of comparison with the long recension, particularly to determine what was considered most essential to the text.

Besides the various editions (and translations) of *Shams al-maʿārif al-kubrá*, the most widely printed of al-Būnī's writings is *Manbaʿ uṣūl al-ḥikmah*, also known as *Miftāḥ uṣūl al-ḥikmah* (Key to the Foundations of Wisdom). This is a collection of four separate texts: *al-Uṣūl wa-al-ḍawābiṭ*, *Bughyat al-mushtāq fī maʿrifah waḍʿ al-awfāq*, *Sharḥ al-barhatīyah al-maʿrūf bi-sharḥ al-ʿahd al-qadīm*, and *Sharḥ al-Juljulūtīyah al-kubrá*. The edition examined for the current study was published in Beirut in 1421/2000 by the same company that printed the 1420/2000 edition of *Shams al-maʿārif al-kubrá*.[208] Even the covers of the two books are nearly identical. Similarly, both are well organized, with each having a comprehensive table of contents at the back clearly listing chapters and sub-sections.

As the title suggests, *al-Uṣūl wa-al-ḍawābiṭ* is intended to impart the basics to the beginner. This makes it an excellent source for a basic overview of al-Būnī's views and practices. The text is primarily dedicated to the manufacture and use of magic squares. Consisting of fifty-seven pages, it is about one-tenth the size of the long recension of *Shams al-maʿārif*. *Al-Uṣūl wa-al-ḍawābiṭ* still mentions many sources of power familiar from other works by al-Būnī, such as Arabic letters, heavenly bodies, angels, jinn, and the Names of God. The reduced length and narrower focus make it much easier to read and more concise than *Shams al-maʿārif*. In addition to the printed version, reference will also be made to BN Tunis 661, copied in 1294 AH/1877 CE by Muḥammad al-Manūbī al-Firātī.

The next text in *Manbaʿ uṣūl al-ḥikmah*, *Bughyat al-mushtāq fī maʿrifah waḍʿ al-awfāq*, is much shorter. It is only ten pages long, and is focused on certain technical issues in the construction of magic squares.

Sharḥ al-barhatīyah al-maʿrūf bi-sharḥ al-ʿahd al-qadīm is another short treatise, only twenty-three pages long. It deals with twenty-eight non-Arabic Names of God which are said to come from ancient sources. Each of these Names is associated with one of the Ninety-Nine Beautiful Names of God. Since there are twenty-eight Names, they are also each connected to a particular Arabic letter and to a particular mansion of the moon.[209] The name *al-Barhatīyah* refers both to this list as a whole and to the first of the Divine Names listed.

At 232 pages, *Sharḥ al-Juljualūtīyah al-kubrá* is the second longest treatise attributed to al-Būnī, and about two-fifths the size of *Shams al-maʿārif*. The text is an extensive commentary on two different but related poems: *al-Ṭarīqah al-kubrá* (The Long Path) and *al-Ṭarīqah al-ṣughrá* (The Short Path). The latter consists of 70 lines, and the former of 434. "The Long Path" is a grand variant of "The Short Path," and *Manbaʿ uṣūl al-ḥikmah* gives extensive commentary on both. The "luminous letters" (discussed below) figure prominently in this interpretation. The "Short Path" corresponds (at least in part) to a poem in chapter 12 of *Shams al-maʿārif*.[210] The rhyme and meter are the same, and several lines appear in both texts. However, the order of lines is not always the same, and at seventy lines the "Short Path" is longer than the poem of fifty-nine lines in *Shams al-maʿārif*.

The commentary on both of the poems consists of instructions on how to use the invocations themselves (or individual lines from them), along with similar instructions for the constituent elements of those lines. For example, the first line of "The Short Path" refers to the *Basmalah*, so the commentary describes the special properties of the *Basmalah* itself, as well as those of the Names of God in the *Basmalah* (*Allah*, *al-Raḥmān*, *al-Raḥīm*) and those of the Arabic letters which make up the phrase (*bāʾ-sīn-mīm-alif-lām-hāʾ-rāʾ-ḥāʾ-nūn-yāʾ*).[211]

Finally, there are two shorter treatises which have been consulted based solely on manuscripts from the Tunisian Bibliothèque Nationale. The first is *Tartīb al-daʿwāt* (The Ordering of Invocations) (BN Tunis 9581). The copyist was Yūsuf ibn Muḥammad, and he produced the manuscript in 1007 AH/1598-99 CE. The hand is "Mashriqī." The text itself is fairly short (thirty-three folios) and primarily consists of a discussion of the Beautiful Names of God, divided into ten groups—nine of 10 Names each, and one of 9 Names. While such groupings are also seen in chapters 21-30 of *Shams al-maʿārif al-kubrá*, the particular groupings are different. (See below, chapter seven, for more information.)

A final text from the Tunisian Bibliothèque Nationale is *Kitāb laṭāʾif al-ishārāt fī al-ḥurūf al-ʿālīyāt*, MS 9755. The manuscript is dated 1023 AH/1614-15 CE and the handwriting is certainly Mashriqī; the catalog describes it as "Egyptian." Notes in the front and back flaps suggest that the manuscript was put to good use. The frontispiece contains a list of the Beautiful Names of God with their *abjad* values, as well as several magic squares. There are also occasional additions in the margins, including a full paragraph added after the last page (apparently taking up a subject from earlier in the text).

Like *Tartīb al-daʿwāt*, *Kitāb laṭāʾif al-ishārāt* is a short (62 folios) and narrowly focused text. Other than some incidental references to other topics, the book is solely concerned with the Arabic alphabet. The latter part of the book is entirely devoted to studies of individual letters.

It is particularly noteworthy in the uses it prescribes for particular letters. Much more so than other texts in al-Būnī's corpus, *Kitāb laṭāʾif al-Ishārāt* recommends specific magical cures for specific pains and ailments, rather than generalized protections and cures. It even includes a list of the different parts of the body and how they correspond to different letters and constellations of the zodiac.[212]

Chapter Five: Magical Means and Methods in al-Būnī's Corpus

Introduction

Having established the context for al-Būnī's works and before going on to the specific uses of Islamic symbols in that corpus, it is necessary to provide an overview of how they are used. In the chapters to come several rituals, tools, and forms will be referred to frequently. These have various connections to Islamic belief and practice and to earlier practices of Muslim and non-Muslim magicians. Specifically, these are Islamic (particularly Sufi) devotional practices, spiritual beings of various types, and magic squares and similar matrices.

Sufi Devotions: Remembrance, Retreat, and Prayer

Besides using religious symbols for power, al-Būnī's corpus also couches their use in religious terms such as *duʿāʾ*, *dhikr*, *khalwah*, and *riyāḍah*. *Duʿāʾ*—prayers or invocations to God or His angels—are common throughout al-Būnī's corpus. Often, these are referred to as *adiʿīyah mustajābah*—"prayers which are answered." Many of the invocations described specifically require ritual purity, fasting, spiritual retreats, or even making donations to the poor in order for them to operate.[213]

Dhikr—recitation and remembrance of God—is praised in the corpus as the "highest discipline of worship." More specifically, such recitation of pious phrases, Names of God, or names of angels is used for specific ends, either on its own or in conjunction with retreats or other ceremonies.

Riyāḍah and *khalwah* describe solitary retreat—a practice associated with Islamic mysticism since the earliest ascetics and Sufis, often in imitation of the Prophet's example. In al-Būnī's corpus, these terms take on additional meaning. They still mean solitary retreat, often with particular disciplines attached. These may include the wearing of particular clothes, fasting of various degrees (i.e., eating very little to nothing, or only certain things), or particular forms of *dhikr*. In the corpus, however, the goal is not so much personal spiritual development as it is the achievement of particular ends. Very often, this involves forcing an encounter with a spirit (sometimes a jinn, but also possibly an angel) and enlisting its assistance. What in Sufi practice had been a discipline to subdue the individual (base) soul—the *nafs*—became a method of subduing spirits outside the individual, that is to say, the *rūḥānīyāt*.

Spirits

The importance of different spirits in al-Būnī's corpus has already been alluded to. Long before the seventh/thirteenth century, even before the advent of Islam, the manipulation and command of spirits was a significant part of magical practice throughout the Mediterranean. Ancient Greek amulets commanded *daemons* or gods; Egyptian magicians called on their own gods; Jewish amulets commanded angels. The purveyors and users of these magical tools lived in a "demon-haunted world," to steal a phrase from Carl Sagan. Demons and other spirits could harm or could be compelled to help. Even angels could be compelled to assist the magician.

Many aspects of this worldview and practice did not change with the advent of Islam. The Quran itself mentions various spirits—angels, jinn, and *shayṭāns* (devils).[214] Furthermore, belief in such entities was an article of faith in Islam from early on.

As mentioned earlier, Ibn al-Nadīm claimed that both "blameworthy" and "praiseworthy" magicians performed their operations by commanding devils, jinn and other spirits. The only major difference was whether they propitiated these spirits with evil acts or compelled them to serve through spiritual disciplines and the Names of God.[215] Angels, devils, jinn, and other spirits are found throughout al-Būnī's corpus, though there are no books or chapters specifically devoted to them. Frequently these spiritual beings—including angels, jinn, and others—are discussed as a means to an end: it is through them that the magician's ends are accomplished, and these spirits are made to serve through the operations that will be detailed here in the succeeding chapters. Such spirits are frequently described as "servants" of particular Names of God or Arabic letters. Malign spirits, particularly devils and jinn, are also present as causes of trouble—something to be kept away or protected from.

Angels

The powers of angels' and spirits' names are mentioned alongside discussions of the Ninety-Nine Beautiful Names of God in al-Būnī's corpus.[216] Those Names of God also have angels specifically associated with them—and very often, an entire hierarchy of angels below them.[217]

The most commonly mentioned angels in al-Būnī's corpus are the four archangels: Gabriel (*Jibrāʾīl* AKA *Jibrīl*), Michael (*Mīkāʾīl*, AKA *Mīkāl*), *Isrāfīl*, and *ʿIzrāʾīl*. Their names are frequently written on talismans, and incantations are addressed to them.[218] These are names well known from Islamic angelology. Gabriel, of course, is the messenger of God, who brought God's revelation to Muḥammad. Mīkāʾīl is one of many variants on the Quranic angel Mīkāl, or the Biblical Michael.[219] ʿIzrāʾīl is the angel of death, and Isrāfīl is the angel who will blow his trumpet on Judgment Day to raise the dead.[220]

Many others are named in al-Būnī's corpus, either as rulers over different spheres of creation or—more importantly for the current study—as agents to be appealed to (or compelled) for assistance. Also, there are numerous discussions on how to produce names of angels. At the end of chapter forty of *Shams al-maʿārif al-kubrá*, it is explained that every letter has servants from both the "high" and "low" angels. In the discussion of letters in *Sharḥ al-Juljulūtīyah al-kubrá*, a "servant angel" is given for each letter, as are 2-5 *iḍmār* (hidden names). Both sets of names are meaningless.[221] Chapter thirty-eight of *Shams al-maʿārif* also gives the name of the servant and the angel of each letter in turn. Most often, regardless of what the specific instructions are for the body of the name, they all end in *-īl*.[222]

Innumerable names of angels are given, and most are meaningless and awkward-sounding in Arabic. However, the use of any language other than Arabic spells disaster for the magician or summoner who wishes to use angels. Doing so will call the wrong angel—specifically, the one associated with the foreign word.

Devils

Many talismans and invocations are directed against devils. However, the nature and power of such beings is implied, rather than being discussed openly. Some of the most frequent phrases in this context are: protection against "the whisperings/temptations of devils," against "every rebellious devil" (*kull shayṭān rajīm*), or "against every devil or sultan" (*min kull shayṭān wa-sulṭān*). In these stock phrases, it is implied that devils may harm either body or soul, and that there are means to protect against them.

One threat particularly worthy of mention is the *qarīnah* (pl. *qarāʾin*). While the Quranic meaning of the world is simply a "companion" (usually a companion devil that tempts one to evil), modern ethnography describes the *qarīnah* as a child-stealing demon, much like Lilith in Jewish folklore.[223] It is clearly this latter use, rather than any temptress, that is indicated in different charms to protect against the *qarāʾin*. The particular defenses against these demons will be taken up in the following chapters.

Jinn

Jinn occupy a middle ground in al-Būnī's corpus. They have the ability both to harm and to help. On the one hand, many of the amulets and incantations in the corpus are for protection against the jinn just as others are intended to protect against devils. On the other, jinn may also be compelled to serve. The most common instructions for obtaining the services of a jinn in al-Būnī's corpus involved taking the numerical values of the letters of the jinn's name and inscribing those into a magic square.[224]

"Servants" and Other "Spiritual Beings"

In addition to angels, jinn, and devils much more generalized "spiritual beings," "servants," "lower spirits," "higher spirits," and the like are described throughout al-Būnī's corpus. Many of these are tied in some way to individual letters, Names of God, or stars and have no other distinguishing characteristics. Their names and associations are described solely in order to command and use them. Often they are referred to by such indistinct terms as "spirits" (*rūḥānīyāt*) or "servants" (*khuddām*). Illnesses may also be personalized. For instance, instructions are given on how to kill an *ʿāriḍ* (misfortune or fit). That same spirit can also be made to serve.[225]

Such indistinct spirits may be the means by which divine or heavenly power is utilized. The influence of the stars, for instance, is mediated through spirits (of an undefined nature).[226] Talismans based on the stations of the moon similarly enlist the aid of the "high" and "low" spirits, though it is unclear just who or what they are. Methods are described to obtain assistance from "the servant of the Two Holy Names"—particularly with regard to money.[227] While it would be logical to assume that this "servant," being attached to Divine Names, is an angel, it is far from certain.

Different tables of the "seven signs" (on which, more later) also list a set of "servants" associated with the different signs. Winkler has attempted to correlate these "servants" with demons and other spirits throughout Arabic folklore, demonology, and occult literature.[228] In chapter thirty-four of *Shams al-maʿārif*, there are complicated rules for deriving the name of a "servant" for each letter based upon alphabetical and numerical manipulations of the letter's own name and the numerical values associated with it and these constituent letters. Through these manipulations, the letters and their associated magic squares and Latin squares are seen as representing the name of the particular angel or "servant." It is by these obscure symbols that these spirits are to be addressed, rather than by their "proper" names.

In *al-Uṣūl wa-al-ḍawābiṭ*, the names of spiritual "helpers" or "servants" are discovered through the Balance of Letters.[229] Letters of the name of the magician (*al-ṭālib*), the object to be influenced (*al-maṭlūb*), and the action (*al-ʿamal*) are manipulated to determine the name of the appropriate "servant." Then, through the act of writing, the "servant" is given its particular task.[230]

Magic Squares and Other Matrices

One magical element not mentioned by Ibn al-Nadīm and not common in pre-Islamic magic is the use of squares or matrices—called *awfāq* (sing. *wafq*) in al-Būnī's corpus. The differences between various squares are explained in detail in the eighth section of *al-Uṣūl wa-al-ḍawābiṭ*. Such matrices (usually squares) can be numerical (*ʿadadīyah*), alphabetical (*ḥarfīyah*), or verbal (*lafẓīyah*). Later, a "mixed" (*mushtarikah*) square is mentioned as a possibility.[231]

A "numerical square" is more commonly known in English as a "magic square." In such a matrix, a set of numbers are arranged so that they will add up to the same sum horizontally across every row, vertically down every column, and in some cases even diagonally. The earliest treatises on their construction were written in the third/ninth century, but these dealt with them solely as a mathematical problem.[232]

There are disputes over the earliest appearance of such squares in occult writings of the Islamic world. Francis Maddison and Emilie Savage-Smith claim that the first Arabic magic square comes from the Jābirian corpus,[233] while Schuyler Cammann asserted that the earliest known Islamic magic squares are found in the *Rasāʾil Ikhwān al-Ṣafāʾ*.[234] Since the dating of both texts are themselves subject to debate, it is sufficient here to note that magic squares are found in Arabic occult literature shortly after their appearance in mathematical texts.

Al-Būnī's corpus contains magic squares of varying complexity. The smallest are third-order, that is to say they have three rows across and three down for a total of nine cells. Others are significantly more complex. *Bughyat al-mushtāq fī maʿrifat waḍʿ al-awfāq* includes instructions on how to construct magic squares of increasingly greater difficulty, up to an order of ten (i.e., ten rows and ten columns).[235]

Alphabetical squares, also known as Latin squares, were an innovation first found in al-Būnī's corpus. In such squares, letters are arranged in such a way that no row or column is repeated; the numerical value of the letters is irrelevant. In the corpus, this is most frequently used to write out one of God's Beautiful Names or some pious phrase (e.g., the *Basmalah* or another Quranic phrase). Without the need for complex arithmetic, these can be much larger than magic squares. For example, *Shams al-maʿārif* includes a Latin square with twenty-five rows and columns.[236]

As the name implies, a "mixed" square combines letters and numerals, usually with the letters of a name or phrase written across the top line and the remaining cells filled with numerals. Finally, "Verbal" squares include entire words or phrases in each cell. Again, this is most often a Name of God or a phrase taken from the Quran.

These matrices—particularly those which manipulate words or letters rather than numbers—can take a number of different forms. Some squares are turned at a forty-five degree angle, looking more like a diamond. Others are also have a different number of cells in each row or column: some have one more, and some have one less. Rectangles, while rare, are also present.

Throughout al-Būnī's corpus, different matrices are associated with various powers, as will be seen in the succeeding chapters. For example, there are squares for each of the Ninety-Nine Beautiful Names of God, and even one for the seven signs of His Greatest Name. Each of the planets has a particular square as well, and there are squares given for each of the letters of the alphabet, particularly groups like the *sawāqiṭ*. Also, there are squares to command particular jinn or angels.

Al-Būnī's corpus is perhaps best known for its use of different kinds of squares or other matrices, and rightly so. While these have some antecedents in earlier magical literature, the fact remains that the variety of such squares and the multitude of uses for which they are prescribed is unprecedented in the previous literature.

Conclusions

In these forms, the religious milieu of the seventh/thirteenth century and the history of magic come together. Some of the vocabulary of al-Būnī's corpus is clearly religious. Various devotional practices familiar from Sufism are used as means to utilize different powers. The corpus also occupies a world in which unseen spirits are very real actors: they have the ability to harm and must be protected against; they have the ability to help as well, and may be compelled to do so. Most of the denizens of this spirit world are taken from an explicitly Islamic cosmology, drawing on the Quran and tradition. Others are somewhat more ambiguous. The use of them, particularly compelling their assistance, is similar to much of the magic being practiced around the Mediterranean up until that time. Finally, the use of magic squares in earlier occult texts appears to have inspired the use of these and similar matrices with greater complexity and variety.

Chapter Six: Numbers and Arabic Letters in al-Būnī's Corpus

Introduction

The study of Arabic letters and their occult properties is elevated, powerful, and ubiquitous in al-Būnī's corpus. In *Sharḥ al-Juljulūtīyah*, al-Būnī's master al-Khwārizmī is quoted as saying that knowledge of Arabic letters and their secrets is the foundation of knowledge, that it is the greatest, strongest, and most praiseworthy science, and furthermore that it is reserved for the wise and the pure.[237] Similarly, in *al-Uṣūl wa-al-ḍawābiṭ* it is asserted that the "science" of transformations effected by the letters of a name can only be understood by a limited few and their students.[238]

Letters are of primary importance in *al-Uṣūl wa-al-ḍawābiṭ*, and are called the most exalted things in all creation.[239] As discussed below, numbers are intimately connected with Arabic letters, and numbers are described as a great and subtle spiritual power *Shams al-maʿārif.*[240] According to *Kitāb laṭāʾif al-ishārāt*, God created the world through the secret of letters. He also planted great power and wisdom in them, including the secrets of His Greatest Name, His speech, and the afterlife.[241] It is claimed in *Sharḥ al-Juljulūtīyah* that anyone who has these secrets revealed to them will achieve all their desires.[242] Meditating on the letters will also reveal great mysteries and wisdom, since all things ultimately proceed from them.[243]

Since the topic here is the originality of al-Būnī's corpus as a set of instructions for using Islamic religious symbols for protection and healing, it is appropriate to address first how and why it is possible to discuss Arabic letters as "Islamic" symbols generally, and specifically in the context of al-Būnī's corpus.

It is almost banal to repeat yet again that the Arabic alphabet is holy in Islam, in part because of the centrality of the revealed Arabic Quran (particularly the "crowing letters" or "luminous letters," which will be discussed in detail later, and in part because of prohibitions of figural imagery in Islamic art (regardless of the fact that such prohibitions were far from universally observed).

In al-Būnī's corpus, the connection is made more explicit: the power and effects of Islamic symbols such as the Names of God and verses of the Quran are frequently directly connected to the powers and constituent letters of these symbols. This relationship can apply in reverse as well, so that letters are given particular significance because of their presence or preeminence in such Islamic symbols. In chapter thirty-one of *Shams al-maʿārif al-kubrá*, one place where the Arabic letters and their special properties are listed and catalogued, it is explained that the secrets of every people are contained in their book, and the secrets of the Quran are contained in Arabic letters.

Besides the large number of instances where the letters themselves are the main subject, letters are connected to virtually every other topic in al-Būnī's corpus. Everything has a name, and all names (including God's Beautiful Names and even the names of the letters themselves) are made up of letters. Throughout al-Būnī's corpus, it is a common assertion that names are connected to and influence the thing named. This also gives power to the name's constituent elements of a name—that is, the Arabic letters which make it up.

Those letters may then establish a link between the thing named and elements such as numbers, Quranic verses, Names of God, or the natural world. With regard to the latter, the Arabic alphabet fortuitously has twenty-eight letters, which makes them evenly divisible among the twenty-eight days of the lunar month (measured by the "stations" of the moon), the four elements (as well as the Elemental Qualities and humors), or the seven days of the week; seven planets; or the "seven signs," as discussed below.

Texts

As mentioned above, the study of the Arabic alphabet is one of the most commonly addressed topics in al-Būnī's corpus, present in at least a dozen texts attributed to al-Būnī, out of approximately sixty known titles.[244] In fact, Arabic letters are such a powerful symbol of his writings that the printed editions of *Shams al-maʿārif* and *Sharḥ al-Juljulūtīyah* published by the Nour Library in Beirut in 1420/2000 and 1421/2000 respectively are adorned on the cover by the "Wheel of Human Existence." This chart, discussed below, displays Arabic letters corresponding with the signs of the zodiac, the elements, and parts of the body.

With regard to the content of the texts examined here, *Kitāb laṭāʾif al-ishārāt* is almost solely concerned with the Arabic alphabet. The latter part of the book is entirely devoted to studies of individual letters. Most (though not all) of these entries describe some magical use of the letters, in formulae which are familiar from other texts attributed to al-Būnī. Unlike the chapters mentioned from *Shams al-maʿārif*, these lists do not cover the entire Arabic alphabet, and there is no discernable organizational principle for those letters which do appear. The actual use of the letters, however, is a relatively minor consideration. The primary focus for the discussion of letters appears to be an explanation of their role in the various spheres of existence. In fact, while the text does include Latin squares and magic squares employing the various letters,[245] most of the book's figures and illustrations are representations of al-Būnī's cosmology.

Seven chapters of *Shams al-maʿārif* are specifically focused on Arabic letters or some group of them,[246] while another six deal significantly with the study of letters as an aspect of some other practice.[247] Chapters 31 and 38 are of greatest interest, since each of these list the entire Arabic alphabet, as well as the combined "letter" *lām-alif.* Their emphases are somewhat different, however.

In chapter 31, much is made of the letters' connection to the four elements and Qualities (a topic to be discussed in further detail below). Most of the time, the operations using Arabic letters are based on or related to their respective elements and Qualities. Each letter is assigned particular elements, Elemental Qualities, and their degrees in each. As will be discussed later, this is a highly nuanced discussion of the topic—in fact, the most highly nuanced discussion of it in al-Būnī's corpus—which allows for various levels of contradiction. In addition, the days and stars corresponding to each letter are given.

In chapter 38, however, the emphasis appears to be more spiritual—literally and figuratively. While some of the letters are assigned their elements and Qualities, all of them have spiritual "servants," an angel, and a prayer, and it is clear that most of the operations described in this chapter are related to these spirit servants of the letters, rather than any intrinsic or natural qualities they might have. It is also worth noting that the two chapters list the letters in slightly different order: while chapter 31 lists them in the same order they are found in a modern dictionary (i.e., *alif, bāʾ* , *tāʾ* , *thāʾ* , *jīm*, etc.), chapter 38 lists the letters in *abjad* order. In fact, chapter 31 is the only place in al-Būnī where the "dictionary order" is used. It may well be that this was selected to obscure the very regular division of the letters into the four elements and/or Qualities by their *abjad* order, but this is purely speculation. A unique aspect of chapter 38 worth noticing is the abundance of what one might call "letter art" in the latter part of the chapter. In the printed editions, the last sixteen entries (*nūn* through *lām-alif*) the letters themselves form part of the sign or square rather than providing matrices for Latin squares or magic squares. In MS Tunis 4920-4921, such letter art is also much more prevalent, though it is found with different letters. While, to be sure, this is not restricted solely to this chapter, it does appear to be more prevalent there than elsewhere.

Shorter discussions of the importance and use of Arabic letters are found in *Bughyat al-mushtāq* and *Sharḥ al-Juljulūtīyah*. Since the former is a brief guide to the construction of magic squares, naturally it is mostly concerned with the importance of numbers and Arabic letters. Lines 60-63 of *al-Ṭarīqah al-kubrá* (The Long Path) of the *Juljulūtīyah* refer to the Arabic alphabet and their powers. In the commentary on these lines, uses are listed for all twenty-eight letters of the Arabic alphabet.

Letters and Numbers

As alluded to earlier, each Arabic letter also has a numeric value. Decimal notation and "Indian numerals" were used in the Arab world since at least the third/ninth century, but still the *abjad* system remained highly important in al-Būnī's corpus. In fact, magical operations were among the few areas where the *abjad* system continued to be used.[248]

The system is called *abjad* because this is how the mnemonic for the order of letters begins. The entire series (in the eastern Arab world) is:

ابجدهوّز حطّي كلمن سعفص قرشت ثخذ ضظغ

(*ABJaD HaWWaZ ḤuṬṬiY KaLaMaN Sa'FaṢ QaRaSHaT THaKHaDH ḌaẒaGH*). In the Maghrib and al-Andalus, the order is slightly different:

.ابجد هوز حطي كلمن صعفض قرست ثخذ زغش

ABaJiD HaWaZ^{in} *ḤuṬiY*^{in} *KaLaMN*^{in} ***Ṣ**a'Fa**Ḍ***^{in} *QuRi**S**aT THaKHuDH* ***Z**a**GHSH***^{in} (Bold letters denote those with different placement in the Maghrib from the rest of the Arab world.)[249] Even though the manuscript was produced in the eastern Arab world, *Kitāb laṭā'if al-ishārāt* claims that the letters in this order, divided into seven words, form the "Holder/Carrier of Power": *A-B-J-D H-W-Z-Ḥ, Ṭ-Y-K-L, M-N-Ṣ-', F-Ḍ-Q-R, S-T-TH-KH, DH-Z-GH-SH.*[250]

This correspondence meant that whole words could be transformed into numbers and vice versa. Throughout the long recension of *Shams al-ma'ārif*, the "numerical" and "alphabetical" forms for Names of God—and even for letters—are constantly distinguished from one another. The language used to distinguish between letters and numbers makes it sound as if there were complete identity between the two. Letters are referred to as the "Arabic form" and numerals as the "Indian form." This language persists even when it is clear that the discussion centers on letters as representing sounds rather than numbers.[251] When a Latin square with the "alphabetical" version is given alongside the "numerical" magic square, the mathematical relationships are the same; they are just written in different notation.[252] For example, *al-Uṣūl wa-al-ḍawābiṭ* contains instructions on how to obtain the service of a jinn by transforming the jinn's name into its numerical value, and from that construct a magic square.[253]

The numerology of a word or name could also be related to the number of letters it had. It was significant, for example, that *Allāh* has four Arabic letters (*alif-lām-lām-hā'*), representing the four elements, the four directions, and the four archangels (Gabriel, Michael, Isrāfīl, and ʿIzrā'īl).[254]

Also, the numerical value of a letter influenced the rituals associated with it. Instructions for inscribing rings and amulets with the letter *ḥā'* (*abjad* value 8) call for it to be repeated eight times.[255] Similarly, the number 5 is important for many operations using the letter *hā'* (*abjad* value 5) in *Kitāb laṭā'if al-ishārāt*. This includes fasting for 5 days, and possibly the use of squares based on the letter which have 5 rows and 5 columns.[256] Similarly, instructions for working with *yā'* (*abjad* value 10) call for the letter to be repeated 10 times on some talismans, or 100 on others.[257] Elsewhere, *Shams al-maʿārif* prescribes that the number of days of retreat for meditation on a particular letter should be determined by subtracting that letter's *abjad* value from 3,030.[258]

The *abjad* values of letters also provide rationales for grouping these letters in various ways. In *Shams al-maʿārif*, one such method is to group them into 9 *marātib* (levels, grades) based on their decimal value: *alif- yā'- qāf- ghayn* (1111), *bā'- kāf- rā'* (222), *jīm-lām-shīn* (333), *dāl- mīm- tā'* (444), *hā'- thā'- nūn* (555), *wāw- sīn- khā'* (666), *zāy-ʿayn- dhāl* (777), *ḥā'- fā'- ḍād* (888), *ṭā'- ṣād- ẓā'* (999).[259] This division is accompanied by detailed descriptions of the first seven and mention of the days, stars, and Names of God associated with eight of them. Along with this description, a talisman is given, based on the *marātib,* that will summon "high" and "low" spirits to achieve one's goals.

It is noted in a few places in al-Būnī's corpus that letters and numbers govern different spheres. The power of numbers is related to the intellect, and that of letters is related to the soul.[260] Both numbers and letters "expose" (*tashshāyir*) each other, but each also "exposes" something different as well. While letters "expose" the physical world, numbers "expose" the spiritual world.[261] For this reason, numbers are said to be more powerful.[262]

While even numbers are good for positive influences, odd numbers have harmful powers, such as the ability to cause an abortion.[263] There are numerous specific examples. Words with four-letter roots are said to be the first in goodness, while those with five-letter roots are said to be the first in evil.[264] Along the same lines, a 4x4 magic square is useful for good actions, but a 3x3 square is most useful for baneful ones.[265]

In addition to the *abjad* values of individual letters, the number of letters in the Arabic alphabet is significant in and of itself in al-Būnī's corpus. The even division of the Arabic alphabet's twenty-eight letters among natural phenomena such as the elements, qualities, humors, seasons, directions, and stations of the moon has already been mentioned. Twenty-eight had also been considered a perfect number in ancient Greek numerology, since it was the sum of the first seven numbers (1+2+3+4+5+6+7=28).[266] Furthermore, it is equal to its half (14) plus its fourth (7) plus its seventh (4) plus its fourteenth (2) plus its twenty-eighth; that is, it is the sum of all the numbers by which it is divisible. It was also seen as the sum of the seven planets, nine spheres of existence twelve zodiacal houses. Twenty-eight was seen as a sign of prophethood in Islamic mysticism.[267]

Also, twenty-eight is the sum of the top row and right column of the *budūḥ* magic square (see below: 4+9+2+7+6=28).

Figure 1: Budūḥ Square, in numbers (left) and transliterated abjad letters (right)

4	9	2
3	5	7
8	1	6

dāl	*ṭāʾ*	*bāʾ*
jīm	*hāʾ*	*zāy*
ḥāʾ	*alif*	*wāw*

The *budūḥ* square is one of the earliest—and still most common—magic squares, and its name comes from the letters on its four corners when written out in *abjad* notation. As can be seen, it is fairly simple mathematically speaking, with only three rows and columns, and a sum of fifteen on the rows, columns, and diagonal. Examples are found not only in al-Būnī's corpus, but in virtually any Arabic text that deals with magic squares as well.

Letters and Names

All names, divine and profane, are made up of letters, and so the manipulation of these names' letters can be important in al-Būnī's corpus. In using letters for magical operations, the names of the practitioner, the object, and the goal all have their special role according to these texts. First, the practitioner should organize one after another the names of the subject, the action, and the practitioner. Then he should break these down into their individual letters to determine the elements involved.[268] According to *al-Uṣūl wa-al-ḍawābiṭ* the practice of inscribing a talisman with the letters of the practitioner's and the subject's names, inscribed in the shape of what is desired, comes from ancient authorities.[269]

Shams al-maʿārif claims that the power of the Ninety-Nine Beautiful Names of God comes from the one thousand letters that make up those Names. A letter need not be the initial one for it to be significant in a Divine Name. For instance, Beautiful Names of God associated with *alif* include *ẒĀhir* and *BĀṭin*, as well as *Awwal* and *Ākhir*. Elsewhere, the Names associated with *dāl* include *WuDūD*.[270] Many other examples abound in chapter thirty-one of *Shams al-ma'ārif al-kubrá*, where the Names of God associated with each letter are listed among the letter's characteristics.[271]

Even the names of the Arabic letters themselves have names which were significant in al-Būnī's operations. In particular, letters spelled out with three Arabic letters were considered especially powerful: *alif*, *jīm*, *dāl*, *dhāl*, *zayn*, *sīn*, *shīn*, *ṣād*, *ḍād*, *'ayn*, *qāf*, *kāf*, *lām*, *mīm*, *nūn*, *wāw*. The latter three were especially singled out because each of these was a palindrome—that is, the first and last letters of each were the same.[272]

These names of the letters (and their associated *abjad* numerical value) were also used to find the "spiritual names" of letters. Specifically, the numerical value of the letter's name was translated into letters representing the decimal values of its sum, then the original letter was added as a prefix and *-īl* as a suffix. For example, the spiritual name of *alif* was *Aqyā'īl*. The numerical value of *alif* is 111: 1+80 +30, so the "decimal *abjad*" version would be 100 (*qaf*) +10+1. Adding the prefix *'a* and the suffix *-īl* to *qyā* makes *Aqyā'īl*.[273]

Letters, Elements, and the Balance

One of the most involved methods for deriving the nature of a thing from the letters of its name in al-Būnī's corpus is the "science of the Balance" (*'ilm al-mīzān*). Based on this system, it is explained in *Laṭā'if al-ishārāt* that all things have the natures they do because of the properties with which God endowed them through the letters of their names.[274] Similarly, the use of letters or numbers for a particular purpose depends on the nature and elemental makeup of those letters.[275] Even heavenly bodies and elements of the Neoplatonic spheres such as the sun, the moon, spirit, and soul all derive their Qualities from their names.[276]

The principles behind the Balance of letters originated in Pythagorean "arithmology" and particularly the cosmology of Plato's *Timeus*.[277] This is supported by the many citations of discussions of ancient Greek authorites such as Aristotle, Pythagoras, Democritus, and "Divine Plato" in discussions of the special properties of Arabic letters in *al-Uṣūl wa-al-ḍawābiṭ*.

The "science of the Balance" was first fully articulated in Arabic in the works attributed to Jābir ibn Ḥayyān (fl. 3rd/9th century).[278] These texts mention several different balances: those of the Intellect, Soul, Nature, Form, the spheres, the planets, the Elemental Qualities, animals, vegetables, and minerals. The "balance of the letters" was a method by which each letter of the Arabic alphabet was assigned an element so that the balance of elements in a thing could be determined by the balance of these elements in the letters of its name.[279] The Jābirian corpus described various "natural sciences" for which the Balance could be used: alchemy, medicine, poison, the special properties (*ʿilm al-khawāṣṣ*) of materials, the manufacture of talismans, and the artificial creation of life (such as the homunculus).[280]

Discussions of the "Balance" in the Jābirian corpus and al-Būnī's relied on the understanding of the elements, Qualities, and humors in Aristotelian physics. According to this system, materials are made up from combinations of the four elements (earth, water, fire, air)—or, alternately, the four elemental qualities (hot, cold, wet, dry). This also corresponds to the four humors of Galenic medicine, namely black bile, phlegm, yellow bile, and blood, as laid out on the table in Figure 2: Elements, Qualities, and Humors.

Figure 2: Elements, Qualities, and Humors

Humor	Element	Qualities
Yellow Bile	Fire	Hot, Dry
Blood	Air	Hot, Wet
Black Bile	Earth	Cold, Dry
Phlegm	Water	Cold, Wet

Since there are twenty-eight letters in the Arabic alphabet, this allows each element or quality to have exactly seven letters. The division of letters among the elements or Qualities comes from setting up the four columns and seven rows, and then writing out the alphabet in *abjad* notation. This is deliberate, as explained in *Bughyat al-mushtāq.*[281] This divides letters into the following groups: 1(*alif* group): *alif, hāʾ, ṭāʾ, mīm, fāʾ, shīn, dhāl*; 2 (*bāʾ* group): *bāʾ, wāw, yāʾ, nūn, ṣād, tāʾ, ḍād*; 3 (*jīm* group): *jīm, zāy, kāf, sīn, qāf, thāʾ, ẓāʾ*; 4(*dāl* group): *dāl, ḥāʾ, lām, ʿayn, rāʾ, khāʾ, ghayn.*

Some versions of the system assigned letters different "grades" or "levels" as well as particular elements, though not every division of letters among the elements included these levels. Wherever they did, however, they corresponded to the arrangement presented below and in Figure 3: Levels and Abjad Values of Arabic Letters. The *martabah* was more powerful than the *darajah*, which was more powerful than the *daqīqah*, which was more powerful than the *thānīyah*, which was more powerful than the *thālithah*, which was more powerful than the *rābiʿah*, which was more powerful than the *khāmisah*. This order is found in *Shams al-maʿārif*, *Bughyat al-mushtāq*, and earlier in the Jābirian corpus.[282] The relative value of letters on different levels of the scale is more specific in *Shams al-maʿārif*: each letter in the *martabah* is equivalent to 7 of the *darajah*, 12 of the *daqīqah*, or 18 of the *thānīyah*. Nothing is said about the last two levels, the *rābiʿah* and the *khāmisah.*[283] These levels for each of the different groups of letters are laid out in Figure 3, below.

Figure 3: Levels and *Abjad* Values of Arabic Letters

	dāl group	*jīm* group	*bāʾ* group	*alif* group
First Level *martabah* (grade)	*dāl* (4)	*jīm* (3)	*bāʾ* (2)	*alif* (1)
Second Level *darajah* (degree)	*ḥāʾ* (8)	*zāy* (7)	*wāw* (6)	*hāʾ* (5)
Third Level *daqīqah* (minute)	*lām* (30)	*kāf* (20)	*yāʾ* (10)	*ṭāʾ* (9)

Fourth Level *thānīyah* (second)	*ʿayn* (70)	*sīn* (60)	*nūn* (50)	*mīm* (40)
Fifth Level *thālithah* (third)	*rāʾ* (200)	*qāf* (100)	*ṣād* (90)	*fāʾ* (80)
Sixth Level *rābiʿah* (fourth)	*khāʾ* (600)	*thāʾ* (500)	*tāʾ* (400)	*shīn* (300)
Seventh Degree *khāmisah* (fifth)	*ghayn* (1000)	*ẓāʾ* (900)	*ḍād* (800)	*dhāl* (700)

Unfortunately, as can be seen below in Figure 4: Assignment of Elements and Qualities to Letter Groups, different texts in al-Būnī's corpus—or even different chapters of the same text—divide the letters up differently. *Kitāb laṭāʾif al-ishārāt* , for example, gives two further tables that assign the letters to different elements and Qualities—though the groups remain the same.

Figure 4: Assignment of Elements and Qualities to Letter Groups

	dāl group	*jīm* group	*bāʾ* group	*alif* group
Quality (Jābir ibn Ḥayyān) [284]	Wet	Dry	Cold	Hot
Element (*Bughyat al-mushtāq;*[285] *al-Uṣūl wa-al-ḍawābiṭ)*[286]	Water (Cold, Wet)	Air (Hot, Wet)	Earth (Cold, Dry)	Fire (Hot, Dry)
Quality (*Laṭāʾif al-isharāt)* [287]	Cold	Dry	Wet	Hot
Quality (*Laṭāʾif al-isharāt)* [288]	Cold (First level of spirit)	Wet (Last level of spirit)	Dry (Last level of soul)	Hot (First level of soul)
Element (*Laṭāʾif al-isharāt)* [289]	Water	Fire	Earth	Air

Chapter thirty-one of *Shams al-maʿārif* probably contains the most nuanced discussion of the division of the letters by their Qualities. Firstly, the chapter mentions dissenting opinions regarding the nature of letters (where appropriate). For instance, it describes *bāʾ* as cold and dry, but mentions that some others regard it as hot and wet.[290] Another example is its mention that *shīn* has different Qualities in the Maghrib than among Indians and Greeks.[291] This may well be related to the different *abjad* order used in the Maghrib, since *shīn* is one of the letters that has a different position and value in Maghribi *abjad* reckoning, versus that in the East.

The chapter also assigns some letters a mixed nature. *Jīm*, for example, is said to be hot and wet—in the first level of heat, but not too far removed from being hot and dry. *Sīn* is hot and wet, but its wetness is "mild" and it is associated with both the elements earth (hot and wet) and water (cold and wet).

Wāw is dry, but has some wetness in it. *Lām-alif* is a water letter, but has some dryness in it.[292]

For the sake of thoroughness, one further variation must be mentioned. At the beginning of chapter nineteen of *Shams al-maʿārif*, another system of dividing the Arabic letters into the four elements is proposed. However, the order is random. The first group (letters of fire) follow dictionary order: *alif*, *bāʾ*, *tāʾ*, *thāʾ*, *jīm*, *ḥāʾ*, *khāʾ*. The next group (water letters) is a bit more confused, even. The first three, then the last four (allowing for the misprint of the second *mīm*) are in dictionary order, though the two halves are not: *lām*, *mīm*, *nūn*, *ṣād*, *mīm*, *ḍād*, *ayn*, *ghayn*. The last group (earth letters) only consists of four letters, and only two follow any recognizable order: *fāʾ*, *qāf*, *sīn*, *yāʾ*. Water is not specifically assigned any letters, though—to give the benefit of the doubt—it could include the ten letters not mentioned anywhere in this section: *dāl*, *dhāl*, *rāʾ*, *zāy*, *shīn*, *ṭāʾ*, *ẓāʾ*, *kāf*, *hāʾ*, *wāw*. Also, a promised "image" explaining all of this is nowhere to be found.

In some parts of the corpus the letters are simply laid out in tables of their elements or Qualities (and sometimes their levels). Elsewhere the theory and practice of the Balance are described in detail. The most lucid explanation of the Balance of Letters in al-Būnī's corpus is in *Bughyat al-mushtāq*. Here the relative values of the different levels are established, as well as the relative values of the elements. According to the text, fire is more powerful than earth, which is more powerful than air, which is more powerful than water. The facing images of the "Balances" actually appear to be arranged in such a way as to balance out the relative values of their letters: for each element (and each group of letters), the *martabah*, the *rābiʿah*, and the *khāmisah* are balanced against the *darajah*, the *daqīqah*, and the *thālithah*, with the *thānīyah* sitting at the balance point.[293]

The images found in the discussion of the Balance of Letters in *Shams al-maʿārif* are less clear. There are four sets of balances, but only two of them have letters described on them, and these letters are far from the whole Arabic alphabet.

In short, there is consistency in the general system, but not in any specific correspondences. This means that before making claims about the natures of letters and the words they make up, it is essential to know what the elemental connections are for letters, according to that particular text (and, perhaps, according to that particular section of that particular text).

Groups of Letters

In addition to their individual significance, Arabic letters are also discussed as groups in al-Būnī's corpus. *Al-Uṣūl wa-al-ḍawābiṭ* gives a list of the letters corresponding to the days of the week. Perhaps not surprisingly, the letter for each day corresponds exactly to the *abjad* value for that day's place in the week (which, except for Friday and Saturday also corresponds to its name in Arabic). Sunday, for example, is the first day of the week, so its letter is *alif*, whose *abjad* value is one. In the list, each day also has its associated star.

Most groups of letters are significant because of their role in the Quran. In *Kitāb laṭāʾif al-ishārāt* , the letters which make up the *Basmalah* (*alif, lām, bāʾ, sīn, mīm, hāʾ, rāʾ, ḥāʾ, nūn, yāʾ)* are called "the most noble letters," and twenty-one folios are devoted to descriptions of each of these letters, along with their uses.[294] Similarly, chapter five of *Shams al-maʿārif al-kubrá* is devoted to the *Basmalah* and the secrets of its individual letters. In *Sharḥ al-Juljulūtīyah*, various other ways of presenting these letters are described. In addition to their individual uses, they are also collected in different ways: in a Latin square of 19 squares, and in the individual Names of God mentioned in the *Basmalah* (*Allah, al-Raḥmān, al-Raḥīm*), collected in a Latin square (Latin rectangle?) 7 cells across and 3 down. They are also the central feature in a circle that "never fails to defend."[295]

Luminous Letters

Another important group of letters are "the luminous letters" (*al-ḥurūf al-nūrānīyah*). These are the unattached letters which appear at the beginning of certain chapters of the Quran. Specifically, they are: *lām, ʿayn, alif, qāf, mīm, yāʾ, kāf, ṭāʾ, ṣād, nūn, ḥāʾ, rāʾ, sīn, hāʾ*.[296] The combinations and related *sūrahs* are as follows: *alif-lam-rāʾ*: 10, 11, 14, 15; *alif-lām-mīm:* 2, 3, 29, 30, 31, 32; *alif-lām-mīm-rāʾ*: 13; *alif-lām-mīm-ṣād:* 7; *ṣād:* 38; *ṭāʾ-sīn: 27; ḥāʾ-mīm-ʿayn-qāf:* 42; *ḥāʾ-mīm:* 41, 41, 43, 44, 45, 46; *ṭāʾ-sīn-mīm*: 26, 28; *ṭāʾ-hā; qāf: 50; kāf-hāʾ-yāʾ-ʿayn-ṣād:* 19; *nūn:* 68; *yāʾ- sīn:* 36.[297] They may also be spelled out the way the letters would be pronounced (e.g. *al-ḥāʾ-wa-al-mīm, al-ṭāʾ-wa-al-sīn*, etc.).[298]

The ninth chapter of *Shams al-maʿārif* is devoted to the special properties of these letters.[299] On the authority of the Prophet, they are described as the root of all that is in the world, seen and unseen.[300] It is also worth noting that the seventeenth chapter is devoted to one group of "luminous letters," specifically *kāf, hāʾ, yāʾ, ʿayn,* and *ṣād.*[301]

While each of the luminous letters begins a Name of God, according to *Shams al-maʿārif* , the text only mentions eleven in the context of the luminous letters: *Allah, Laṭīf, Mālik, Ṣādiq, Rabb, Karīm, Ṭayyib, Samīʿ, Ḥamīd, Qadīr, Nūr.*[302] Missing are any Names for *hāʾ, ʿayn,* or *yāʾ*. Nine of the luminous letters (*alif, lām, rāʾ, ḥāʾ, qāf, mīm, kāf, lām,* and *ṣād)* are supposed to be even better than the other five, as they represent the seven heavens, the Seat, and the Throne.

In contrast, those letters not part of the luminous letters are, naturally, the "dark" letters. These are further divided into the "low" and "lower" letters. The first group consists of *dhāl, wāw, qāf, ḍād, dāl, ghayn,* and *bā'*; the letters of the second group are *khā', shīn, fā', yā', khā', tā ', ẓā',* and *zayn.*[303]

The Sawāqiṭ

Another Quranically-derived group is the "7 *sawāqiṭ*," the letters which are not present in the *Fātiḥah: fā', jīm, shīn, thā', ẓā', khā', zāy*. According to al-Būnī's corpus, these letters have great power for good or ill. Their correspondences to the "seven signs" are given, as are their correspondences to different qualities (hot and wet/air: *jīm*; hot and dry/fire: *shīn;* hot and wet/air: *thā', ẓā', zāy*; cold and wet/water: *khā').*[304] This is laid out not only in *Shams al-ma'ārif,* but also in the discussion of the "Long Path" in *Sharḥ al-Juljulūtīyah.*[305]

The thirteenth chapter of *Shams al-ma'ārif al-kubrá* is entirely devoted to the *sawāqiṭ*. It includes Names of God and Latin squares associated with each of the seven letters. Each of the Latin squares associated with each of the seven letters begins with its assigned letters in the upper right corner and contains no letters other than the *sawāqiṭ*. It must be noted, however, that the chapter is still quite short: only just over four pages in the Beirut, 1420/2000 edition. Along with the Latin squares, are the days of the week and the planet associated with each of the *sawāqiṭ*.

Also, Names of God associated with the *sawāqiṭ* are mentioned both in chapters eleven and thirteen. In chapter eleven, each letter has a single Name of God associated with it. One list corresponds with the list of Names of God associated with these letters in a table of the "seven signs": *al-Thābit, al-Jabbār, al-Khabīr, al-Zakī, al-Ẓāhir, al-Fard, al-Shakūr, al-Shahīd.*[306] Another, more detailed list, gives several Names of God for at least some of the *sawāqiṭ*, along with Quranic support for the use of these Names: *Khabīr, al-Shahīd, al-Shahādah, al-Mushāhid, al-Shuhadā', al-Shurb, al-Shifā', al-Ẓull al-Mudūd, al-Ẓuhūr, al-Ẓu'ūn li-al-Marghūb, al-Ẓāhir, al-Fiṭr, al-Fākihah, al-Futṭūr.*[307] With regard to actual use, however, *Shams al-maʿārif* only mentions the harmful power of the *sawāqiṭ*, explaining how they can punish and inflict pain.[308]

Letters and Stars

Another art for the use of Arabic letters was *zāʾirjah*, the art of correspondences between Arabic letters and the signs of the zodiac. The rules of *zāʾirjah* were based on: the letters' numerical value, their divinatory use (Ar. *faʾl*), their disposition in rhythmic versification (*rajaz*), and their use in Latin squares and (because of the first item) magic squares.[309]

Various tables in *Shams al-maʿārif* assign groups of letters to the signs of the Zodiac. These are the same four groups of seven that were divided among the four elements: 1) *alif*, *hāʾ*, *ṭāʾ*, *mīm*, *fāʾ*, *shīn*, *dhāl*; 2) *bāʾ*, *wāw*, *yāʾ*, *nūn*, *ṣād*, *tāʾ*, *ḍād*; 3) *jīm*, *zāy*, *kāf*, *sīn*, *qāf*, *thāʾ*, *ẓāʾ*; 4) *dāl*, *ḥāʾ*, *lām*, *ʿayn*, *rāʾ*, *khāʾ*, *ghayn*.[310]

This is followed by a table assigning four letters to each of the planets. Saturn: *alif- bāʾ-jīm-dāl*, Jupiter: *hāʾ- wāw- zāy- ḥāʾ*, Mars: *ṭāʾ- yāʾ- kāf- lām*, the Sun: *mīm- nūn- sīn- ayn*, Venus: *fāʾ-ṣād- qāf- rāʾ*, Mercury: *shīn- tāʾ- thāʾ- khāʾ*, the Moon: *dhāl-ḍād-ẓāʾ- ghayn*.[311] The table also assigns Elemental Qualities, days of the week, or metals, or "servants" to some planets, while leaving others without such qualifications.

In similar charts, metals are also associated with letters and with planets—particularly in charts of the *sawāqiṭ*. *Al-Uṣūl wa-al-ḍawābiṭ* specifically asserts that letters and numbers are related to metals and are interdependent, just as the soul is dependent on the body.[312]

As mentioned earlier, the third chapter of *Shams al-maʿārif* is devoted to the connections between Arabic letters and the twenty-eight *manāzil* (stations) of the moon.[313] *Kitāb laṭāʾif al-ishārāt* further explains that just as the moon has 14 stations "above the earth" and 14 "below" it, so do the 28 Arabic letters have 14 with dots, and 14 without.[314]

The stations of the moon, like the signs of the zodiac are a series of divisions along the ecliptic. Only, instead of twelve, there are twenty-eight since the sidereal revolution of the moon takes a little more than twenty-seven days (twenty-seven days, seven hours, forty-three minutes, eleven and a half seconds). Each station in medieval Arabic astrology was identified with a single star, but actually represented one twenty-eighth of arc in the ecliptic (12°, 51').[315] The stations of the moon had their origin in Indian astrology, and were combined with the Arabic folklore concerning the *anwāʾ* stars.[316] The Lunar stations were unimportant for timekeeping, since they were eclipsed (as it were) by the Islamic calendar based on the moon's phases.[317] The continuing significance of the Lunar stations was primarily that employed by al-Būnī: discussions of favorable and unfavorable days under particular stations, along with proper activities for particular days. All this is relevant to the current discussion because, fortuitously, the twenty-eight stations of the moon correspond to the twenty-eight letters of the Arabic alphabet. In chapter three of *Shams al-maʿārif*, each of the moon's stations was assigned to a particular Arabic letter.

The chart summarizing this correspondence also mapped out the relationship between the stations of the moon and the signs of the zodiac: Just as in the night sky, each station of the moon takes up approximately two and one-third zodiacal signs.

Uses

Al-Būnī's corpus mentions all sorts of tasks which can be accomplished with Arabic letters. One can use them for love, for bringing near, for keeping away, for binding tongues, for learning, for keeping away harm and sorcery, for opening treasures, and "whatever pops into your head."[318] As mentioned earlier, due to the nature of the material and the state of the corpus, almost every discussion of the significance and use of Arabic letters must be considered on a case by case basis for each text, and often even for particular sections of each text.

Shams al-maʿārif's thirty-first chapter, *Fī al-ḥurūf wa-mā la-hā min al- khawāṣṣ* (Regarding the letters and their special properties) focuses on the letters' natural properties such as their elemental Qualities and the days and planets associated with them. Chapter thirty-eight, *Fī istakhdām al-ḥurūf wa-khawātihā wa-mā la-hā min al-asrār* (Regarding using the letters and their seals and [regarding] their secrets), focuses more on the spiritual qualities of the letters: the angels and "servants" associated with each one (though, to be sure, Elemental Qualities and the like are sometimes mentioned).

Chapter thirty-two of *Shams al-maʿārif* is devoted to a chart of "The Secrets of the Human World," which lays out the correspondences between signs of the Zodiac, parts of the human body, and letters of the Arabic alphabet.[319] Unfortunately, this chart is useless for determining any relationship between the Arabic letters and the actual uses prescribed for them in adjacent chapters of the text and elsewhere in the corpus. First of all, the letters listed for each sign of the zodiac are not so much individual letters as groups similar to those for each of the elements (see above). Therefore individual letters do not specifically correspond to individual zodiacal signs and their respective parts of the body. Each letter—along with the other six in its group—is assigned to three signs of the zodiac and the parts of the body corresponding to those signs. Furthermore, none of the parts of the body mentioned in the chart correspond to any uses proposed for the Arabic letters in *Shams al-maʿārif.*

Finally, the various versions of this chart in different copies of *Shams al-maʿārif* disagree as to which letter groups are assigned to which zodiacal signs. Half of the signs have different letters assigned to them in BN Tunis 4921 and the printed editions. Specifically, the signs which differ are Libra, Scorpio, Sagittarius, Capricorn, Aquarius, and Pisces. The charts also differ with regard to the elements assigned to each sign, although they do agree on the correspondences between the signs and parts of the body.[320] Though it is of little significance for the reasons outlined above, the Tunis manuscript appears to be more reliable than the printed editions in this regard, since the charts in the printed editions contradict a similar chart.

In the Tunis manuscript, the same letter groups are always associated with the same element, but the printed editions include contradictory charts regarding which letters are assigned to which element.[321] Also, the "Wheel of Human Existence" in the printed editions does not distribute the elements evenly among the signs of the zodiac. In those editions, four signs are assigned to water, while only two are assigned to air. (Three are also assigned to earth and fire.)[322]

In chapters thirty-one and thirty-eight of *Shams al-maʿārif*, there is little in common between the two lists as far as the uses of letters for protective and healing magic. Chapter thirty-one mentions such uses for 13 letters: *lām**, *bāʾ*, *ḥāʾ**, *khāʾ*, *dhāl*, *rāʾ*, *sīn**, *shīn*, *ẓāʾ**, *fāʾ**, *mīm*, *hāʾ*, *lām-alif*. Chapter thirty-eight mentions eleven: *alif*, *ḥā**, *ṭāʾ*, *yāʾ*, *kāf*, *lām**, *sīn**, *ʿayn*, *tāʾ*, *fāʾ**, *ẓāʾ**. Five letters (marked here with asterisks) are held in common between the two lists, but this is almost certainly nothing more than a coincidence.

Chapter thirty-one of *Shams al-maʿārif* gives detailed information on the elemental composition of each letter, as mentioned above. However, this information is only specifically relevant for four cures. *Bāʾ*, a cold and dry letter, protects against illnesses of the blood, and blood is hot and wet. *Dhāl* is a fire (hot and dry) letter, and can cure phlegm, which is cold and wet. Perhaps one of the most interesting uses is of *rāʾ*. The letter is cold and wet (i.e., of water), and if one inscribes it on a sheet of tin and places that sheet under the tongue, it will relieve thirst. *Ḥāʾ* is a cold letter, and can be used to cure hot illnesses, though none are mentioned by name. Chapter eight also mentions that repeating the Names of God beginning with *ḥāʾ* will protect a traveler against heat and thirst. [323]

One general principle that applies in both the above-mentioned chapters is that the uses prescribed for the letters are usually for specific ailments rather than generalized protection. Such generalized protection is only mentioned four times in these two chapters. Interestingly, both chapters claim that *lām* is effective in this regard. In chapter thirty-one, it says that whoever carries a sheet with the letter written thirteen times will be protected from all misfortune. Chapter thirty-eight prescribes cures for all sorts of illness: either rinse the letter's ink and drink it or invoke the "servant" of the letter. Other letters associated with broad power to protect and cure are *ḥā'*, *lām-alif* and *ẓā'*.[324]

For whatever reason, certain problems are mentioned multiple times in one chapter without being mentioned in the other. Chapter thirty-one contains various preventions and remedies for different poisons. *Sīn* will cure poison, *ẓā'* will cure venomous stings and bites, and *fā'* will keep snakes and scorpions out of a house.[325] While less dramatic, chapter thirty-eight has the only cures for headaches in the two chapters: one involves writing and binding the letter *ṭā'*; the other uses the letter *sīn*.[326]

Since chapter thirty-eight is mostly concerned with influencing spirits to achieve one's ends, it should not be surprising that so many of the uses for protection and healing in that chapter involve healing the soul in one way or another. Write the seal given for *alif* on a knife and point it at an epileptic to kill the jinn causing the fit. A ring inscribed with the letter *ḥā'* and the name of its angel will suppress lust in the wearer. Drinking ink used to write ten letter *yā'*"s and every Name of God beginning with it will also cure excessive lust; repeating the letter a hundred times will also cure excessive drinking. A sheep's skin with 20 *kāf*'s written on it will cure whoever carries it from melancholy or fear of spirits. The discussion of *'ayn* mentions a Name of God (*'Ālim al-Ghayb wa-al-Shahādah*, "The Revealer of Secrets and the Witness") which will relieve depression. Writing *tā'* 400 times will keep somebody from "seeing phantoms and dreaming." A figure derived from *fā'* will help a child speak who has not done so yet.[327]

Similarly, in chapter thirty-one, the magic square based on *lām* can protect against fear. A magic square using *khā'* can not only cure literal heart palpitations, but also strengthen the heart of a coward. Writing *rā'* and its numerical value (200) will cure insomnia. A 4x4 square of the letter *hā'* will cure fear of the dark.[328]

Chapter thirty-eight states that every letter has its own prayer, angel, "servant," and retreat (*khalwah*). Chapter forty further explains that every letter has a "servant" from the high and low angels, a charm (*ruqá*), a spell (*ʿazīmah*, pl. *ʿazāʾim*), and appropriate incenses (*bakhūr*).[329] This recalls Ibn al-Nadīm's list of materials common to both "forbidden" and "praiseworthy" magicians, though Ibn al-Nadīm did mention a few other materials.[330]

Arabic letters and their associated numbers may also be used with the "Tables of Life and Death" to determine if a sick person or somebody not present will live or die. Add the day they fell ill or departed, the *abjad* value of the subject's name, their mother's name, the number of days that have passed in the "Arab" month, and 20. From this, keep subtracting 30 until you have a remainder between 1 and 30. Then look this number up on the accompanying tables of life and death; both possible outcomes have 15 numbers laid out in somewhat irregular order.[331]

Unlike the above-mentioned chapters of *Shams al-maʿārif*, *Sharḥ al-Juljulūtīyah* only contains generalized discussions of what each letter is best used for rather than a detailed discussion of particular rituals appropriate for each letter. Some of these uses—though certainly not all—are relevant for protection and healing. Of the twenty-eight letters, sixteen (*bāʾ*, *jīm*, *ḥāʾ*, *ṭāʾ*, *kāf*, *lām*, *nūn*, *sīn*, *ʿayn*, *fāʾ*, *rāʾ*, *tāʾ*, *thāʾ*, *ḍād*, *ẓāʾ*, *ghayn*) have some sort of protective or healing use. Five of these (*ṭāʾ*, *lām*, *nūn*, *sīn*, *ʿayn*) have multiple uses. *Sīn* in particular is noteworthy, since almost all of the uses ascribed to it are for protection and healing, whereas most of the others include many further uses and applications.

The uses to which the letters are put are manifold. As in other texts, the applications of Arabic letters are very specific. Three (*ṭāʾ*, *sīn*, *rāʾ*), for example, are useful for headaches. Appropriately enough, *ʿayn* can treat eye pain, as can *nūn*. Both *jīm* and *thāʾ* prevent and cure fevers. *Jīm*, *ḥāʾ*, and *ṭāʾ* are helpful in traveling. *Jīm* relieves thirst, *ḥāʾ* relieves heat and thirst, and *ṭāʾ* gives strength while walking. Some cures are related to more psychological than physical problems. *Kāf* prevents melancholy, *ʿayn* prevents depression (lit. "tightness of the soul"), and *tāʾ* prevents bad dreams.

Five of the letters (*jīm*, *ṭā'*, *lām*, *sīn*, *ẓā'*, *ghayn*) relate to different women's concerns. Both *jīm* and *sīn* ease childbirth, while *ṭā'*, *lām*, and *ẓā'* will protect children in different ways. *Lām* and *ghayn* also protect against the *qarā'in*—demons that follow women. It kills these demons and keeps them from humanity. While the uses for *nūn* are not specifically restricted to women, it is worth mentioning here, since it undoes witchcraft and the "knots" of witches, just as *lām* and *ghayn* protect against demons.

While those three letters operate directly on spirits, five of the letters' uses are related to the elements, humors, and Qualities. *Bā'* is effective against cold, dry illnesses. *Jīm* relieves thirst and hot fever, *ḥā'* relieves heat and thirst, and *kāf* is effective against [excessive] black bile. Even though neither this section nor any other of *Sharḥ al-Juljulūtīyah* establishes strict correspondence between Arabic letters and particular elements and Qualities, it is impossible to conceive of any arrangement that would make both *jīm* and *ḥā'*, which are in separate columns, both effective against heat and wetness. Similarly, since *jīm* and *kāf* are in the same column, how could one be effective against heat and wetness, and the other against black bile, which is cold and dry?

Some protections and remedies are attributed to the luminous letters as a group. When inscribed on the bezel of a ring, they have many useful properties. Specifically in the realm of healing, this ring will help a woman in labor to deliver immediately. It can cure an epileptic who is having a fit. Similarly, the text recounts how a man drove away the jinni causing his wife's epileptic fit by reciting the luminous letters over her.[332]

Two different methods are prescribed in *Kitāb laṭā'if al-ishārāt* for protective and healing applications of Arabic letters. First, there is a list of the Arabic letters describing their properties and uses. Second, there is an independent system of "spiritual medicine" (*ṭibb rūḥānī*). The individual discussions of the letters in *Kitāb laṭā'if al-ishārāt* are somewhat haphazard. Not all of the letters are included, and those which are do not appear in any particular order.

Like in *Shams al-maʿārif*, some cures are said to work because of the Balance of letters. A ring inscribed with the letter *ḥāʾ* and Names of God associated with it—*Ḥayy* (Living), *Ḥalīm* (Forbearing), *Ḥanān* (All-Merciful), *Ḥakīm* (Wise)—will protect the wearer from fever and can actually be used to cure a fever. This is not so much because of the connotations of these Beautiful Names of God, but because *ḥāʾ* (according to this text, at least) is a cold letter, and its elemental cold cancels out the heat of a fever.[333]

There are also magical protection and cures with little or no explanation or external referent. An 8 X 8 magic square with a sum between 250 and 260 protects against disease and scorpion stings.[334] A ring stone inscribed with five *nūn*'s can cure stomach pains or heart palpitations.[335] The letter *ṭāʾ* can cure headaches if bound to a sufferer.

The book also lays out an entire system of "spiritual medicine" (*ṭibb rūḥānī)*, which is supported with quotations from the Quran and the *sunnah* of the Prophet. This is based, interestingly enough, on the signs of the zodiac and the connections between each sign and the limbs of the body. These connections are explicitly laid out on a chart which follows the introductory text.[336]

The Latin square of *dāl* has a variety of practical uses. It helps relieve chest pain, and (significantly, when the moon is in Scorpio) it can cure scorpion sting. The magic square derived from the letter (4 X 4, with a sum of 34) also will help with scorpion stings. Furthermore, it will cure madness, ease the pain of childbirth, and protect against swords.

Inscribing *wāw* will cure phlegm in the mouth or protect against "quartan ague." Significantly, the *abjad* value of *wāw* is six, and a piece of paper with the letter written on it six times will protect against headaches.

Arabic letters may be used to protect not only the soul, but the body as well. The magic square of *yāʾ* protects against the temptings of Satan as well as hunger (which itself might be a spiritual as well as a physical hindrance).[337] There are many similar uses prescribed throughout al-Būnī's corpus for Arabic letters.

Conclusions

Nowhere is it more evident than in the study of letters that while al-Būnī's corpus relies upon systems of correspondences and relations, the exact relations are not consistent in different texts, editions, or even different parts of the same texts. Arabic letters are connected to the elements and Elemental Qualities, and the letters which are so grouped together are always the same. However, the precise elements and Qualities to which they are connected are not always the same. Similarly, different discussions of the "seven signs" assign each sign an Arabic letter, an angel, a demon, a day of the week, and a Divine Name. However, the angels, demons, days, and Names are not always the same group, and they are not always assigned to the same symbols. Perhaps it is because of these elaborate systems of correspondences that the uses ascribed to letters involve more protections against and cures for specific ailments than general issues of health and well-being.

Approaches to Arabic letters in al-Būnī's corpus are contradictory in another way. Letters are ascribed importance and power because of their role in the Quran or holy names—particularly the Beautiful Names of God. However, many of the actual uses prescribed for the letters operate not by these holy forces but rather by their connection to natural phenomena (as understood at the time), such as the influence of heavenly bodies or the elemental composition of earthly ones. Those uses which look toward the realm of the spirit more often than not command angels and other less holy (and less well defined) spirits in a manner that recalls earlier practices, going back to before the advent of Islam.

Chapter Seven: The Names of God in al-Būnī's Corpus: The Beautiful and the Greatest

Texts and Organization

Shams al-maʿārif declared in several places that one of the text's precious, hidden treasures was the study of the Names of God—both His Ninety-Nine Beautiful Names and His Greatest Name.[338] In fact, these topics are prominent throughout al-Būnī's corpus. From a list of more than sixty works attributed to al-Būnī gleaned from Brockelman and various other sources,[339] at least eleven (including those under study here) deal with the Names of God, including His Greatest Name. Most of these apparently are exclusively devoted to the topic.

With regard to *Shams al-maʿārif*, fourteen separate chapters of the "long recension" deal primarily with the Names of God in one way or another. These chapters provide three full lists of all Ninety-Nine Beautiful Names of God, as well as an entire chapter devoted to God's Greatest Name (on which more later). The text also mentions Individual Names of God in various other contexts. Discussions of the power of letters, for example, also mention which Divine Names they appear in. Similarly, the Names of God are invoked in prayers and talismans throughout the book.

There are some discrepancies in the lists of Names given in different locations, but these appear to be fairly minor. God's Names *al-Shāfiʿ* (The Intercessor) and *Shadīd* (Strong) do not appear in chapter sixteen's listing of the Names of God, but they are among the Names discussed later in the series of *anmāṭ* (modes or ways, sing. *namaṭ*) spread over chapters 21-30. This dispersal of the topic is another indication that *Shams al-maʿārif* is a compilation of al-Būnī's other writings, and that he had addressed the same topic many times in these different works.

Two of the texts collected in *Manbaʿ uṣūl al-ḥikmah* are specifically devoted to poems concerning the Beautiful Names of God. Not only do these poems explicate the Names of God, but they also are claimed to be invocations in and of themselves which can command spirits by their usage of those Names.[340]

The first of these, *al-Barhatīyah*, deals with twenty-eight non-Arabic Names of God which are said to come from ancient sources. Each of these Names is associated with one of the Ninety-Nine Beautiful Names of God. Naturally, since only twenty-eight Names are contained and they are not in Arabic, this list is very different from that contained in the *ḥadīth* attributed to Abū Hurayrah (see below). Furthermore, since there are twenty-eight Names, they are also each connected to a particular Arabic letter and to the planets associated with these letters.[341]

The *Juljulūtīyah* actually deals with two poems: the "Long Path" and the "Short Path." The latter consists of 70 lines, and the former of 434. The "Long Path" is a grand variant of "The Short Path," and *Manbaʿ uṣūl al-ḥikmah* gives extensive commentary on both. The "luminous letters" (discussed below) figure prominently in this interpretation. The "Short Path" corresponds (at least in part) to a poem in chapter 12 of *Shams al-maʿārif.*[342] The rhyme and meter are the same, and several lines appear in both texts. However, the order of lines is not always the same, and at seventy lines the "Short Path" is longer than the poem of fifty-nine lines in *Shams al-maʿārif.*

History of the Names of God

Al-Būnī's extensive discussion of the Names of God in these texts explicitly draws support from the Quran, the *ḥadīth* of the Prophet, and the works of Sufi masters. Frequently, Quranic verses are cited which admonish worshippers to pray to and address God by "His Beautiful Names." The most important *ḥadīth* for al-Būnī's study of the Names of God was attributed to al-Tirmidhī, on the authority of Abū Hurayrah:

> To God belong ninety-nine Names, a hundred less one; for He (the Unique) likes (to be designated by these enumerated Names) one by one; whosoever knows the ninety-nine Names will enter paradise.[343]

This general admonition is followed by a complete list of all Ninety-Nine of the Beautiful Names of God. This tradition (sometimes with the list, sometimes without) was widely accepted and repeated by Sufis such as al-Ghazālī and Ibn al-ʿArabī. Interestingly, Louis Massginon described al-Tirmidhī as the first mystic to display Hellenistic influences and use literary "cabbala" in Islamic mysticism.[344]

Long before al-Būnī's time, the study of the Names of God—particularly their powers and special properties—was closely associated with Sufism. In the fifth century AH/eleventh century CE, Abū Maslamah al-Majrīṭī had claimed in his *Ghayāt al-ḥakīm* that Sufis were able to effect great transformations and conjurations by the Greatest Name of God, and further that Sufis debated amongst themselves as to the legitimacy of this enterprise. For further discussion of these topics, he referred the reader to another book of his that is, unfortunately, lost to us.[345]

Muḥyī al-Dīn Ibn al-ʿArabī (d. 638/1240) is one of the Sufi authorities best known for his meditations on the Names of God. According to him, it is only through the study of God's names that the worshipper gets close to God. It is worth noting that Ibn Khaldūn, in his *Muqaddimah*, specifically accused Ibn al-ʿArabī of practicing the same kind of *sīmīyā'* (letter-magic) as al-Būnī, very probably for just these sorts of speculations.[346]

Ibn al-ʿArabī and other Sufi authorities are cited throughout al-Būnī's corpus in support of studying the Names of God.[347] Ḥasan al-Baṣrī is particularly prominent in *al-Uṣūl wa-al-ḍawābiṭ*.[348] It is also asserted in al-Būnī's corpus that the study of the Names of God—particularly of His Greatest Name—is a discipline taken from the Sufis.[349] Even when specific authorities are not mentioned by name, the approach in al-Būnī's writings to the Names of God corresponds with Ibn al-ʿArabī's advice concerning the study of the Names of God and with the methods for which al-Ghazālī had criticized the Sufis—namely, combining literary study with awaiting divine revelation.

According to al-Būnī, one only acquires knowledge of the Beautiful Names of God through a combination of perseverance and good luck—in contrast to al-Ghazālī's insistence on reason and faith alone.[350] Furthermore, it is also claimed that one finds God's Beautiful Names solely through Divine grace and that each person must find the appropriate Name for himself at a given time within himself.[351]

Nature of the Names of God

One of the most important questions for al-Būnī or any Muslim dealing with the Beautiful Names of God is: What does it mean to have a single God referred to and prayed to by His Ninety-Nine different Beautiful Names? On a purely practical level, there are various lists of the Beautiful Names of God in different parts of al-Būnī's corpus, as discussed above.

Even though there are many Names, al-Būnī's writings assert that they are all joined by something strange and wondrous and furthermore they all ultimately have a single meaning. At the same time, they are different from each other, as each Name has its special properties and characteristics, related to its alphabetical (and therefore numeric) makeup.[352] One set of letters with a special relationship with the Names of God is the so-called "luminous letters"—that is, the unattached letters which precede certain *sūrahs*.[353] *Shams al-ma'ārif* cites Ibn 'Abbās as saying that each of these letters comes from a Divine Name, while citing Abū al-'Āliyah as saying that each of these letters is the "key" to a Divine Name starting with that letter (e.g., alif="Allāh," lām="Laṭīf," etc.).[354]

Furthermore, al-Būnī's writings also refer to the *ẓāhir* (external, visible) and *bāṭin* (esoteric, invisible) elements of the Names of God. Sometimes a Name is referred to in al-Būnī's writings without explicitly stating what that Name is. For instance, it is claimed that *Sūrat Yā-Sīn* contains a Name which would help anybody "be he virtuous or libertine," though it is never spelled out just what this Name is.[355]

Regarding the number of God's Beautiful Names, Toufic Fahd has suggested that the term "ninety-nine Names of God" simply signifies for al-Būnī that there are a great many—perhaps even innumerable—Names.[356] It is true that there are an exceptionally large number of Names discussed throughout al-Būnī's corpus. However, in most instances the listing of

Names is specifically restricted to ninety-nine. This is emphasized when the Beautiful Names of God are divided into groups, as discussed below. Furthermore, the mention of God having "one hundred less one" Beautiful Names in the *ḥadīth* attributed to Abū Hurayrah fuelled speculation in al-Būnī's corpus about what the hundredth Name might be. Different texts report assertions that it is different Names such as *Allah* or *Huwa* (Him). *Kitāb laṭā'if al-ishārāt* explicitly states that The Greatest Name is the hundredth Name of God[357] and the assertion is found elsewhere as well.

As Muḥammad was the "Seal of the Prophets," his name also has special significance. It is asserted in *Shams al-ma'ārif* that Muḥammad's name is the hundredth Name of God.[358] According to *Tartīb al-da'wāt*, writing the Prophet's name fifty-three times after the Friday prayers could preserve one from insanity.[359] In *Shams al-ma'ārif*, though, it is claimed that Muḥammad's name must be left out of a charm, for the mention of Muḥammad's name would then take precedence over the request being made.[360]

Groups of Names of God

As mentioned above, sometimes the Names of God are organized into different groups in al-Būnī's writings. At one point, *Shams al-ma'ārif* organizes the Names into several groups of *laṭā'if* (subtleties, sing. *laṭīfah*).[361] As mentioned above, in chapters twenty-one through thirty, the various Names are organized by their respective *anmāṭ* (modes or ways, sing. *namaṭ*). In each case, the Names collected under a particular *laṭīfah* or *namaṭ* have certain common properties and uses.[362] It should be noted that, while none of these groupings is centered on protection or healing, individual Names in the groups may (in the discussion of the groups themselves) be described as having special properties in these areas. For example, the Name *al-Shāfī* (The Healer) is listed in a group of Names devoted to affection and union between people, yet the same discussion explains how the Name by itself may be used to cure leprosy.[363]

Tartīb al-daʿwāt also divides the Names of God into ten groups (nine of ten Names each, and a final one of nine Names). Furthermore, the Names are frequently discussed in pairs in the text. Finally, towards the end of the text, there is an extensive discussion of a group of ten Names: *al-Shadīd* (The Strong), *Dhū al-Quwwah* (The Holder of Strength), *al-Matīn*, (The Firm), *al-Sharīʿ* (The Path), *al-Raqīb* (The All-Observant), *al-Muqtadir* (The All-Determiner), *al-Qāhir* (The Victorious), *al-Qawī* (The Strong), *al-Bāʿith*,(The Raiser of the Dead), *al-Wārith* (The Inheritor). Taken together, these form the basis of a massive Latin square, 15 squares across and 12 down. Unfortunately, the example in MS Tunis 9581 is incomplete.[364]

The Greatest Name of God

Besides the Ninety-Nine Beautiful Names of God, His Greatest Name was also a topic of great importance in al-Būnī's writings, as in much of Islamic mystical speculation. According to *Shams al-maʿārif*, the Greatest Name is as superior to all the other Names of God as Laylat al-Qadr is to all other nights in the Islamic calendar, or as Friday is to all other days of the week.[365] Ironically, the text also states that insight into the Greatest Name is not something to be written down but rather should be revealed solely by God to the individual.[366]

Al-Būnī's corpus gives conflicting information as to the identity of the Greatest Name. According to these writings, The Greatest Name contains within itself the germ of all the other Divine Names, and even of creation itself. In some places it is asserted that all of the Ninety-Nine Beautiful Names of God are Great,[367] and no one Name is closer than the other to His Greatest Name. It is said to be different for each individual, or even different for the same individual in different circumstances.[368] It is claimed that knowledge of this Name is revealed only by God to the individual; knowledge of it is dependent on one's progress on the Path towards God.[369] Whoever knows God by the unique Name appropriate to his own state and station has learned the Greatest Name that is especially for him.[370]

Even so, some Names are apparently closer to the Greatest Name than are others. In chapters twenty-one through twenty-nine of *Shams al-maʿārif*, al-Būnī takes pains to identify which of the Ninety-Nine Beautiful Names of God contain one, two, or more letters of the Greatest Name of God. This is also mentioned in other discussions of the Names of God throughout the book, though not as regularly or as prominently.[371] Elsewhere, it is simply asserted that the Greatest Name is *Huwa* (He) or *Allah.*[372] In other instances, prescriptions appeal to God's Greatest Name by writing *al-Ism al-Aʿẓam* (The Greatest Name). This latter may well be a case often documented in magical recipes where the practitioner would know what to replace the phrase *al-Ism al-Aʿẓam* with.)

As mentioned earlier, *Tartīb al-daʿwāt* organizes the Beautiful Names of God into groups. One of these groups of Names in is said to be the Greatest Name itself. This is the tenth group of Names, and even though the text says there are ten in the list, the Tunis manuscript only has eight (unless *Dhū al-Jalāl wa-al-Ikrām* counts as two, rather than one as it usually does): *al-Hādī* (The Guide), *al-Khabīr* (The All-Knowing), *al-Mubīn* (The Illuminator), *ʿIlām al-Ghuyūb* (Revealer of the Hidden), *Dhū al-Jalāl wa-al-Ikrām* (The Lord of Majesty and Generosity), *al-Quddūs* (The Holy), *al-Salām* (Peace), *al-Muʾmin* (The Faithful).[373]

According to the corpus, the Quran and the Prophet Muḥammad may also contain the Greatest Name of God as well as being sources for the study of this Name. In *Shams al-maʿārif*, the Greatest Name is said to be taken from *Āyat al-Kursī* [374] (the "Throne Verse" of the Quran, 2:255; see below, chapter eight). Elsewhere, the Greatest Name of God is connected to the fourteen "luminous letters" of the Quran. Specifically, these fourteen letters are each connected with a Divine Name, and these Names can produce the same effects as the Greatest Name of God. In fact, *Shams al-maʿārif* reports that these Names were inscribed on Solomon's ring, with which he subdued the jinn.[375] Elsewhere it is claimed that the opening letters of the *sūrah*s consist of the Greatest Name of God in and of themselves.[376] Similarly, although not the Greatest Name itself, al-Būnī reports that Muḥammad said the Basmalah is as close to the Greatest Name as the white of the eye is to the pupil.[377]

Nor does the Greatest Name of God have to be an Arabic name—or even a comprehensible one. On at least one occasion, the Greatest Name of God is said to be a particular Hebrew phrase: "אהיה אשר אהיה אדון' צבאות אל שד'" (*Ehyeh esher ehye Adonai Tsvuot El-Shaddai*)[378]. Fahd has explicitly connected the Hebrew name *El-Shaddai* with the Arabic *Al-Shadīd* (The Strong).[379]

The Greatest Name was also expressed in a set of indecipherable symbols, commonly (and inaccurately) referred to as "The Seven Seals of Solomon" or "The Seven Solomonic Seals."[380] These symbols are known by various names in al-Būnī's corpus and in the secondary literature. *Sharḥ al-Juljulūtīyah* refers to the seven signs as the "talismans" associated with the *sawāqiṭ* or (collectively) as the "Solomonic talisman."[381] By the early twentieth century, they were also known as the "*Juljulūtīyah* seals" (*khawātim Juljulūtīyah*) in the Maghrib.[382] Here they will simply be called "the seven signs."

Both the "Short Path" from *Sharḥ al-Juljulūtīyah* and the poem given in chapter 12 of *Shams al-ma'ārif al-kubrá* describe the seven signs as representing the Greatest Name of God. In *Shams al-ma'ārif*, the poem is preceded and followed by different discussions of the seven signs as symbols of the Greatest Name of God.[383] Later in the same chapter, an invocation addresses God by His Greatest Name, as represented by the seven signs:

> O, God, I pray to you by the *hā'* from your Greatest Name and the three rods, and the valued *alif*, and the closed; shortened *mīm*, and the ladder and by the four [strokes], which are like a paw with no wrist, and by the divided *hā'*, and the glorified *wāw*, image of Your Greatest, Honored Name...[384]

While, as discussed below, there are numerous variants of the seven signs, this invocation describes them very well (See Figure 5). The only major difference is that instead of the star, an *alif* is mentioned.

Figure 5: The Seven Signs Representing the Greatest Name of God

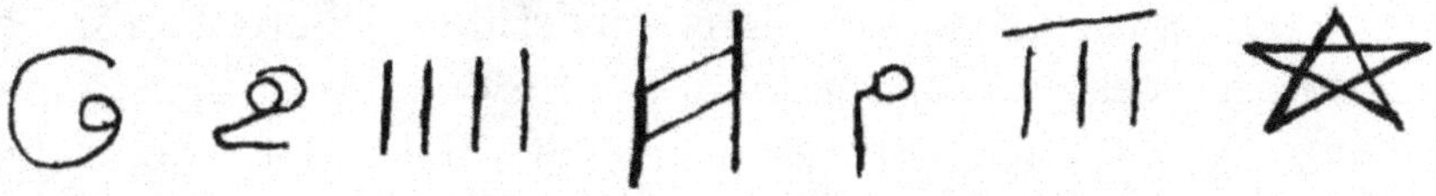

The most extensive scholarship on these signs individually and as a group is still H. A. Winkler's *Siegel und Charaktere in der Muhammedanischen Zauberei*. The second section of this book is entirely devoted to the "seven signs." Here Winkler gives variant versions of the signs, as well as tables of them and their relationships with letters, angels, demons, astrological bodies, and elements and Elemental Qualities.[385]

Winkler presented twenty-three variants of the different basic forms and various combinations in which they may be found, taken from talismans and various texts. Among the texts are eleven manuscripts and printed books attributed to al-Būnī, including the oldest known manuscript of *Shams al-maʿārif*.[386] The history and comparisons of the various individual symbols is fascinating and erudite, if occasionally speculative. The earliest example of the "seven signs" used together is a block-printed talisman from the fourth/tenth fifth/eleventh century.[387]

To be sure, there are variants across different manuscripts (to say nothing of different texts or the difference between such manuals and talismans), but it is possible to identify seven basic symbols, with variant versions of each. Winkler developed the most useful typology of the "seven signs," dividing them into these seven categories: The Star (pentagram, hexagram), The Ladder, The Four Strokes, The Three Strokes (surmounted by another line), The *Mīm*, The *Hāʾ*, and The *Wāw* (usually with a curving "tail").

While Winkler noted many variations of these symbols in different manuscripts, the sources consulted here, especially the printed works, are fairly consistent in their representations of the symbols. In Winkler's presentations, for example, the star is sometimes a pentagram, sometimes a hexagram. In the printed editions of *Shams al-maʿārif* and other texts, the star consistently is a pentagram (usually right-side up, but occasionally upside-down).

The appropriate seven signs may still be different in some circumstances. In *Shams al-maʿārif*, different sets of figures are given for what the Greatest Name of God is that should be inscribed,[388] how it should be inscribed for curses,[389] and how one shaykh said the Greatest Name should be inscribed for good or for ill.[390] Compounding the complication further is the fact that various editions of *Shams al-maʿārif* have copied these symbols differently. Tewfik Canaan has seen this as damning evidence that the copyists themselves do not believe in their efficacy.[391] Such an assertion is too presumptuous. There are many occasions where authors have sincerely believed in what they were writing and believed that it was important to get it exactly right, and yet somehow they have produced divergent copies.

The most interesting division of the seven signs into individual elements presented by Winkler is a table, reproduced from the oldest known copy of *Shams al-maʿārif.*[392] This table gives the Arabic letters, Divine Names, angels, "servants," qualities and days of the week corresponding to each of the signs.

No such table exists in any of the printed editions of *Shams al-maʿārif*; in fact, those editions never deal with the seven signs individually. *Sharḥ al-Juljulūtīyah* does contain such a table.[393] In comparing this table with that reproduced in Winker, once again the idea of correspondences existing is consistent, but the exact correspondences themselves are not the same. The table in *Sharḥ al- Juljulūtīyah* includes nine categories, while the one in the Paris manuscript of *Shams al-maʿārif* includes seven (which, of course, turns the table into a square seven rows across and seven rows down). Of these categories, six are identical in the two texts: the signs themselves, their Arabic letters, Names of God, days of the week, angels, and their other spirits.

With regard to the letters in the table, one interesting fact is that the letters associated with the seven signs are the *sawāqiṭ*. In fact, the table in *Sharḥ al-Juljulūtīyah* is included in that text's discussion of those letters.[394]

As to the last set of spirits mentioned, there are slight differences in the interpretation of these spirits. The Paris manuscript of *Shams al-maʿārif* reproduced in Winkler calls these spirits *khuddām*, a term which literally means "servants," but which Winkler translates as *Planetendämonen* (demons of the planets). [395] *Sharḥ al-Juljulūtīyah* calls them *aʿwān arḍī* (earthly helpers). Doutté described these "servants" as kings of the jinn.[396]

In addition, the Paris manuscript of *Shams al-maʿārif* gives the "natures" (i.e., elemental Qualities) associated with each symbol. *Sharḥ al-Juljulūtīyah* gives the planet associated with each symbol, the symbol's planet, and fumigations associated with the symbol.

Within the categories, there is broad agreement between the two on what to include. However, as with correspondences between Arabic letters and the elements or Qualities, the exact relationships are not identical. Both of them share six of the seven symbol types mentioned above. Even their order is largely the same. The only difference, apart from the stylistic variations which are so common in the presentation of these symbols, is that the sixth symbol in *Sharḥ al-Juljulūtīyah* is the *hāʾ*, while in *Shams al-maʿārif*, that place is held by a second "ladder," without the projections above and below. Similarly, six of the seven angels referred to are identical, as are six of the seven "servants." In these cases, as well, the order is the same and the mismatched items are in the same place in the order.

The letters included in the two tables are identical, which is not surprising since those are the *sawāqiṭ*. The first three letters in the series are paired with the same signs in both texts, while the last four are in a different order.

The same is true of the seven (Arabic) Beautiful Names of God associated with each of the "seven signs," respectively. Since each of these Names begins with the Arabic letter corresponding with the given sign, the order of these Names is matched (and mismatched) in the same order as the Arabic letters. Six of the seven Names of God in the series are the same, except for the Names connect to *shīn*. The Paris manuscript of *Shams al-maʿārif* connects *Shahīd* with the letter, while *Sharḥ al-Juljulūtīyah* connects *Shakūr* with the letter. Naturally, both texts have the same set of days of the week to work with for each table, so those are the same. And in both the list of days follows the same order (going through the charts from beginning to end, starting with Sunday and going through to Saturday).

It is also worth noting that references to the seven signs in *Sharḥ al-Juljulūtīyah* contain minor variations. First of all, there are not always seven; the texts specifically states that a square using the signs may have either seven or eight columns and rows, and examples are given of both. In every instance, the additional sign is a further pentagram; there is usually one on either side of the symbols when they are listed as eight.[397]

Using the Names of God

Al-Būnī's corpus does not discuss the Names of God for their own sake alone, but also for their practical uses. In examining these applications, the most important questions are: who could use these Names, what form did they take, and what ends were they used for?

Who can use them?

It would be natural to assume that, since al-Būnī's writings were widely known and distributed, they were intended for a broad audience. The logical conclusion would then be that anybody with sufficient capacity to read and understand and follow the directions given should be able to use the Names of God in the manner prescribed. However, in some places, these same writings state that particular uses of the Names of God are restricted to the prophets and saints; they are essentially a kind of miracle.[398] Also, the *awliyā'* (saints) are said to have special insight into these Names as a result of Divine grace and inspiration—insight which cannot be achieved through rational study.[399] In a further connection, the number of saints in the world is also ninety-nine, presumably because that is the number of the Beautiful Names.[400]

It is also mentioned in *Shams al-maʿārif* that the prophets have special knowledge of God's Greatest Name and His Hidden Names, and it is through these Names that they were able to work miracles.[401] This access is given them by revelation.[402] At the same time, the chapter on the Names by which Jesus raised the dead (chapter seven of *Shams al-maʿārif*) not only describes how he used these names to raise the dead and perform other miracles, but also how the ordinary reader can use these Names.[403] Elsewhere in the book there are instructions on how to copy and use the Names of God which were on Moses' staff.[404]

Methods for Using the Names of God

Throughout al-Būnī's writings, many different images related to the Names of God are said to be infused with Divine power. In *Tartīb al-daʿwāt*, al-Būnī frequently mentions the *rasm* (image) of each Name, and further states that each Name has its own *rasm* on the "Preserved Tablet [in Heaven]" (*al-Lawḥ al-maḥfūẓ*),[405] in addition to whatever specific images (*rasm*) are mentioned. In chapters sixteen and thirty-nine of *Shams al-maʿārif*, both Latin squares and magic squares are given for each of God's Beautiful Names. There is even a Latin square inscribed with the Seven Solomonic Signs representing the Greatest Name of God.[406]

The numerical value of each of the Names of God, derived from their *abjad* value, was important for both Latin squares and magic squares. The value for magic squares was obvious: the numerical value of each Name determined the content of the magic square.[407] For instance, if a Name's value is divisible by 3, then place a number equal to one-third of the Name's value in the center square. Taking *Allah* as an example, its *abjad* value is 66:

(*Allah* =الله= ا [*alif*:1] +ل [*lām*:30] +ل [*lām*:30] +ه [*hā*ʾ:5]).[408]

At the same time, as with any name, special properties of the Beautiful Names of God could be derived from each Name's constituent letters and the particular element associated with each letter, in proportion to its numerical value. Instructions on how to derive the mathematical value of the Beautiful Names of God were very detailed. The definite articles for Names should not count towards their numerical value,[409] for instance, nor should repeated letters in a series of Names be counted towards their numerical value.[410]

The numerical value of the Beautiful Names of God was also influential in other rituals. When different kinds of *dhikr* were prescribed in al-Būnī's writings, the number of repetitions was explicitly specified, often quite large, and frequently related to the numerical value of the Name in question. One set of instructions specified that the reader should begin by repeating a particular Name of God a number of times equal to the number of letters in the Name or the Name's *abjad* value. The number of repetitions in the next series would be the number of letters in the Name multiplied by its *abjad* value. The last set of repetitions would be equal to the square of the *abjad* value.[411]

Different kinds of *dhikr* were discussed, including *riyāḍah*, recitation of Names at a specific time, during a retreat over a number of days with night-vigils and limited fasting (i.e., eating only certain things and eating very little in general).[412] Other kinds of retreat were prescribed in the corpus as well. *Shams al-maʿārif* explains that each Name has its own particular *khalwah* (solitary retreat) as well as its own servant and its own special truths.[413] The discussion of the Names of God in chapter 39 describes how to conduct a retreat upon particular Names—what to eat, how much to sleep, etc.[414] Many other rituals associated with using the names of God were taken from Sufi practice. Various magic squares, prayers, and other talismans and invocations required retreats to operate, as well as ritual purity and sometimes even fasting or donation of alms to the poor. [415] In other places, the Greatest Name is prescribed to summon some great spirit or angel, but only after extensive fasting and other spiritual exercises.[416]

Purposes of the Names of God

All of these instructions are meant to guide the reader to a successful application of the Names of God. Some uses are very specific and limited, while others are extremely broad. The intended uses affect the Names of God chosen and the way in which they are to be used. *Al-Uṣūl wa-al-ḍawābiṭ* instructs the reader to choose one suitable to one's request, action, and intention of the user.[417] The numerical value of one's own name might even be added to that of the thing desired, after which one would find the Beautiful Name of God that matches the pair of them. As a result of these kinds of instructions, the uses prescribed for the Ninety-Nine Beautiful Names of God are usually related to their literal meanings in Arabic.

For instance, the Name *al-Bāri'* (He Who Creates *Ex Nihilo*) comes from the same Arabic root as the verb meaning "to recover from a disease" and whoever repeats this Name will be cured cure of any illness by God.[418] Similarly, the Name *al-ʿĀlīm* (The All-Knowing) can be used to recover special knowledge.[419] Repeating the Names *al-Sāmiʿ* (The [All-] Hearing) and *al-Baṣīr* (The [All-] Seeing) will cure weak vision and hearing, and may also be used to increase the user's knowledge and understanding.[420]

The Names *al-Ilāh* (a variant of *Allāh*) and *al-Muḥyī* (The Life-Bringer) are said to have great healing power, especially when inscribed in a 7 x 7 square.[421] A magic square made from the Name *al-Bāʿith* (The Raiser of the Dead) has great power to heal any ill.[422] Two Names which appear to be related to beginning or creation—*al-Muṣawwir* (The Shaper) and *al-Mubdiʾ* (The Creator, The Originator)—can be used to cure a headache: write the Names down and bind them to the patient's head.[423]

Not all uses of the Names of God are obviously related to their literal meanings. Inscribing the Names *al-Kāfī* (The Sufficient) and *al-Ghanī* (He Who Brings Wealth) will protect against the evils of men and jinn.[424] A gold ring inscribed with the Name *al-Muqtadir* (The Powerful), or a magic square based on the Name, will strengthen the wearer's spirit and protect against plague, as well as making others obey him.[425] If the Names *al-Sarīʿ* (The Swift), *al-Raqīb* (The Watcher) and *al-Matīn* (The Firm) are inscribed on a door and all the members of the household are obedient to God, those people will be protected from eye injuries.[426]

Tartīb al-daʿwāt's massive Latin square has many uses directly related to protection and healing. It can turn away the evil eye; inscribed on a table, it can protect whoever eats off it from any pain from their food; it can prevent a pregnant woman from miscarrying; it can cure colic; it can cure headache; it can cure epilepsy; it can protect against bad dreams; and, finally, it can cure illnesses for which there is no other cure.[427]

Some other protective uses of the Beautiful Names of God, while not strictly medical, are worth noting. A magic square based on the Name *al-Ṣamad* (The Eternal) will protect from hunger and keep one safe in battle. Among other things, *al-Ṣamad* means enduring hunger, according to al-Būnī.[428] *Al-Ghāfir* (The Pardoner) is another Name which, worn as a magic square, will protect the wearer in battle—in this case, specifically from losing his head (literally, that is).[429]

As with any of the Beautiful Names of God, al-Būnī discusses the practical applications of God's Greatest Name. In different places, it is associated with the power of the prophets. According to *Shams al-maʿārif*, the Greatest Name of God was inscribed on the heart of Adam and on Solomon's ring,[430] possibly the source for the appellation "seven seals of Solomon." It also claims that Jesus was able to bring the dead back to life by the power of the Greatest Name.[431]

The Greatest Name of God can also ward off pain or disease, make friendship fast, tame any animal, find buried treasure, expel, bind, loose, or even set a tyrant's house on fire.[432] Similarly, a Latin square consisting of the seven signs can accomplish anything.[433] Another figure (revealed to al-Būnī in Aleppo) with the seven signs set in the four corners is said to be a source of great power and knowledge.[434]

In addition to these worldly benefits, the Greatest Name of God also will protect the bearer from the "punishment of the grave" when written and carried. The Latin square representing the Greatest Name of God protects against sorcery, but can also accomplish a number of other tasks, such as freeing people from prison or making all things easy.[435] The Greatest Name will bring these blessings to whoever pronounces it, even if that user has no idea of what he has said.[436]

Sharḥ al-Juljulūtīyah lists a number of specific uses for the seven signs representing the Greatest Name of God. While not all are positive or related to healing, many are. Inscribing the seven signs in one way or another can achieve the following ends: protect dead from the punishment of the grave, make sorcery ineffective, undo witchcraft (lit., "knots"—*ḥall ʿuqūd*), cure a fit, cure plague, protect versus man: jinn; the childbed demon; the demons following women; and all misfortune; cure any illness, cancel any witchcraft, remove the evil eye's influence, cure pain, cure hemorrhages, cure the bewitched, cure colic.[437]

Specific Uses: Scorpion Sting and Obstetrics

It is also worth nothing that there are certain problems which a number of different Names of God can cure or protect against. For example, numerous cures are given for scorpion sting throughout the corpus. In *Tartīb al-daʿwāt*, several different pairs of Names are given to cure scorpion sting or ease the pain. In three cases, the pairs of Names should be written, then the Names effaced and then the liquid used to efface the ink should be drunk. In two out of the three, oil is the substance that is prescribed to efface the Names.[438] The prevalence of cures for scorpion sting is interesting, since in many *aḥādīth* it is one of the few ailments which Muḥammad explicitly says that verses of the Quran (or Names of God) could legitimately be used to cure. However, since the *ḥadīth* itself is never mentioned, nor the Prophet cited in such cases, it may be just a coincidence.

Among other specific uses of Names of God, one sees often uses that have to do with childbirth in one way or another. The Names *al-Khāliq* (The Creator) and *al-Muḥyī* (The Life-Giver), when inscribed on a lead tablet and carried by a pregnant woman, will prevent miscarriage.[439] As noted earlier, the uses of Names of God are frequently connected with their literal meanings in Arabic, so it is not surprising that Names associated with creation and giving life would be used in this way.

Elsewhere, the birth of a child is perceived not so much as related to creation and giving life, but to accumulating wealth and power. In the discussion of the Names *al-Rabb* (The Lord) and *al-Mujīb* (He Who Answers [Prayers]) in *Tartīb al-daʿwāt*, they are generally associated with lordship and victory. At the same time, however, not only will repeating them bless one's material wealth in other ways, but they will also make one's wife pregnant.[440]

Such uses were not restricted to people. The Names *al-Awwal* (The First) and *al-Qawī* (The Strong) have a talisman associated with them that will ease a difficult pregnancy for an animal.[441]

The Names of God and Graeco-Islamic "Scientific" Medicine

Tartīb al-daʿwāt is unique in the works examined in that it explicitly discusses how to use the special properties of the Beautiful Names of God in a manner which relies on Graeco-Islamic medicine and the humoral system. One basic example is mention of how frequent repetition of the Names *al-Khāliq* (The Creator) and *al-Muḥyī* (The Life-Giver) allow one to penetrate the deepest secrets of doctors.[442]

Other uses of the Names of God in the humoral system are connected to their alphabetical-elemental makeup. A Name has certain qualities if the letters which make it up have those qualities, or if certain qualities predominate. A Latin square made from hot, moist Names was said to cure illnesses that bring flatulence (*amrāḍ rīḥīyah*) if bound to a patient.[443] Presumably, such Names would be useful because elemental air (*rīḥ*) was also hot and wet. This is somewhat problematic, since it contradicts the notion of balance in humoral medicine. One would expect instead a cold, dry remedy to counter a hot, wet illness.

There are several more examples, mostly near the end of the text. A Latin square of seventy-two Names related to fire (which is hot and dry) will combat all wet, cold ailments; one with Names that are cold and dry will cure illnesses related to phlegm (which is cold and wet); and one with fifty-four Names, all of which are moist, will cure cold and dry illnesses.[444]

Unfortunately, in the Tunis manuscript of *Tartīb al-daʿwāt*, it is difficult to see the connection between the instructions given and the Latin squares presented. It appears that at some point an extra row or column was added to each of the Latin squares, so they do not even have the right number of Names.

Religious Uses

At the same time, while spirits may be commanded to improve the user's worldly lot through the use of the Beautiful Names of God, these Names may also be used to dispel devils who plague the pupil with doubt or temptation[445] as well as those who subject their victims to literal plague. Other Beautiful Names of God would provide concrete benefits in the spiritual realm as well as the temporal.

In the short recension of *Shams al-maʿārif*, it is written that God's forgiveness is granted through His Names: *Huwa Allah alladhī lā ilāha illá huwa, al-Wāḥid, al-Aḥad, al-Fard, al-Watr, al-Ṣamad, al-Rabb, Anta, Anta* [sic]).[446] According to *al-Uṣūl wa- al-ḍawābiṭ*, if one simply repeats *Allāh* enough, then "The Two Kingdoms" (i.e., of this life, and the afterlife) will be revealed, and the user will be able to influence all things (by the grace of God).[447] The long recension of *Shams al-maʿārif* asserts some Names would preserve one on Judgement Day if one repeated them, as alluded to earlier.[448]

Like their uses for protection and healing, the uses of the Beautiful Names of God for these religious ends were also often connected to the literal Arabic meaning of the Names. Repeating the Names *al-Dā'im* (The Everlasting), *al-Qadīm* (The

Ancient), and *al-Azalī* (The Eternal) will help one remain ascetic if one continues to repeat them.[449] In the discussion of the Name *al-Rashīd* (He Who Directs), *Shams al-maʿārif* recommends carrying a Latin square inscribed with the Name so that God will correct the carrier's state both internally and externally.[450]

Sometimes the texts go so far as to discuss the Names of God as objects of pure contemplation rather than something to be used as tools. Such discussions are found throughout al-Būnī's corpus, but are most prominent in chapter thirty-nine of *Shams al-maʿārif.* Along similar lines, the instructions in *al-Uṣūl wa-al-ḍawābiṭ* urge the reader not to abandon a particular Name after achieving his goal, since this Name will continue to act as an intermediary between God and the worshipper.[451]

Chapter Eight: The Power of the Quran and Its Verses in al-Būnī's Corpus

Introduction

Reverence for the text of the Quran and attributing power to it had been generally accepted in Islam long before the seventh/thirteenth century, so it is unsurprising that there are appeals to the authority of the Quran throughout al-Būnī's corpus. It is claimed in *Shams al-maʿārif* that the letters and numbers of the Quran are the key to revealing the secrets of the Names of God. Furthermore, every Quranic verse is said to have its own power and a shape that will compel spirits to give their assistance.[452] Of particular interest for this dissertation, the Quran is also described as a healing for both bodies and the truth of souls.[453] The healing power of the Quran is further supported with a quote from the Quran itself, "And of the Quran has descended that which is healing and a mercy to the believers,"[454] as well as a *ḥadīth* of the Prophet: "The healing of my community comes from three things: A verse of God's Book, or a spoonful of honey, or a cup from the cupper's hand."[455]

There was nothing unusual about using sacred texts for magical ends, even in the Abrahamic traditions. Certain psalms recurred frequently in Jewish magic, and Christian magic employed both the Psalms and stories from the Gospel, as well as other elements from the New Testament.

Texts

Direct appeals to power held by the Quran itself or individual verses are relatively rare in al-Būnī's corpus. Compared with the large numbers of works devoted to the study of Arabic letters and the Names of God, only four texts devoted to the magical uses of the Quran itself have been attributed to al-Būnī.[456]

The *Basmalah* is briefly discussed in *Sharḥ al-Juljulūtīyah al-kubrá* and in *Laṭā'if al-ishārāt*, but the most extensive discussion of Quranic verses in the texts examined here is in *Shams al-ma'ārif*. Specifically, chapter five is devoted to the *Basmalah*, chapter eighteen is devoted to the "Throne Verse" (*Āyat al-Kursī*, 2:255), and chapter twenty is devoted to *Sūrat Yā-Sīn* (36).[457]

This last chapter of *Shams al-ma'ārif* deserves a brief introduction. The list of topics at the beginning of the text states that the twentieth chapter deals with *Sūrat Yā-Sīn*. However, the chapter is not distinguished from the previous chapter in most printed editions of the text, suggesting that this is an error in the original manuscript on which all of the current printed texts were based. The undated "saffron-paged" Beirut edition does note a distinction between the chapters, but since this text is careful in other respects (e.g., providing verse and chapter for Quranic quotes) it seems likely that the editor would correct such a mistake found in the original.[458]

Extensive discussion of Quranic verses is not restricted to these chapters, either. Chapter fourteen of *Shams al-ma'ārif* is dedicated to *rīyāḍāt* (retreats with spiritual disciplines). These disciplines are described in extensive detail, including what one needs to wear, what verses to recite, and how to fast or what to eat. The purpose, explicitly outlined in this chapter, is to make spirit "servants" appear. These can be either jinn or angels, depending on the retreat. Most of the prayers specified in this chapter refer to Quranic verses. However, most of them also fall outside the purview of this dissertation, as they deal with issues not directly related to health and healing—wealth, preservation of position, and victory over enemies. This is perhaps most vividly illustrated in an account given of a wazir living under constant threat of death from the sultan, who managed to preserve his favor with the sultan (and, thereby, his life) through recitation of Quranic verses.[459]

Uses

These texts include instructions on how to use Quranic verses for protecting and restoring health, for general well-being or to cure particular ailments. Usually this is achieved by reciting the verse, carrying a written version, or drinking or anointing ink used to write the verse.

Instructions to recite verses for protection generally specify that they should be recited as one is going to sleep (perhaps a set number of times) and promise that God will protect the reciter from all manner of harm. Different verses and recitations can protect against different things. Some protect against any harm, others against spirits such as jinn or devils, and others against particular physical problems (e.g., blindness or paralysis).

Another common method is for the user to drink water which in some way has been infused with the *barakah* of the verse (though the term *barakah* is not always used). One might recite the verse over a bowl of water, or write the verse on a vessel and rinse out the ink to drink, or one might infuse water with a sheet inscribed with the verse, or even a ring. Some Quranic verses are sovereign remedies for any illness when used in this way, while others cure particular problems. Similarly, water or oil may be used to rinse away the verse and then either wash or anoint the afflicted person. Such uses are usually cures for specific parts of the body, and the water or oil is applied to the affected area. However, this kind of application is never used for simple protection. While water from rinsing a Quranic verse may be used for ends not related to healing—such as enhancing one's memory or becoming loved or admired[460]—most of the uses for healing apply this method and conversely it is used more often for healing than for any other purpose.

Finally, Quranic verses or their individual letters can be written on talismans—either directly or in some square, circle, or other pattern—to be worn or carried. These show some of the greatest variations in use. Talismans based on different Quranic verses are prescribed for both protection and healing, for general well-being and specific problems.

Specific Verses

Like the Names of God, verses of the Quran may be selected for particular uses because of their literal meaning—in this case, because of words or incidents in particular verses. For example, a talisman inscribed with verses about the Sleepers of the Cave (Quran 18:25, 18) is said to contain a "name" that can ease the pain of one who is suffering and can bring sleep, particularly mentioning a crying infant.[461] However, this is not the only verse prescribed for this purpose. Another talisman consists of the *Fātiḥah*, *Āyat al-Kursī*, and other verses bound to an infant to stop it from crying.[462]

Verses employed for protection included words of the root *ḥāʾ-fāʾ-ẓāʾ* (to preserve, protect), for instance 12:64, 13:11, 15:9, 37:7, 85:19-22, 86:4. *Shams al-maʿārif* lists some twenty "verses of preserving," which not only include those verses with the root *ḥāʾ-fāʾ-ẓāʾ*, but also two with the verbs *najjā* (to save, deliver, rescue) and one with the word *tawakkaltu* (I relied upon God).[463]

A set of Quranic verses that mention healing *shifāʾ* (healing) and related terms (9:14, 10:57, 16:69, 17:82, 26:78-80, 41:44) are said to be able to cure any pain of the body in conjunction with the "Throne Verse." However, this power is far from exclusive. In fact, in the same section it is said the "Throne Verse" alone has the power to cure headache.[464]

Quranic verses which mentioned jinn and devils (*shayṭāns*) were to be used for protection against these spirits. These included 2:6, 6:46, 36:65, 42:24, 45:23 for use against jinn and 29:18, 33:97, 113:1, 114:1 for use against devils.[465]

Another set of verses, called the "verses of protection" (*Āyāt al-ḥaras*) seemed to be grouped with no such restriction on holding a particular word, phrase, or root. These included 5:1-5, 2:255 (*Āyat al-Kursī*), 2:256-57, 2:284-286, 7:54-56, 37:1-11, 17:110, 55:33-35, 59:21-24, 72:3-4. These verses hold the power to heal "a hundred ills," and leprosy is particularly mentioned.[466]

Other named verses have power in their own right. Surprisingly, the *Muʿawwidhatān* (the two verses of refuge) also are hardly ever referred to in the corpus. Their place in Quranic commentary has been mentioned above, in chapter two on Islamic perspectives on magic. However the *Fātiḥah*, the *Basmalah*, and *Āyat al-Kursī* all are accorded significant power and effectiveness in al-Būnī's corpus.[467]

The Basmalah

It is widely known that Muslims are enjoined to commence every significant undertaking with the *Basmalah* (*bi-ism Allāh al-Raḥmān al-Raḥīm*, "In the name of God, the Merciful, the Compassionate"). This is reinforced by a famous *ḥadīth*, also quoted in *Shams al-maʿārif*, to the effect that any action that does not begin with the *Basmalah* will come to naught.[468] Of course, in al-Būnī's corpus, there are even more blessings and special uses ascribed to the *Basmalah*.

According to another *ḥadīth* quoted in *Shams al-maʿārif*, the *Basmalah* attracts angels, repels devils, and keeps away poison.[469] The *Basmalah* also has a role attributed to it in the works of the great Quranic prophets. It is claimed that the phrase was written on Adam's brow, Gabriel's wing as he approached Abraham, Moses' staff when he parted the Red Sea, the tongue of Jesus when he raised the dead, and the famous ring of Solomon.[470] Furthermore, the meaning of all God's revealed books is said to be in the Quran, all the meaning of the Quran is said to be in the *Fātiḥah*, all of the *Fātiḥah* in the *Basmalah*, and all of the *Basmalah* in *bāʾ*—its very first letter.[471] It is claimed that reciting the *Basmalah* has special virtues and power to protect one after death—to stave off the punishment in the grave, or to ensure entry to heaven. This is attributed to various *ḥadīths*, and also to the *Injīl*.[472]

Many other uses are given for the *Basmalah* that are more specific in their instructions and their ends. For example, if a woman whose children always die writes it one hundred and ten times and binds this to her child, it will live; the same talisman, bound to a sterile woman, will enable her to become pregnant.[473] When the *Basmalah* is written out seventy times and placed in a dead person's grave, they will be safe from the punishment of Munkar and Nakīr until Judgment Day.

As with many of the Quranic verses mentioned, the *Basmalah* can be recited on sleeping to protect one from all sorts of things: devils, theft, sudden death, or any misfortune.[474] Similarly, anybody who recites it every morning on waking will never wake up half paralyzed.[475] Elsewhere, the reader is more generally admonished to begin every action with the *Basmalah*, or else it will come to naught.

The phrase can also be dissolved in liquid to convey its blessing. Not only can one obtain the blessing by drinking the liquid, but it may also be used to fumigate somebody with a fever to cure them. There appears to be an idea of literally fighting fire with fire in this prescription. The inscription with the *Basmalah* refers to the infernal origins of fever, and the inscription is to be dissolved in a solution of hot oil (including spider and coriander).[476]

Also, even more than other verses, the *Basmalah* is connected to its Arabic letters and to the Names of God in texts attributed to al-Būnī. To be sure, all Quranic verses are made up of letters, but the letters of the *Basmalah* are examined separately in more detail than those of any other verse, specifically in *Shams al-maʿārif*, *Laṭāʾif al-ishārāt*, and *Sharḥ al-Juljulūtīyah*.[477] These letters, in turn, are connected to the Names of God. Not only are Names associated with each of the individual letters of the *Basmalah* but it is also asserted that the Greatest Name of God is actually contained in the *Basmalah* itself.[478]

The letters of the *Basmalah* may be written out individually, or in squares, circles, and other patterns. These may be either for protection or for healing specific ailments. They can cure any illness, ensure a swift birth for a woman in labor, keep away jinn and devils, protect a prosperous shop from the evil eye, make a woman pregnant who has been sterile or had miscarriages. They can protect against the punishment in the grave or cure somebody who has been poisoned.[479]

The Fātiḥah

There is little variation in discussions of how to use the *Fātiḥah* for protection or healing. In almost every case, the verse is used to bless a liquid in some way, and thereby to bring its benefits to the patient. This may be water, or sometimes oil; the verse may be recited over the liquid, or the liquid my erase the written verse; the liquid may be drunk or used to wash or anoint the patient—or perhaps the afflicted area. However, the general principle remains the same: the blessing of the *Fātiḥah* is physically transmitted to the subject. Some of these are cures for specific illnesses, but more than anything else, the verse is used to cure any illness or generally to make a patient well.[480] One cure is notable only because it specifies that among other things it could cure any wet or dry illness.[481] This is one of the few occasions where the humoral evaluation of an illness is mentioned at all in relation to cures based on verses from the Quran.

Āyat al-Kursī (The Throne Verse)

Āyat al-Kursī (The Throne Verse) is verse 255 of *Sūrat al-Baqarah* (The Sūrah of the Cow, the second sūrah of the Quran). An entire chapter of *Shams al-maʿārif* is devoted to the verse—and a fairly substantial one at that.[482] The length of the chapter may be related to the fact that the instructions for using the verse are very long, sometimes covering an entire page.[483]

Most of the uses prescribed for this verse involve either carrying or binding some written form of it, or reciting the verse. Reciting the verse is particularly associated with protection. Most often, this involves reciting the verse at night to be kept safe from evil spirits and other frightening things—devils, jinn, *mārid*, *ʿifrīt*, and even sultans.[484] One unique prescription calls for reciting the verse over seven pieces of salt, which are then to be eaten to cure problems related to phlegm.[485] While not explicitly stated, this may be connected to phlegm's cold, wet nature—a rare example of Galenic humors being important for an application of a Quranic verse for healing.

The verse may also be written to protect against demons, particularly demons that plague women. Specifically, these are the *qarā'in*—which are particularly known as childbed demons—and the *tawābi'*—which are demons that follow women.[486] All the other relevant uses prescribed for writing the verse—whether that writing is worn or drunk—are to cure actively. Most of these uses are to cure particular ailments. If there is any common thread, all are concerned with relieving pain. For whatever reason, none of them are specifically for concerns of pregnancy or childbirth.

Sūrat Yā'-Sīn

Sūrat Yā'-Sīn (36) is called the "Heart of the Quran" in *Shams al-ma'ārif* and elsewhere.[487] While an entire chapter is devoted to prayers and invocations using this *sūrah*, most of them are directed towards wealth or power over others in various ways. The latter may include being well-liked or overpowering one's enemies. In fact, only one prayer in the chapter deals with healing at all. Typical of the prayers in the chapter, it is about a page long. It is fairly broad in application, intended to prevent all sorts of pain. The *sūrah* is also mentioned in other parts of the text. For instance, reciting the verse with *Sūrat al-Ikhlāṣ* (112), *Sūrat al-Dukhān* (44), and other verses will get a believing jinni to heal one.[488] It is worth noting that while many instructions are given on how to use Quranic verses to enlist the aid of angels, jinn, and other spirits, most of those are generalized to get them to do one's bidding in any or all sorts of tasks. It is rare for jinn or other spirits to be actively enlisted in healing.

Conclusions

The Quran is constantly referred to in al-Būnī's corpus for legitimation, and by the seventh/thirteenth century the Quran was seen by many Muslims as a real, legitimate source of power—particularly for protection and healing. However, neither the Quran as a whole nor individual verses are as prominent in al-Būnī's corpus as are the Names of God, numbers, or Arabic letters. They are certainly present and prescribed for protection and healing, however, and their uses include both general and specific issues of health. Some verses are used more than others in particular manners or for particular uses, but no broad patterns in their use are apparent.

One factor that is true of all discussions of the Quran and individual verses in al-Būnī's corpus is that, unlike the Names of God or Arabic letters, there is no attempt in al-Būnī's corpus to classify Quranic verses by their elemental content, and references to their influences on the humors or illnesses caused by humoral imbalance are extremely rare. The Quran and its verses are presented as self-sufficient cures in and of themselves.

Conclusions: al-Būnī's Corpus: "Magic," "Religion," or "Science"?

The study of "Islamic magic" is complex and contentious, beginning with the extensive debates over how (or whether) to even use the word "magic," how Western scholars have understood the term, and how Muslims had understood such practices up until the seventh/thirteenth century. The life of al-Būnī himself is also something of a mystery, and it may well be that many later authors falsely attributed their writings to him. Looking at the corpus, then, as an eclectic collection of authors and texts in conversation with each other, certain patterns emerge in the treatment of health and well-being, as promoted through the use of Islamic symbols.

There is broad agreement across the corpus that the special properties of the Names of God, verses of the Quran, and even letters of the Arabic alphabet have the power to change the world. This may be done directly or through spiritual agents, such as angels or jinn. Even if one skirts blasphemy by saying that God Himself cannot be compelled, then at the very least He may be relied upon to answer certain prayers or favor those who wear, drink, or otherwise connect themselves to His Names or His holy book.

Furthermore, this power may be used by any one capable of performing the assigned rituals correctly. Taking the intellectualist approach, it is clear that such operations are "magic" in the way such rituals automatically work under such conditions. At the same time, al-Būnī's corpus is very much Islamic.

The focus here has been on which Names of God, Quranic verses, or Arabic letters may be used for which purposes according to al-Būnī's corpus. The purpose behind this method has been to document the emergence of "Islamic magic" in these writings. However, the rituals described in these writings are "Islamic" in numerous other ways as well. Many are specifically associated with Sufi Islam, such as the performance of *dhikr* and different kinds of retreats. The images of the spirit world are largely derived from Islamic sources as well. Furthermore, the ritual purity that must be maintained for many of them is Islamically derived, as are the ideas of right action (e.g., the need to donate alms as a part of many rituals).

A particularly interesting example of this Islamic morality at work is in the attitude towards curses—at least some of them—in the corpus. Curses brought about by Quranic verses or the Names of God are accompanied by warnings that if the victim died, the perpetrator would be called to account on Judgement Day.[489] At the same time, it must be acknowledged that not all curses were so limited. Non-fatal curses, such as to bind an enemy's tongue, or even his urine carried no warnings about the magician's soul.[490] Also, older techniques—such as the manipulation of letters and numbers—with closer connections to the Hellenistic world and to "natural" magic seem to have fewer restraints than those which manipulate more explicitly Islamic religious elements. When curses—even fatal ones—employ Arabic letters, warnings about the fate of the magician's soul are much rarer than among those which utilize the Names of God or verses of the Quran. This remains true even when those letters supposedly derive their power from their placement in those very sources.

Al-Būnī's corpus also justifies, explains, and supports its rituals through reference to the great prophets of the Quran. Naturally, Solomon is frequently mentioned, but Moses and Jesus are also important figures. The means by which these prophets performed their miracles are explained, and it is implied or even stated directly that the reader can duplicate such feats through the rituals described. Their effectiveness and holiness is emphasized by also placing them in the context of other great holy men of Islamic history or those known to al-Būnī himself. This assessment of the religious credentials of the corpus is repeated in Sufi biographies that praise al-Būnī for his understanding and discussion of God's secrets. It should be noted, though, that such a view was not universally accepted. Perhaps most famously Ibn Khaldūn claimed that al-Būnī and similar practitioners of *sīmīyāʾ* (including Muḥyī al-

Dīn Ibn al-ʿArabī) were actually practicing forbidden, harmful sorcery (*siḥr*), while disguising it through their use of Islamic symbols.

Returning to al-Būnī's corpus as such, even the concepts of protection and healing in the corpus are conditioned by Islam. That is to say, the worldview derived from the Quran and Islamic tradition influences the idea of what needed to be healed or protected against. Physical problems like plague or epilepsy are said to be caused by jinn. Similarly, demons and the evil eye are blamed for the death of infants and other misfortune. Thus, to protect the body, the magician must do also attend to the spiritual realm. In addition to these problems of the body, the idea of protection includes protecting the soul. Techniques are prescribed to keep away whispering, tempting devils in life and even in death, magic may be useful, protecting against Munkar and Nakīr and their torment of the dead in their grave.

The Islamic identity of al-Būnī's magic supports Daniel O'Keefe's assertions about the historical relationship between "magic" and "religion." In particular his eighth postulate, "Religion is the institution that creates or models magic for society,"[491] provides an appropriate model for understanding the writings under study.

The Historical Context: Continuities and Innovations

Besides the question of whether or not al-Būnī's corpus may properly be called "Islamic" or "magic," there is also the issue of how it related to other, similar practices and to the social and religious history of the Islamic world more generally. While it is important to note the changes brought into the understanding and practice of magic, it must be remembered that there were continuities as well. Firstly, the new "Islamic magic" promulgated by al-Būnī supplemented but did not supplant the Neoplatonic and celestial magic which had come before. Manuscripts of *Ghāyat al-ḥakīm*, for instance, continued to be produced through the eleventh and twelfth centuries hijri (seventeenth and eighteenth centuries of the Common Era).[492]

With regard to al-Būnī's corpus itself, it must be acknowledged that since the use of Islamic symbols is what distinguishes the corpus from previous magical literature, that aspect has been emphasized here. However, it should be remembered that celestial bodies such as the moon, stars, and planets also have their own role in these writings. The use of such elements links al-Būnī's corpus to the earlier literary occult tradition in Arabic, as represented by *Ghāyat al-ḥakīm*, the Jābirian alchemical corpus, and others, with a provenance of occult ideas stretching back into antiquity. It is interesting to note that the *Rasā'il Ikhwān al-Ṣafā'* explicitly state that astrology and knowledge of the stars are the foundation of the occult arts.[493] Similarly, it must be acknowledged that the long recension of *Shams al-maʿārif* also gives pride of place to astrology, by commencing the text with a discussion of the planets, stars, and constellations.

The continued importance of the physical *khawāṣṣ*, or special properties, of physical materials, represents another continuity with earlier traditions. In fact, it is entirely possible that the great importance attached to the *khawāṣṣ* of the Beautiful Names of God throughout the Būnī corpus is connected to this older tradition. The *khawāṣṣ* of materials related to their special relationship with the various celestial spirits (seen in the stars) who were the intermediaries in transmitting the power of The One to the magician. In the Islamic literature, particularly al-Būnī's corpus, the Beautiful Names of God represented God Himself and were also the means by which the magician could acquire and use divine power.

This was not simply a substitution of one set of names (or Names) for another. The explicitly Islamic nature of the magic described in al-Būnī's corpus resulted in real changes in the way magic was understood and practiced. Earlier occult writings from the Islamic world, as represented by the Ikhwān al-Ṣafā' and *Ghāyat al-ḥakīm*, took the Neoplatonic One as the ultimate source of all power and magic. Al-Būnī and his successors, however, took the Islamic Allah as the ultimate source of power (and authority). On the one hand, this change signaled that Neoplatonism had been islamicized through the medium of Sufism. With respect to the magic itself, this theoretical change resulted in changes both in the form of magic employed and in the kinds of goals it could be used for.

With the identification of Allah as the source of magical power in al-Būnī's corpus, the methods for accessing that power changed. Instead of relying on ceremonies derived from Ḥarrārian ritual, methods to utilize divine power were taken from those who were already trying to get close to God in another sense—namely, the Sufis. Islamic ritual purity, fasting, superogatory prayers, *dhikr*, and solitary retreat took the place of prayers to the stars. Lory has suggested that since al-Būnī was a Sufi, it was a natural consequence for him and those who attributed their writings to him to pursue divine power as a part of achieving union with God.[494] Regarded this way, the Islamic magic of the corpus is less like sorcery or witchcraft, and more like a kind of sainthood for the masses, making God's blessings in this world available to all.

Directions for Future Research

As pointed out in chapter four, there is still a great deal to be learned about al-Būnī's corpus, even down to who wrote particular books, chapters, or passages and when. The deeper question for the study of these works is not why did the authors invent a new Islamic magic. Quite simply, they did not. Material evidence shows that the Names of God and verses of the Quran had been used for magical power since at least the fourth/tenth century. Nor is the question even why did people suddenly start writing about "Islamic magic." Ibn al-Nadīm's *Fihrist* clearly mentions several authors whose works and methods—as best as we can understand from Ibn al-Nadīm's fragmentary reports—closely correspond with those of al-Būnī's corpus. Rather, the question needs to be: Why did al-Būnī's name take on such a prominent role as the author of these works? For whatever reason, al-Būnī's corpus represents the earliest surviving literature devoted to the magical uses of Islamic symbols.

While magical texts like those of this corpus are important sources, a full understanding of the role of magic in medieval Islamic societies requires that scholars look beyond prescriptive manuals to evidence of actual practice. This will be a much more complicated task, requiring the collection of numerous small pieces of evidence from scattered sources such as contemporary reports and material evidence.[495] This may be difficult and time-consuming, but it is the only way to learn about the importance of such practices for the great mass of illiterate and semi-literate people at this time.

In 1996, Toufic Fahd pointed out that despite an abundance of Arabic sources very little serious scholarly attention had been paid to the study of magic in Islamic societies.[496] Progress is being made in this area, but the above statement is still largely true. Fortunately, for those who wish to pursue the subject further, there are not only numerous primary sources available, but also a large number of models for how to approach the topic. The study of magic is drawing great interest in the history of numerous regions, periods, and groups. Particularly worthy of note is the Pennsylvania State University Press series *Magic in History* and the burgeoning scholarship on Jewish magic and magic in Late Antiquity. It is hoped that the present work is will not only contribute to the study of magic in medieval Islam, and the historical study of magic more generally, but also that it will serve as an inspiration and resource for other scholars who wish to expand on the issues raised here.

BIBLIOGRAPHY

Primary Sources

Ibn al-ʿArabī, Muḥyī al-Dīn (d. 638/1240). *al-Futūḥāt al-Makkiyah*, ed. ʿUthmān Yaḥyā and Ibrāhīm Madkūr. Cairo: al-Ḥayʾat al-Miṣriyyah, 1972-1987/88.

al-Būnī, Aḥmad ibn ʿAlī (d.622/1225). *Kitāb laṭāʾif al-ishārāt fī al-ḥurūf al-ʿālīyāt*. BN Tunis 9755: Fols. 1-62.

———. *Shams al-maʿārif al-kubrá*. 4 vols. in 1. Beirut: Muʾassasat al-nūr al-maṭbūʿāt, 1420/2000.

———. *Shams al-maʿārif al-kubrá*. 4 vols. in 1. Beirut: al-Maktabah al-shaʿabīyah, 1405/1985.

———. *Shams al-maʿārif al-kubrá*. 4 vols. in 1. Beirut: al-Maktabah al-ʿilmīyah, n.d.

———. *Shams al-maʿārif al-kubrá*. 4 vols. in 1. Cairo: al-Maṭbaʿah al-Ḥusaynīyah, n.d. (1905?).

———. *Shams al-maʿārif al-kubrá*. 4 vols. in 2 manuscripts. BN Tunis 4920, 4921.

———. *Shams al-maʿārif wa-laṭāʾif al-ʿawārif [al-ṣughrá]*. BN Tunis 6711.

———. *Shams al-maʿārif al-wusṭá*. BN Tunis 7401.

———. *Tartīb al-daʿwāt*. BN Tunis 9581: Fols. 1-33.

———. *al-Uṣūl wa-al-ḍawābiṭ*. In *Manbaʿ Uṣūl al-ḥikmah*. Beirut: Manshūrāt Muʾsasah al-Nūr al-maṭbūʿāt, 1421/2000.

———. *al-Uṣūl wa-al-ḍawābiṭ*. BN Tunis 661.

al-Ghazālī, Abū Ḥāmid (d. 505/1111). *al-Maqṣad al-Asnā*, ed. Fadlou Shehādī. Beirut: Librairie Orientale, 1986.

Ibn Khaldūn, Walī al-Dīn ʿAbd al-Raḥmān ibn Muḥammad (d. 784/1382). *The Muqaddimah: An Introduction to History*. Tr. Franz Rosenthal. Bollingen Series XLIII. New York: Bollingen Foundation, Inc., 1958.

al-Majrīṭī, Abū Maslamah (fl. 5th/11th century). *Ghāyat al-ḥakīm* (BN Tunis 9758).

———. *Ghayāt al-ḥakīm* [Das Ziel des Weisen]. tr. Helmut Ritter. Studien der Bibliothek Warburg 12. Leipzig: B.G. Teubner, 1933.

Ibn al-Nadīm, Muḥammad Abū al-Faraj (fl. 987 CE). *The Fihrist of al-Nadim*. ed. and tr. Bayard Dodge. Records of Civilization: Sources and Studies LXXXIII. New York: Columbia University Press, 1970.

———. *Kitāb al-Fihrist*. ed. Gustav Flügel. Leipzig: F.C.W. Vogel, 1871. 2 vols. in 1.

Ibn al-Ṣabbāgh, Muḥammad ibn Abī al-Qāsim (d. 724/1323). *The Mystical Teachings of al-Shadhili*. (Arabic title: *Durrāt al-asrār*). Tr. E. H. Douglas. Ed. Ibrahim M. Abu Rabiʿ. Albany: State University of New York Press, 1993.

Tāmir, ʿĀrif, ed. *Rasāʾil Ikhwān al-Ṣafāʾ*. Beirut: Manshūrāt ʿAwīḍāt, 1415/1995.

Secondary Sources

Bağdatli, İsmail Paşa. *Hadīyat al-ʿĀrifīn: Asmāʾ al-muʾallifīn wa-athār al-muṣannafīn*. Istanbul: Milli egitim basimevi, 1951-55.

Balghrād, Muḥammad. "Min aʿlām ʿAnnābah." *al-Aṣalah* V:34-35 (Jumādī II-Rajab 1396/June-July 1976): 64,244.

Bencheneb, H. "al-Sanūsī, Abū ʿAbd Allah Muḥammad b. Yūsuf b. ʿUmar b. Shuʿayb." *EI*². s.v.

Benmansour, Abdelwahab. *Aʿlām al-Maghrib al-ʿArabī*. Rabat: al-Maṭbaʿat al-Malikīyah, 1406/1986.

Bousquet, G. H. "Fiqh et sorcellerie: Petite contribution l'étude de la sorcellerie en Islâm," *Annales de l'Institut des Études Orientales* 8 (1949-50), 230-234.

Brockelmann, Carl. *Geschichte der arabischen Literatur*. 2nd ed. Leiden: E.J. Brill, 1943-49, repr. with new English introduction by Jan Just Witkam, Leiden: E.J. Brill, 1996. 1st ed. Weimar: E. Felber, 1898-1902.

Cammann, Schuyler. “Islamic and Indian Magic Squares.” *History of Religions* VIII (1969): 181-209, 271-299.

Canaan, Tewfik, “The Decipherment of Arabic Talismans I-II,” *Berytus* IV (1937): 69-110; V (1938): 141-151. Repr. in *Magic and Divination in Early Islam*, ed. and intro. Emilie Savage-Smith, 125-177. The Formation of the Classical Islamic World 42. Wiltshire, England: Ashgate Publishing, Ltd., 2003.

Conrad, Lawrence. “Arab Islamic Medicine,” in *Companion Encyclopedia of the History of Medicine*, eds. W. F. Bynum and Roy Porter. London: Routledge, 1993. s.v.

Cunningham, Graham. *Religion and Magic*. Cambridge: Cambridge University Press, 1999.

Dār al-Kutub al-Qawmīyah (Tunisia). *al-Fihris al-ʿām li-al-makhṭūṭāt* [*Catalogue général des manuscrits*]. Tunis: al-Jumhūrīyah al-Tūnisīyah, Wizārat al-thaqāfah, Dār al-kutub al-waṭanīyah, 1975-1999. 8 vols.

Dietrich, A. “al-Būnī,” *EI*[2], supp. (vol. XII). Leiden: E. J. Brill, 2004. sv.

Douglas, Mary. *Purity and Danger*. London: Ark Paperbacks. Originally published London: Routledge and Kegan Paul, 1966.

Doutté, Edmond, *Magie et religion dans l'Afrique du Nord*. Alger: Typ. A. Jourdan, 1908. Repr. Paris: J. Maisonneuve et P. Geuthner S. A., 1994.

Druart, Therese-Anne. “Al-Farābī, Emanation, and Metaphysics.” In *Neo-platonism and Islamic Thought*, ed. Parviz Morewedge, 127-148. Studies in Neoplatonism; Ancient and Modern, vol. 5. R. Baine Harris, general editor. Albany, NY: SUNY Press, 1992.

El-Ğawhary, Mohammed. “Die Gottesnamen im magischen Gebrauch in den al-Buni zugeschriebenen Werken,” PhD diss. Bonn: Rheinischen Friedrich-Wilhelms-Universität zu Bonn, 1968.

Ernst, Carl. *The Shambhala Guide to Sufism*. Boston: Shambhala Publications, Inc., 1997.

Fahd, Toufic. "L'Agriculture nabatéene en Andalousie," *Ciencias de la Naturaleza en al-Andalus* IV. Ed. C. Álvarez de Morales. Granada: CSIC, 1996. 41-52. repr. In *L'Agriculture nabatéene vol. III: Articles et index arabe,* 311-324. Damascus: Institut français de Damas, 1998.

———. "Anges, demons et djinns en Islam." In "Génies, anges, et demons." Eds. Denise Bernot et al. Special issue of *Sources orientales* VIII (1971):153-214.

———. *La Divination Arabe.* Leiden: E.J. Brill, 1966.

———. "Djafr." *EI*². s.v.

———. "Ḥurūf, ʿIlm al-." *EI*². s.v.

———. "Magie comme 'source de la sagesse' dans l'oeuvre d'al-Būnī" in "Charmes et sortileges. Magie et magicians," special issue, *Res Orientales* XIV (2002):61-108.

———. "Matériaux pour l'histoire de l'agriculture en Irak: *al-Filâḥa n-nabaṭiyya,*" *Handbuch der Orientalistik,* I, Abt. 6, Band 6. Absch., Teil 1 (1977), 276-377. repr. in *L'Agriculture Nabatéene,* ed. Toufic Fahd, vol. II: *Articles et index arab.* Damascus: Institut Français de Damas, 1998. 175-277.

———. "Le monde du sorcier en Islam," in "Le monde du sorcier," special issue, *Sources Orientales* VII (1966): 155-204.

———. "Nabaṭ--2. The Nabaṭ al-ʿIrāḳ," *EI*². s.v.

———. "Ṣābiʾa," *EI2*, s.v.

———. "Sciences naturelles et magie dans *Ġayat al-ḥakīm* du pseudo-Maŷrīṭī." In *Ciencias de la naturaleza en al-Andalus: Textos y estudios I.* ed. Garcia Sanchez. Granada: Consejo superior de investigaciones científicas escuela de estudios arabes, 1990.

———. "Tamīma," *EI*². s.v.

———. "Ibn Waḥshiyya," *EI*². s.v.

———. "Zāʾirdja," *EI*², s.v.

Fakhry, Majid. *A History of Islamic Philosophy.* New York: Columbia University Press, 1983.

Frazer, James George. *The Golden Bough.* 1-volume abridged edition. London: MacMillan Publishing Company, 1922; repr., New York: Touchstone, 1996.

———. *The Golden Bough: A Study in Magic and Religion,* 3rd ed. London: MacMillan and Company Ltd., 1911. 12 vols. repr. 1966.

———. *The Golden Bough: A New Abridgement of the Classic Work.* ed., notes, and foreword Theodor H. Gaster. New York: Criterion Books, 1959.

Gardet, L. "Asmā' al-Ḥusnā'," *EI*². s.v.

Geertz, Hildred. "An Anthropology of Religion and Magic I." *Journal of Interdisciplinary History* VI:1 (Summer 1976): 71-89.

Goldziher, Ignaz, "Le culte des saints chez les musulmans." *Revue de l'histoire des religions* II (1880): 257-351.

Goode, William J. *Religion among the Primitives.* Glencoe, IL: The Free Press, 1951.

Goody, Jack. "Religion and Ritual: The Definitional Problem" in *British Journal of Sociology* 12 (1961): 142-164.

Gordon, Richard. "Reporting the Marvellous: Private Divination in the Greek Magical Papyri," in *Envisioning Magic,* eds. Peter Schäfer and Hans G. Kippenberg, 65-92. Leiden: Brill, 1997.

Graefe, E. and D.B. Macdonald [M. Plessner], "Djadwal." *EI*². s.v.

Graham, William A. "Basmala," *Encyclopaedia of the Quran.* ed. Jane Damman Mc Auliffe. Leiden: Brill, 2000. s.v.

Hoffman, C. A. "Fiat Magia." In *Magic and Ritual in the Ancient World,* eds. Paul Mirecki and Marvin Meyer, 179-186. Leiden: Brill, 2002

Horton, Robin. "Levy-Bruhl, Durkheim and the Scientific Revolution." In *Modes of Thought* , eds. Robin Horton and Ruth Finnegan, 249-305. London: Farber and Farber, 1973.

Kippenberg, Hans G. and Peter Schäfer. "Envisioning Magic: A Princeton Seminar and Symposium." In Peter Schäfer and Hans G. Kippenberg, eds. *Envisioning Magic*, vii-xi. Leiden: Brill, 1997.

Kraus, Paul. *Jābir ibn Ḥayyān: Contribution à l'histoire des idées scientifiques dans l'Islam*, vol. II: *Jābir et la science Grecque*. Memoires de l'Institut de l'Egypt, vol. 45 (Cairo: 1942-43).

Lory, Pierre. "La magie chez les Iḫwān al-Ṣafāʾ." In "Sciences occultes et Islam," eds. Annick Regourd and Pierre Lory, special issue, *Bulletin d'études orientales* XLIV (1992): 147-159.

———. "La magie des lettres dans le *Šams al-maʿârif* d'al-Bûnî." *Bulletin d'études orientales* XXXIX-XL (1987-88): 97-111.

———. "al-Shādhilī, Abū al-Ḥasan ʿAlī b. ʿAbd Allah b. ʿAbd al-Djabbar (ca. 593-656/ca. 1196-1258)," *EI²*. s.v.

———. "Shādhiliyya," *EI²*. s.v.

MacDonald, Duncan Black. "Ḳarīn." *EI²*, s.v.

———. *Religious Attitude and Life in Islam*. University of Chicago: the Haskell Lectures on comparative religion, 1906; repr. Khayats Oriental Reprints 9. Beirut: Khayats, 1965.

Maddison, Francis and Emilie Savage-Smith, with contributions from Ralph Pinder-Wilson and Tim Stanley. *Science, Tools, and Magic*. Nasser D. Khalili Collection of Islamic Art 12. London: The Nour Foundation in association with Azimuth Editions and Oxford University Press, 1997.

MacDonald, Duncan Black. "Siḥr," *Encyclopaedia of Islam*. First edition. Leiden: E.J. Brill and Luzac & Co, 1915-38; repr. Leiden: E. J. Brill, 1987. s.v.

Malinowski, Bronislaw. "Magic, Science, and Religion," in *Magic, Science, and Religion and Other Essays*. The Free Press, 1948; reprint, with an introduction by Robert Redfield, Garden City, NY: Doubleday Anchor Books, 1954. Originally published in *Science, Religion and Reality*. ed. James Needham. n.p., 1925.

Marquet, Yves. "Ikhwān al-Ṣafā'," *EI*[2]. s.v.

Massignon, Louis. *Origines du lexique technique de la mystique musulmane*. Paris: Libraire Philosophique J. Vrin, 1954.

Mauss, Marcel. *A General Theory of Magic*. Tr. Robert Brain. Foreword by D. F. Pocock. London: Routledge and Kegan Paul, 1972. Repr. Routledge Classics 2001, 2002.

———. "Théorie genérale de la magie." *Sociologie et anthropologie*. Paris: Presses Universitaires de France, 1950. Originally published, in collaboration with Henri Hubert, in *Année sociologique* (1902).

Muḥsin Muḥammad Nazīl Sāmarra, *Dharī'ah ilá taṣānīf al-Shī'ah*. Najaf, Iraq, 1936-1986.

Muṣṭāfá ibn 'Abd Allah Kâtip Čelebī Ḥajjī Khalīfah (1017-67/1609-57). *Kashf al-ẓunūn*. Istanbul: Maarif Matbaasi, 1941-43. 2 vols.

al-Nabhānī, Yūsuf ibn Ismail (1849/50-1932). *Jāmi' karamāt al-awliyā'*. Cairo: n.p., 1911; repr. Beirut: n.p., 1970.

Netton, Ian Richard. *Muslim Neoplatonists: An Introduction to the Thought of the Brethren of Purity*. London: G. Allen and Unwin, 1982.

Nuwayhiḍ, 'Ādil. *Mu'jam al-a'lām al-Jazā'ir*. Beirut, 1400/1980.

O'Connor, Kathleen. "The Alchemical Creation of Life (takwin) and Other Concepts of Genesis in Medieval Islam." PhD. diss., University of Pennsylvania, 1994.

O'Keefe, Daniel. *Stolen Lightning: The Social Theory of Magic*. New York: Continuum, 1982.

"Openburhan—The Quran Browser." <http:// www.openburhan.com>. Last updated January 16, 2004. Accessed April 15, 2005.

Perho, Irmeli. *The Prophet's Medicine: A Creation of the Muslim Traditionalist Scholars.* Studia Orientalia 74. Helsinki: The Finnish Oriental Society, 1995.

Pettersson, Olaf. "Magic—Religion: Some Marginal Notes to an Old Problem." *Ethnos* 3-4 (1957): 109-119.

Pickthall, Mohammed Marmaduke. *The Meaning of the Glorious Koran.* New York: New American Library), n.d.

Pielow, Dorothée Anna Maria. *Die Quelle der Weisheit. Die arabische Magie im Spiegel des Uṣūl al-Ḥikma von Aḥmad Ibn ʿAlī al-Būnī.* Arabistische Texte und Studien, Band 8. Hildesheim: Georg Olms Verlag, 1995.

Pingree, David. "Some of the Sources of the *Ghāyat al-ḥakīm.*" *Journal of the Warburg and Courtauld Institutes* XLIII (1980), 1-15.

Plessner, M. "Balīnūs," *EI*², s.v.

———. "Hirmīs," *EI*². s.v.

Rehaya, M. "al-Maʾmūn b. Hārūn al-Rashīd," *EI*². s.v.

Ritner, Robert K. "The Religious, Social, and Legal Parameters of Traditional Egyptian Magic." In *Ancient Magic and Ritual Power*, eds. Marvin Meyer and Paul Mirecki, 43-60. Leiden: E. J. Brill, 1995.

Ruska, J. "Die Alchimie ar-Razi's" *Der Islam* XXII (1934): 281-319.

———. "Wafḳ."*Encyclopaedia of Islam.* First edition. Leiden: E.J. Brill and Luzac & Co, 1915-38; repr. Leiden: E. J. Brill, 1987. s.v.

Sabra, A. I., "ʿIlm al-Ḥisāb," *EI*², s.v

al-Said, Mansour Solyman, "Medicine in Islam," *Encyclopaedia of the History of Science, Technology, and Medicine in Non-Western Cultures*, ed. Helaine Selin. Dordrecht: Kluwer Academic Publishers, 1997, 695-968.

Sālim, Muḥammad ʿAdnān and Muḥammad Bassām Rushdī. *al-Muʿjam al-mufarras al-maʿānī al-Quran al-ʿaẓīm* (*The Indexing Dictionary of the Meanings of the Great Quran*). Beirut: Dār al-Kutub al-Muʾāsir, 1416/1995.

Savage-Smith, Emilie, ed. *Magic and Divination in Early Islam*. The Formation of the Classical Islamic World, edited by Lawrence Conrad, vol. 42. Wiltshire, England: Ashgate Variorum, 2004.

Schimmel, Annemarie. *Mystical Dimensions of Islam*. Chapel Hill, NC: University of North Carolina Press, 1975.

Sesiano, J. "Wafḳ." in *EI²*. s.v.

Sezgin, Fuat, *Geschichte des Arabischen Schriftums*. Band IV (Alchimie-Chemie, Botanik-Agrikultur). Leiden: E.J. Brill, 1971.

Shakir, M. H., tr. *Holy Qurʾan*. Published with facing English and Arabic text. Elmhurst, NY: Tahrike Tarsile Qurʾan, Inc., 1982.

Ṣiddīqī, Muḥammad Zubayr. *Ḥadīth Literature: Its Origin, Development, and Special Features*. Ed. and revised by Abdal Hakim Muʿad. Cambridge: The Islamic Texts society, 1993.

Skorupski, John. *Symbol and Theory: A Philosophical Study of Theories of Religion in Social Anthropology*. Cambridge: Cambridge University Press, 1976.

Slane, William MacGuckin de. *Catalogue des manuscripts arabes*. Paris: Imprimerie nationale, 1883-1895.

Smart, Ninian. *Dimensions of the Sacred: An Anatomy of the World's Beliefs*. London: Fontana Press, 1997.

Smith, Jonathan. "*Adde Parvum Parvo Magnus Acervus Erit*." In *Map is Not Territory: Studies in the History of Religions*, 240-264. Leiden: E. J. Brill, 1975. Repr. Chicago: University of Chicago Press, 1993. 240-264. Originally published in *History of Religions* XI:1 (August 1971): 67-90.

———. "The Temple and the Magician." In *Map is Not Territory: Studies in the History of Religions*. Leiden: E. J. Brill, 1975. Repr. Chicago: University of Chicago Press, 1993. 172-189. Originally published in *God's Christ and His People*, eds. Jacob Jervell and Wayne A. Meeks, 233-247. Oslo: Oslo Universitetsforlaget, 1976.

———. "Trading Places." In *Ancient Magic and Ritual Power*, eds. Marvin Meyer and Paul Mirecki, 13-27. Leiden: E. J. Brill, 1995.

———. "When the Bough Breaks." In *Map is Not Territory: Studies in the History of Religions*, 208-239 with afterword. Leiden: E. J. Brill, 1975. Repr. Chicago: University of Chicago Press, 1993. Originally printed in *History of Religions* Vol. 12, No. 4 (May 1973), 342-371.

Thomas, Keith. "An Anthropology of Religion and Magic II." *Journal of Interdisciplinary History* VI:1 (Summer 1976): 91-109.

———. *Religion and the Decline of Magic*. New York: Scribner, 1971.

Tylor, Edward B. *Primitive Culture: Researches into the Development of Mythology, Philosophy, Religion, Language, Art, and Culture*. New York: Brentano's Publishers, 1924. 1st ed. 1871.

Ullmann, Manfred. *Islamic Medicine*. Islamic Surveys 11. tr. Jean Watt. Edinburgh: Edinburgh University Press, 1978.

———. *Die Natur- und Geheimwissenschaften im Islam*. Handbuch der Orientalistik. Erste Abteilung. Ergänzungsband VI, 2. Abschnitt. Leiden: E. J. Brill, 1972.

Vadja, J. "Quelques éléments juifs et pseudo-juifs dans l'encyclopédie magique de Bûnî." In *Goldziher Memorial Volume*, eds. Samuel Löwinger and Joseph Somogyi, I:387-392. Budapest: n.p., 1948.

Varisco, Daniel Martin. "The Magical Significance of the Lunar Stations in the 13th Century Yemeni *Kitāb al-tabṣira fī ʿilm al-nujūm* of al-Malik al-Ashraf," in "Divination, Magie, Pouvoirs au Yémen," ed. Anne Regourd, special issue, *Quaderni di Studi Arabi* 13 (1995), 19-40.

Vickery, John B. *The Literary Impact of The Golden Bough*. Princeton: Princeton University Press, 1973.

Watt, W. Montgomery and R. Bell. *Bell's Introduction to the Quran*. Islamic Surveys 8. Edinburgh: Edinburgh University Press, 1970. Paperback ed. 1977; repr. 1990.

Weil, G—(G.S. Colin). "Abdjad." *EI²*, s.v.

Wensinck, A. J. *A Handbook of Early Muhammadan Tradition*. Leiden: E. J. Brill, 1960.

Wensinck, A. J. "Isrāfīl," *EI²*, s.v.

———. "Mīkāl" *EI²*, s.v.

Wiet, G. "Akhmīm." *EI²*, s.v.

Winkler, H. A. *Siegel und Charaktere in der Muhammedanischen Zauberei*. Studien zur Geschichte und Kultur des Islamischen Orients VII, general editor C. H. Becker. Berlin: Walter de Gruyter & Co., 1930.

Zwemer, Samuel Marinas. "The Familiar Spirit or Qarina." *Moslem World* VI (1916): 360-374.

———. *The Influence of Animism in Islam*. London: Central Board of Missions and Society for Promoting Christian Knowledge, 1920.

Supplemental Bibliography

The works listed below were either published after 2005 or were otherwise unavailable to me when I completed the original dissertation. However, I believe these will be of particular use to those interested in Aḥmad al-Būnī and the works attributed to him.

Bailey, Michael D. "The Meanings of Magic." *Magic, Ritual, and Witchcraft* 1, no. 1 (summer 2006): 1-23.

Coullaut Cordero, Jaime. El Kitāb Šams al-Maʻārif al-Kubrà (al-ŷuz' al-awwal) de Aḥmad b. ʿAlī al-Būnī: Sufismo y ciencias ocultas." Ph.D. diss., Universidad de Salamanca, 2009.

Coulon, Jean-Charles. "La magie islamique et le *corpus* bunianam au Moyen Âge." PhD. diss., Université Paris IV Sorbonne, 2013.

———. "Magie et politique: événements historiques et pensée politique dans le *Šams al-maʿārif* attribué à al-Būnī (mort en 622/1225)." In "Islamicate Occultism: New Perspectives," eds. Matthew Melvin-Koushki and Noah Gardiner, special issue, *Arabica* Supplement Volume 1 (2017--forthcoming).

———. "Orthodoxie et magie dans l'oeuvre d'al-Bûnî." In *Magie et divination dans les cultures de l'Orient: actes du colloque organisé par L'Institut du Proche-Orient Ancien du Collège de France, La Société Asiatique et le CNRS (Umr 7192), les 19 Et 20 Juin 2008. Paris-Collège De France*, edited by Jean-Marie Durand and Antoine Jacquet, 213-30. Paris: Éditions Jean Maisonneuve, 2010.

Davies, Owen. *Grimoires: A History of Magic Books*. Oxford: Oxford University Press, 2009.

Gardiner, Noah. "Esotericism and the Early Circulation of the Sufi Occultist Aḥmad al-Būnī's Works." In "Islamicate Occultism: New Perspectives," eds. Matthew Melvin-Koushki and Noah Gardiner, special issue, *Arabica* Supplement Volume 1 (2017--forthcoming).

———. "Forbidden Knowledge? Notes on the Production, Transmission, and Reception of the Major Works of Aḥmad Al-Būnī." *Journal of Arabic and Islamic Studies* 12 (2012): 81-143.

Graham, Lloyd D. "A Comparison of the Seven Seals in Islamic Esotericism and Jewish Kabbalah." Published electronically February 9, 2014. https://www. academia.edu/ 5998229/A_comparison _of_the_ Seven_ Seals_in _ Islamic_esotericism_ and_ Jewish _Kabbalah.

———. "In Islamic Talismans, Repeat-Letter Ciphers Representing the 'Greatest Name' Relate to an Early Prototype of the Seven Seals and May Link the Seals with the Pleiades." *Epigraphy Society Occasional Papers* 29 (2011): 70-91.

———. "The Seven Seals of Revelation and the Seven Classical Planets." *The Esoteric Quarterly* 6, no. 2 (2010): 45-58.

Hamès, Constant. "Al-Būnī." In *The Encyclopaedia of Islam Three*, edited by Kate Fleet, Gudrun Krämer, Denis Matringe, John Nawas and Rowson. Everett. Leiden: Brill, 2011.

Knight, Michael Muhammad. *Magic in Islam*. TarcherPerigree, 2016.

Lory, Pierre. *La Science Des Lettres En Islam*. Paris: Editions Dervy, 2004.

Martin, John D. "Theurgy in the Medieval Islamic World: Conceptions of Cosmology in Al-Būnī's Doctrine of the Divine Names." Master's thesis, American University in Cairo, 2011.

Nomanul Haq, S., and S. Nomanul Haq. "Occult Sciences and Medicine." In *The New Cambridge History of Islam*. Edited by Michael Cook. Vol. 4, *Islamic Cultures and Societies to the End of the Eighteenth Century*, edited by Robert Irwin. 640-67. Cambridge: Cambridge University Press, 2010.

Saif, Liana. "From Ġāyat Al-Ḥakīm to Šams Al-Maʿārif Wa-Laṭā'if Al-ʿawwārif: Ways of Knowing and Paths of Power in Medieval Islam." In "Islamicate Occultism: New Perspectives," eds. Matthew Melvin-Koushki and Noah Gardiner, special issue, *Arabica* Supplement Volume 1 (2017--forthcoming).

Varisco, Daniel Martin. "Illuminating the Lunar Stations (Manāzil Al-Qamar) in Al-Būnī's Šams Al-Maʿārif."

In “Islamicate Occultism: New Perspectives,” eds. Matthew Melvin-Koushki and Noah Gardiner, special issue, *Arabica* Supplement Volume 1 (2017--forthcoming).

Witkam, Jan Just. “Gazing at the Sun: Remarks on the Egyptian Magician Al-Būnī and His Work.” In O Ye Gentlemen: Arabic Studies on Science and Literary Culture, in Honour of Remke Kruk, edited by Arnoud Vrolijk and Jan P. Hogendijk. Islamic Philosophy, Theology, and Science Leiden: Brill, 2007.

NOTES

[1] Aḥmad ibn ʿAlī al-Būnī (d. 622/1220), *Shams al-maʿārif al-kubrá* (Beirut, 1420/2000), II:252.

[2] Cf. al-Būnī, *Shams al-maʿārif al-kubrá* (Cairo, n.d. [1905?]), IV:19; al-Būnī, *al-Uṣūl wa-al-ḍawābiṭ* (BN Tunis 661), fols. 35v, 36v.

[3] The contemporary spread and influence of al-Būnī's corpus will be discussed in greater detail in chapter four.

[4] e.g, al-Būnī, *Shams al-maʿārif al-kubrá* (BN Tunis 4920), p. 243.

[5] Rheinischen Friedrich-Wilhelms-Universität zu Bonn, 1968.

[6] For a brief history of the various theories about the nature and definition of magic, see below, chapter one.

[7] Edward B. Tylor, *Primitive Culture: Researches into the Development of Mythology, Philosophy, Religion, Language, Art, and Culture* (New York: Brentano's Publishers, 1924; 1st ed. 1871), I:115-116.

[8] Tylor I: 424.

[9] Sorcery: Tylor II:112-113; demons and disease: Tylor II:126-128,129,139, 146ff; divination: Tylor II:131-32, 134,135;

[10] Tylor, II:144.

[11] Exorcism: Tylor, II:111; hagiolotry: Tylor, II:120-23.

[12] Graham Cunningham, *Religion and Magic: Approaches and Theories* (Cambridge: Cambridge University Press, 1999), 18.

[13] The discussion of Frazer's scholarship on magic and religion is based on the twelve-volume third edition of *The Golden Bough*. For a history of the various editions of *The Golden Bough* and the fate of Frazer's theses in each edition, see Jonathan Smith's "When the Bough Breaks," *History of Religions* Vol. 12, No. 4 (May 1973), 342-371; reprinted with afterword in *Map is Not Territory: Studies in the History of Religions* (Leiden: E. J. Brill, 1975; repr. Chicago: University of Chicago Press, 1993), 208-239.

[14] James George Frazer, *The Golden Bough: A Study in Magic and Religion*, 3rd ed. (London: MacMillan and Company Ltd., 1911, 12 vols; repr. 1966), I:222.

[15] Frazer, *Golden Bough*³, I: 52. cf. I:52-54, 174-175. Weapon salve: I:202-03.

[16] Frazer, *Golden Bough*³, I:111-113.

[17] Frazer, *Golden Bough*³, I:221-222, 224.

[18] Frazer, *Golden Bough*³, I:224-225.

[19] Egyptian and Babylonian magic and religion: Frazer, *Golden Bough*³, I:67 78; cult of saints: Frazer, *Golden Bough*³, I:78, etc.

[20] Frazer, *Golden Bough*³, I:223.

[21] See below for an explanation of the structural-functionalist distinction between religion and magic.

[22]Jack Goody, "Religion and Ritual: The Definitional Problem," *British Journal of Sociology* 12 (1961): 156, 157.

[23]Marcel Mauss, "Théorie genérale de la magie," in *Sociologie et anthropologie* (Paris: Presses Universitaires de France, 1950), 118-119.

[24] Goody, 157, 159.

[25] Goody, 157, 159.

[26] Goody, 154; citing T. Parsons, *The Structure of Social Action* (New York: n.p., 1937), 429ff.

[27] John Skorupski, *Symbol and Theory: A Philosophical Study of Theories of Religion in Social Anthropology* (Cambridge: Cambridge University Press, 1976),, 125.

[28] Skorupski, 156.

[29] Skorupski, 155, 180; cf. 134 ff.

[30] Skorupski, 127.

[31] Skorupski, 155; cf. 127-30.

[32] C. A. Hoffman, "Fiat Magia" in *Magic and Ritual in the Ancient World*, eds. Paul Mirecki and Marvin Meyer (Leiden: Brill, 2002), 180, 194.

[33] Hoffman, 188-190.

[34] See the discussion of Olaf Pettersson's work, below.

[35] Émile Durkheim, *Elementary Forms of the Religious Life*, tr. Joseph Ward Swain (London: George Allen and Unwin), 47, cited in Cunningham, 44.

[36] Durkheim, 44, cited in Cunningham, 44.

[37] Durkheim, 300, 301, cited in Cunningham, 44.

[38] Mauss, 12-13.

[39] Mauss, 12.

[40] Mauss, 15-16.

[41] Mauss, 118-119.

[42] Mauss, 14.

[43] Mauss, 134.

[44] Marcel Mauss and Henri Hubert, *A General Theory of Magic*, tr. Robert Brain (London: Routledge and Kegan Paul), 20, cited in Cunningham, 48.

[45] Kathleen O'Connor, "The Alchemical Creation of Life (takwin) and Other Concepts of Genesis in Medieval Islam," (Ph.D. diss., University of Pennsylvania, 1994), 333.

[46] Bronislaw Malinowski, "Magic, Science, and Religion," in *Magic, Science, and Religion and Other Essays by Bronislaw Malinowski* (n.p.: The Free Press, 1948; reprint, with an introduction by Robert Redfield; Garden City, NY: Doubleday Anchor Books, 1954), 86-87.

[47] Malinowski, 29-31.

[48] Malinowski, 87.

[49] Malinowski, 38.

[50] Malinowski, 88.

[51] Daniel O'Keefe, *Stolen Lightning: The Social Theory of Magic* (New York: Continuum Publishing Co., 1982), 25.

[52] O'Keefe, 33.

[53] O'Keefe, 14.

[54] O'Keefe, 211ff; cf. Weber, *The Sociology of Religion*, tr. Ephraim Fischoff (Boston: Beacon Press, 1964).

[55] O'Keefe, 11-12.

[56] O'Keefe, 210ff.

[57] O'Keefe, 235ff.

[58] O'Keefe, 559.

[59] O'Keefe, 26.

[60] O'Keefe, 39ff.

[61] Olaf Pettersson, "Magic-Religion," *Ethnos* (1957), 113-119.

[62] Petterson, 111, 119.

[63] Mary Douglas, *Purity and Danger* (London: Ark Paperbacks, 1984; originally published London: Routledge & Kegan Paul, 1966), 58ff.

[64] Cunningham, 61; see also Douglas, 64, 69ff.

[65] Cunningham, 67

[66] Ninian Smart, *Dimensions of the Sacred* (London: Fontana Press, 1997), 108.

[67] Smart, 107.

[68] Smart, 123.

[69] Hildred Geertz, "An Anthropology of Religion and Magic I," *Journal of Interdisciplinary History* VI:1 (Summer 1976), 71-72.

[70] Keith Thomas, "An Anthropology of Religion and Magic II," *Journal of Interdisciplinary History* VI:1 (Summer 1976), 94-95; cf. Keith Thomas, *Religion and the Decline of Magic* (New York: Scribner, 1971).

[71] Jonathan Z. Smith, "Trading Places," *Ancient Magic and Ritual Power*, eds. Marvin Meyer and Paul Mirecki (Leiden: E. J. Brill, 1995), 16-17.

[72] Smith, "Trading Places," 16.

[73] Smith, "Trading Places," 20.

[74] Robert K. Ritner, "The Religious, Social, and Legal Parameters of Traditional Egyptian Magic," *Ancient Magic and Ritual Power*, eds. Marvin Meyer and Paul Mirecki (Leiden: E. J. Brill, 1995), 59-60.

[75] Ritner, 44-45.

[76] Ritner, 44-45.

[77] Ritner, 44-45.

[78] Ritner, 44-45.

[79] All references to Quranic verses are based on the numbering of the "Egyptian edition." Where other authors' citations according to the Flügel edition are mentioned, the original numbering will be followed by the Egyptian numbering in square brackets. All English renderings are my own, except where another translation is specifically cited.

[80] e.g., Quran 43:30 (Abraham); 7:109, 10:76-77, 26:30-34, 27:10-14, XXVIII:36, 40:24, 51:39 (Moses); 5:110, 56:6 (Jesus); 74:24 (Muḥammad).

[81] e.g., Quran 17:47, 101; 25:8

[82] Quran 7:116-119, 10:80-82, 20:66-70.

[83] *Rasāʾil Ikhwān al-Ṣafāʾ* (Beirut: Manshūrāt ʿAwīdāt, 1415/1995), IV:240, 256.

[84] *Rasāʾil Ikhwān al-Ṣafāʾ* (Beirut, 1415/1995), IV:264. Curiously, this was kept in general terms; no specific connection was made between these claims and the actions of specific individuals (e.g., Pharaoh's magicians).

[85] *Rasāʾil Ikhwān al-Ṣafāʾ* (Beirut, 1415/1995), IV:274.

[86] ʿAbd Allāh ibn Muslim Ibn Qutaybah (d. 889 CE), *Mukhtalif al-ḥadīth*; Abū Jaʿfar Muḥammad ibn Jarīr al-Ṭabarī (d. 923 CE), *Tafsīr* (n.p., n.d.), I:1347,$_{23}$-348,$_{10}$; Aḥmad ibn Muḥammad Thaʿlabī (d. 1035 CE), *Qiṣāṣ al-anbiyāʾ* (Cairo: n.p., 1314/1896-97), 30, $_{16\ sqq}$; Fakhr al-Dīn al-Rāzī, *Mafātiḥ al-ghayb al-mushahhar bi-al-Tafsīr al-kabīr*, 434, $_{19-28}$; Sarīshī, commentary on Ḥarīrī's *Maqāmāt* (Cairo, 1314/1896-97), I:211; all of the above cited in D. B. MacDonald, "Siḥr," in *The Encyclopaedia of Islam*, ed. M.Th. Houtsma et al. (Leiden: E.J. Brill, 1913-1936), s.v.;

[87] re: the angels who are driven away, Quran 15:16-18.

[88] al-Bukhārī, *Ṣaḥīḥ*, ed. L. Krehl and Th. W. Juynboll (Leiden: E. J. Brill, 1907-08), "Ṭibb," *bāb* 36; Muslim, *Ṣaḥīḥ* (Cairo: n.p., 1238/1822-23), "Salām," trads. 41, 42; cf. idem, trad. 59; Abū Daūd, *Sunan* (Cairo, n.p., 1292/1875-76), "Ṭibb," *bāb* 15; al-Tirmidhī, *Ṣaḥīḥ* (Cairo: n.p., 1292/1875-76), "Ṭibb," *bābs* 17-19; Ibn Mājah, *Sunan* with Muḥammad ibn ʿAbd Allah, *Miftāḥ al-ḥājah* (Lucknow: n.p., 1315/1897-98), "Ṭibb," *bāb* 32; Mālik ibn Anas, *Muwaṭṭaʾ* with commentary by Zurqānī (Cairo: n.p., 1279/1862-63), "al-Wuḍūʿ min al-ʿayn," trads. 1-3; Aḥmad ibn Hanbal, *Musnad* (Cairo: n.p., 1313/1895-96), vol. I, pp. 274, 294; vol. II, pp. 222, 289, 319, 420, 439, 487; vol. IV, p. 67, vol. V, pp. 70, 379; al-Ṭayālisī, *Musnad* (Hyderabad: n.p., 1321/1903-04), trad. 1760; all cited in A.J. Wensinck, *A Handbook of Early Muhammadan Tradition* (Leiden: E.J. Brill, 1960), 139.

[89] al-Bukhārī, *Ṣaḥīḥ*, "Ṭibb," *bābs* 17, 19, 42-45, 54; "Riqāq," *bābs* 21, 50; Muslim, *Ṣaḥīḥ*, "Imān," trads. 371, 372, 374, 375; "Salām," trads. 103, 107, 116, 121; Abū Daūd, *Sunan*, "Ṭibb," *bābs* 9, 24; cf. Aḥmad ibn Ḥanbal, *Musnad*, vol. I, pp. 274, 321, 401, 403, 454; vol. IV, pp. 436, 441, 443; cf. vol. V, pp. 60bis, 447, 447f, 448, 448f, 449bis; all cited in Wensinck, *Handbook*, 138.

[90] Abū Daūd, *Sunan*, "Ṭibb," *bābs* 17, 24; al-Nasāʾī, *Sunan*, "Taḥrīm al-dam," *bāb* 19; cf. Aḥmad ibn Ḥanbal, *Musnad*, vol. I, pp. 389, 438, 440; vol. II, p. 220; all cited in Wensinck, *Handbook*, 139.

[91] Aḥmad ibn Ḥanbal, *Musnad*, vol. I, pp. 190, 191; al-Tirmidhī, *Ṣaḥīḥ*, "Ḥudūd," 27; Muslim, *Ṣaḥīḥ*, "Īmān," 144; al-Bukhārī, *Ṣaḥīḥ*, "Waṣīyah," 23; "Ṭibb," 40; "Ḥudūd," 44; all cited in Toufic Fahd, "Siḥr," *EI*², s.v.

[92] Toufic Fahd, "La connaissance de l'inconnaissable et l'obtention de l'impossible dans la pensée mantique et magique de l'islam," in "Sciences occultes et l'islam," eds. Annick Regourd and Pierre Lory, special issue, *Bulletin d'études orientales* XLIV (1992), 40.

[93] Aḥmad ibn Ḥanbal, *Musnad*, vo. I, pp. 38, 381, 397, 439; al-Nasāʾī, *Sunan*, *Zīnah* (n.p., n.d.), 17; Abū Daūd, *Sunan*, (n.p., n.d.), "Khātam," 3; all cited in Toufic Fahd, "Tamīma," *EI*², s.v.

[94] Abū Daūd, *Sunan*, (n.p., n.d.), "Ṭibb," 17; Ibn Mājah, *Sunan*, "Ṭibb," 39; cf. Aḥmad ibn Ḥanbal, *Musnad*, vol. I, p. 381; vol. IV, p. 156. All cited in Fahd, "Tamīma," *EI*². cf. Edward Lane, *Arabic-English Lexicon* (London: Williams and Norgate, 1867), I:316.

[95] G. H. Bousquet, "Fiqh et sorcellerie: Petite contribution à l'étude de la sorcellerie en Islâm," *Annales de l'Institute des Études Orientales* 8 (1949-50), 232-34.

[96] Shirnūbī, commentary on Ibn Abī Zayd al-Qayrawānī (d.386/996), *Risālah* (n.p., 1319/1901-02), cited in Bousquet, p. 231, n. 4.

[97] al-Ghazālī, *Iḥyāʾ ʿulūm al-dīn* (Cairo, 1334/1915-16), 15, 26; cited in D. B. MacDonald, "Siḥr."

[98] Chernoûbî, 188, cited in Bousquet, p. 231, n. 4.

[99] Bousquet, 230.

[100] Bousquet, 231.

[101] Wensinck, *Handbook*, 22, 110-111, 112.

[102] Bousquet, 232-33.

[103] Bousquet, 232.

[104] Bousquet, 232.

[105] Muḥammad Abū Ḥāmid al-Ghazālī (d. 1111), *Munqidh min al-ḍalāl* (n.p., Rajab 1385/1965-66), 145.

[106] *Rasāʾil Ikhwān al-Ṣafāʾ* (Beirut, 1415/1995), IV:248-50; 257ff.

[107] *Rasāʾil Ikhwān al-Ṣafāʾ* (Beirut, 1415/1995), IV:263-64.

[108] *Rasāʾil Ikhwān al-Ṣafāʾ* (Beirut, 1415/1995), IV:242, 274-75; Lory, "La magie chez les Iḫwān al-Ṣafāʾ," 151-52.

[109] *Rasāʾil Ikhwān al-Ṣafāʾ* (Beirut, 1415/1995), IV:263-64. Conspicuous by its absence from their discussion of *siḥr* is any mention of *jafr*, either as the particular foresight granted members of the Prophet's line or as divination by letters.

[110] *Rasāʾil Ikhwān al-Ṣafāʾ* (Beirut, 1415/1995), IV:262-63; cf. *Rasāʾil Ikhwān al-Ṣafāʾ* (Beirut: n.p., 1376-77/1957), IV:332, cited in Lory, "La magie chez les Iḫwān al-Ṣafāʾ," 150. Regarding the "false magic" used by the ignorant, see above.

[111] *Rasāʾil Ikhwān al-Ṣafāʾ* (Beirut,1376-77/1957), IV:407, cited in Lory, "La magie chez les Iḫwān al-Ṣafāʾ," 150.

[112] *Rasāʾil Ikhwān al-Ṣafāʾ* (Beirut: n.p., 1415/1995), IV:263-64, cited in Lory, "La magie chez les Iḫwān al-Ṣafāʾ," 148, 154.

[113] *Rasāʾil Ikhwān al-Ṣafāʾ* (Beirut: n.p., 1415/1995), IV:263-64.

[114] *Rasāʾil Ikhwān al-Ṣafāʾ* (Beirut, 1415/1995), IV:244, 245-46, 247; cf. *Rasāʾil Ikhwān al-Ṣafāʾ* (Beirut: n.p., 1376-77/1957), IV:291-92, 292-93, 293-94, 310, 314, 325-26 ; cited in Lory, "La magie chez les Iḫwān al-Ṣafāʾ," 153-54.

[115] *Rasāʾil Ikhwān al-Ṣafāʾ* (Beirut, 1415/1995), IV:264

[116] Manfred Ullmann, *Islamic Medicine*. Islamic Surveys 11, tr. Jean Watt (Edinburgh: Edinburgh University Press, 1978), 111ff.

[117] Lawrence Conrad, "Arab Islamic Medicine," in *Companion Encyclopedia of the History of Medicine*, eds. W. F. Bynum and Roy Porter (London: Routledge, 1993), 699; Ullmann, *Islamic Medicine*, 107ff.

[118] Pingree, "Some of the Sources of the *Ghāyat al-Ḥakīm*," *Journal of the Warburg and Courtauld* Institutes XLIII(1980), 15.

[119] Quran 2:62, 5:69, 22:17.

[120] Toufic Fahd, "Ṣābiʾa," *EI*^{2}, VIII:675a ff.

[121] Muḥammad Abū al-Faraj ibn al-Nadīm (fl. 987), *Kitāb al-Fihrist*, ed. Gustav Flügel (Leipzig: F. C. W. Vogel, 1871), I:308-313 (*maqālah* VIII, *fann* ii). Alchemy is dealt with in a separate chapter (*maqālah* X: vol. I, pp. 351ff). Cf. Ibn al-Nadīm, *The Fihrist of al-Nadīm*, ed. and tr. Bayard Dodge (New York: Columbia University Press, 1970), II:725-733.

[122] Ibn al-Nadīm (fl. 987 CE), I: 309.

[123] Ibn al-Nadīm, I:309; cf. Duncan Black MacDonald, "Siḥr," *Encyclopaedia of Islam,* First edition (Leiden: E.J. Brill and Luzac & Co, 1915-38; repr. Leiden: E. J. Brill, 1987), s.v.

[124] Ibn al-Nadīm, 309.

[125] Ibn al-Nadīm, I:311-312; cf. Dodge, 730-732. The authors are: Ibn Mundhiryanī (AKA Aḥmad ibn Jaʿfar), Khalaf ibn Yūsuf al-Dastumīsānī (AKA Ibn Qinān), Ḥammād ibn Murrah al-Yamānī, Abū al-Qāsim al-Faḍl ibn Sahl ibn al-Faḍl al-Ḥarīrī, Aḥmad Abū Bakr ibn

Waḥshīyah al-Kaldānī, Aḥmad Abū al-Ṭālib ibn al-Ḥusayn ibn ʿAlī ibn Aḥmad ibn Muḥammad ibn ʿAbd al-Mālik al-Zayyāt.

[126] Ibn al-Nadīm, I:312-313. Authors: Qālishtānus, Bulīnās al-Ḥakīm, Arūs Rūmī, Hermes [Trismegistus]; cf. Dodge, pp. 732-733.

[127] M. Plessner, "Hirmis," *EI*², s.v.

[128] Manfred Ullmann, *Die Natur- und Geheimwissenschaften im Islam* (Leiden: E. J. Brill, 1972), 375.

[129] Ullmann, *Die Natur- und Geheimwissenschaften im Islam*, 374-75.

[130] Ullmann, *Die Natur- und Geheimwissenschaften im Islam*, 375.

[131] Ar. فريقويوس (vocalization [and pointing on one letter] uncertain).

[132] Ullmann, *Die Natur- und Geheimwissenschaften im Islam*, 375-76; cf. Ibn al-Nadīm, I:313.

[133] M. Plessner, "Balīnūs," *EI*², s.v.; Ibn al-Nadīm, I:312.

[134] Ullmann, *Die Natur- und Geheimwissenschaften im Islam*, 404-405.

[135] Ullmann, *Die Natur- und Geheimwissenschaften im Islam*, 380.

[136] Ullmann, *Die Natur- und Geheimwissenschaften im Islam*, 380-81.

[137] Ibn al-Nadīm, I:312.

[138] Ibn al-Nadīm, I:310, 312.

[139] Fuat Sezgin, *Geschichte des Arabischen Schriftums, Band IV (Alchimie-Chemie, Botanik-Agrikultur)* (Leiden: E.J. Brill, 1971), IV:68.

[140] Gustav Flügel, ed., *Fihrist* II:154, n. 11 (ref. to I:312); II:190, n. 19 (ref. to I:353).

[141] Ibn al-Nadīm, I:310, 312.

[142] Ullmann, *Die Natur- und Geheimwissenschaften im Islam*, 407.

[143] Cf. Ullmann, *Die Natur- und Geheimwissenschaften im Islam*, 303.

[144] Toufic Fahd, "Ibn Waḥshīyya," *EI*², s.v. ; cf. David Chwoldson, "Über die Überreste der altbabylonischen Literatur in arabischen Übersetzungen," *Mémoires des Savants Etrangers présentés à l'Académie Impériale des Sciences de St. Pétersbourg* VIII (1859), 329-524; Alfred von Gutschmid, "Die Nabatäische Landwirtschaft un ihre Geschwister," *ZDMG* 15 (1861), 1-110, repr. in *Kleine Schriften* II (n.p., n.d.), 568-716; Theodor Nöldeke, "Noch Einiges über die 'nabatäische Landwirtschaft," *ZDMG* 29 (1875), 445-55.

[145] Toufic Fahd, "Ibn Waḥshīyya," *EI*², s.v.

[146] Toufic Fahd, "Ibn Waḥshīyya," *EI*², s.v.

[147] Toufic Fahd, "Nabaṭ--2. The Nabaṭ al-ʿIrāḳ," *EI*², s.v.

[148] Toufic Fahd, "Matériaux pour l'histoire de l'agriculture en Irak: *al-Filâḥa n-nabaṭiyya*," *Handbuch der Orientalistik* I, Abt. 6, Band. 6. Absh. Teil 1 (1977), 289, 368; repr. in *L'Ariculture Nabatéene*, ed. Toufic Fahd (Damascus: Institut Français de Damas, 1998), III:189, 268.

[149] Fahd, "Matériaux pour l'histoire de l'agriculture en Irak," 300 ; repr., 200.

150 Not to be confused with the mathematician Abū al-Qāsim Maslamah al-Majrīṭī (d. ca. 398/1007)

151 Sezgin, IV:295.

152 Pingree, "Some of the Sources of the *Ghāyat al-Ḥakīm*,", 2-3.

153 Pingree, "Some of the Sources of the *Ghāyat al-Ḥakīm*," 2, 4.

154 Pingree, "Some of the Sources of the *Ghāyat al-Ḥakīm*," 13,

155 Pingree, "Some of the Sources of the *Ghāyat al-Ḥakīm*," 15.

156 Pingree, "Some of the Sources of the *Ghāyat al-Ḥakīm*," 15.

157 Toufic Fahd, "Sciences naturelles et magie dans *Ġāyat al-ḥakīm* du pseudo-Maŷrīṭī," *Ciencias de la naturaleza en al-Andalus: Textos y estudios* I, ed. Garcia Sanchez (Granada: Consejo superior de investigaciones científicas escuela de estudios arabes, 1990), 16; citing *Ghāyat al-ḥakīm*, ed. Hellmut Ritter (Leipzig: Teubnor, 1933), 333-35?; ed. and German tr. H. Ritner and M. Plessner (London: The Warburg Institute, 1962), 348-50?.

158 Ullmann, *Die Natur- und Geheimwissenschaften im Islam*, 389-90.

159 *Rasā'il al-Ikhwān al-Ṣafā'* (Beirut, 1415/1995), IV:237.

160 *Rasā'il Ikhwān al-Ṣafā'* (Beirut, 1415/1995), IV: 240-41.

161 Ian Richard Netton, *Muslim Neoplatonists: An Introduction to the Thought of the Brethren of Purity* (Ikhwān al-Ṣafā') (London: George Allen & Unwin, 1982), 42.

162 *Rasā'il Ikhwān al-Ṣafā'* (Beirut, 1415/1995), IV: 251.

163 *Rasā'il Ikhwān al-Ṣafā'* (Beirut, 1415/1995), IV:324-371.

164 *Rasā'il Ikhwān al-Ṣafā'* (Beirut, 1415/1995), IV:242, 274-75; Lory, "La magie chez les Iḫwān al-Ṣafā'," 151-52.

165 Ibn al-Nadīm, 308-309.

166 Ibn al-Nadīm, I:310-311; cf. Dodge, 728-730. Ancient authors: Ariyūs al-Rūmī, Lawhaq ibn ʿArfaj. Muslim authors: Abū Naṣr Aḥmad ibn Hilāl al-Bakīl, Ibn al-Imām, Ṣāliḥ al-Mudaybirī, ʿUqbah al-Adhraʿī, Abū Khālid al-Khurasānī, Abū ʿAmr ʿUthmān ibn Abī Raṣṣāṣah.

167 J. Walker (P. Fenton), "Sulaymān b. Dāwūd," *EI*², s.v.

168 Ibn al-Nadīm, 309-310.

169 Ibn al-Nadīm, I:310.

170 See Perho for a more detailed treatment of this issue, especially pp. 145-46.

171 Perho, 53-54.

172 Perho, 53. citing Maḥmūd Nāẓim al-Nasīmī, *al-Ṭibb al-nabawī wa-ʿilm al-ḥadīth*, 2nd ed. (Beirut: n.p., 1407/1987), I:30, 188; Ömer Recep, "Ṭibb an-nabī, Die Prophetenmedizin bei Ibn as-Sunnī und Abū Nuʿaim unter besonderer Berücksichtigung der Kapitel über den Kopfschmerz, die Augen-, Nasen-, Zahnkrankheiten und die Hämaorrhoiden," diss., Philippos-Universität (Marburg, 1969), p. 4, item 2; *GAL*², I:156.

[173] Perho, 54. citing Recep (1969), pp. 4-5, item 3.

[174] Perho, 58-61.

[175] Variants include Taqī al-Dīn and Shihāb al-Dīn (A. Dietrich, "al-Būnī," *EI*², supp. [vol. XII] [Leiden: E. J. Brill, 2004], s.v.)

[176] Ibn al-Zayyāt (fl. 14th-15th century CE), *al-Kawākib al-sayyārah fī tartīb al-ziyārah fī al-Qarafatayn al-kubrá wa-al-ṣughrá* (Baghdad: Maktabat al-muthanná, 1968[?] repr. of Cairo 1907 ed.), 268, cited in Dietrich, s.v.

[177] E.g., ʿAdil Nuwayhiḍ, *Muʿjam al-aʿlām al-Jazāʾir* (Beirut, 1400/1980), 47.

[178] Yūsuf b. Ismāʿīl al-Nabhānī, *Jāmiʿ karāmāt al-awlīyāʾ* (Cairo: n.p., 1911; repr. Beirut: n.p., 1970), 508.

[179] Balghrād, 244.

[180] Abdelwahab Benmansour, *Aʿlām al-Maghrib al-ʿArabī* (Rabat: al-Maṭbaʿah al-Malakīyah, 1406/1986), IV:57.

[181] e.g., Carl Ernst, *The Shambhala Guide to Sufism* (Boston: Shambhala Publications, Inc., 1997), 92.

[182] Mohammed El-Ğawhary, "Die Gottesnamen im magischen Gebrauch in den al-Buni zugeschriebenen Werken," Ph.D. thesis. (Bonn, 1968),15; citing al-Būnī, *Shams al-maʿārif al-kubrá* (Cairo, 1900 or 1905), III:302, lines 26f.; IV:413, lines 27ff.

[183] Wiet, "Akhmīm," *EI*², s.v.

[184] El-Ğawhary, p. 14, n. 5; citing Muḥammad Muḥsin, *Dharʿīah ilá taṣānīf al-Shīʿah* (Najaf, 1936-1961, 14 vols.), I:27, lines 14-17; XIV:226.

[185] Benmansour, IV:57.

[186] Al-Būnī, *Shams al-maʿārif al-kubrá* (Beirut, 1415/2000), 557.

[187] Muḥammad Balghrād, "Min aʿlām ʿAnnābah," *al-Aṣalah* vol. 5, nos. 34-35 (Jumādá II-Rajab 1396/June-July 1976), p. 245.

[188] For a list of the works attributed to al-Būnī beyond those listed in the Bibliography, see: Carl Brockelman, *Geschichte der arabischen Litteratur*, 2nd ed. (Leiden: E.J. Brill, 1942-49; repr. with new English introduction by Jan Just Witkam, Leiden: E.J. Brill, 1996), I:655-656 (=1st ed., [Weimar: E. Felber, 1898-1902], I:497-498); supp. I:910-911; İsmail Paşa Bağdatli, *Hadīyat al-ʿĀrifīn: Asmāʾ al-muʾallifīn wa-athār al-muṣannafīn* (Istanbul: Milli egitim basimevi, 1951-55), I:90-91; Toufic Fahd, *La Divination arabe* (Leiden: E.J. Brill, 1966), 231-232, 237-238, 243; Ullmann, *Die Natur- und Geheim-wissenschaften im Islam*, 390-391. Al-Būnī and his works are not found in Fuat Sezgin's *Geschichte des arabischen Schrifttums* (Leiden, E.J. Brill, 1967-1984) since that work only covers Arabic literature through the mid-fifth century AH (mid-eleventh century CE).

[189] Emilie Savage-Smith, "Magic and Islam," in Maddison and Savage-Smith, vol. I, p. 66, cat. 21, n. 4.

[190] Fahd, T. "Djafr," *EI*², s.v. [II:375-77].

[191] J. Ruska, "Die Alchimie ar-Razi's," *Der Islam* xxii (1934), 307-310.

[192] El-Ǧawhary, 17.

[193] El-Ǧawhary, 17-25.

[194] El-Ǧawhary, 17; no mention of specific instances in *Shams al-maʿārif*.

[195] El-Ǧawhary, 29.

[196] Toufic Fahd, "Magie comme 'source de la sagesse' dans l'oeuvre d'al-Būnī," 104-105 ; citing al-Būnī, *Shams al-maʿārif al-kubrá* (Cairo, 1349/1928), 530-532; Pierre Lory, "La magie des lettres dans le Šams al-maʿârif d'al-Bûnî," 98-99; citing al-Būnī, *Shams al-maʿārif al-kubrá* (Cairo, n.d.), 481; cf. al-Būnī, *Shams al-maʿārif al-kubrá* (Beirut, 1420/2000), 554-556.

[197] Lory, "La magie des lettres dans le Šams al-maʿârif d'al-Bûnî," 98-99 ; citing al-Būnī, *Shams al-maʿārif al-kubrá* (Cairo, n.d.), 60, 143, 144.

[198] Aḥmad ibn ʿAlī al-Būnī, (d.622/1225), *Shams al-maʿārif al-kubrá* (Beirut: Muʾassasat al-nūr al-maṭbūʿāt, 1420/2000), 362.

[199] Toufic Fahd, *La divination arabe*, p. 231, notes 1-4.

[200] Ismet Parmaksızoğlu, *Manisa Genel Kütüphanesi tarihcoğratya yezınaları kataloğu*, Kütüphaneler kataloguri yayımlarından, ser. 3, no. 1 (Istanbul: Millî Eğitim Basımevi, 1952), [no.] 1445, cited in Fahd, *Divination arabe*, p. 231, n.1.

[201] William MacGuckin de Slane, *Catalogue des manuscrits arabes* (Paris: Imprimerie nationale, 1883-1895), p. 478.

[202] Dietrich, "al-Būnī," *EI*², supp., s.v.

[203] El-Ǧawhary, 16.

[204] Manfred Ullmann, *Die Natur- und Geheimwissenschaften im Islam*, p. 35, nn. 4, 5; p. 391, p. 413; citing Shihāb al-Dīn Aḥmad ib ʿAbd al-Wahhāb ibn Muḥammad al-Nuwayrī (d. 732/1332), *Nihayat al-ʿArab*, XII:225; cf. *GAL* II:139ff.

[205] Ibn Khaldūn (d. 784/1382), *The Muqaddimah: An Introduction to History*, Bollingen Series XLIII, tr. Franz Rosenthal (New York: Bollingen Foundation, Inc., 1958), III:181 [=Arabic ed. III:145-46].

[206] Ibn Khaldūn (tr. Rosenthal), III:177, 178, 181 (=Arabic text, III:142, 143, 145).

[207] Rosenthal, tr. *Muqaddimah*, III:177, n. 818.

[208] Muḥarram 1, 1421 AH (The first day of the year 1421 AH) was April 6, 2000 CE.

[209] al-Būnī, *al-Barhatīyah* in *Manbaʿ uṣūl al-ḥikmah* (Beirut, 1420/2000), 69-76.

[210] al-Būnī, *Sharḥ al-Jaljalūtīyah al-kubrá* in *Manba' uṣūl al-ḥikmah* (Beirut, 1421/2000), 97-99 ; al-Būnī, *Shams al-ma'ārif al-kubrá* (Beirut, 1420/2000), 99-101.

[211] al-Būnī, *Sharḥ al-Jaljalūtīyah al-kubrá* in *Manba' uṣūl al-ḥikmah* (Beirut, 1420/2000), 101-119.

[212] al-Būnī, Aḥmad ibn 'Alī (d.622/1225), *Kitāb laṭā'if al-Ishārāt fī al-ḥurūf al-'ālīyāt* (BN Tunis 9755), 21v, 22r.

[213] cf. al-Būnī, *Shams al-ma'ārif al-kubrá* (BN Tunis 4920), pp. 193,194.

[214] See below, chapter eight, for more information on the mention of jinn and devils in the Quran, and the importance of these discussions for al-Būnī's corpus.

[215] Ibn al-Nadīm, I:309-310.

[216] al-Buni, *Shams al-ma'ārif al-kubrá* (Cairo, n.d. [1905?]), I:51.

[217] al-Būnī, *Shams al-ma'ārif al-kubrá* (Beirut, 1405/1985), 271. In chapters 21-30 (pp. 268-304) on the *anmāṭ* of the Names of God, each Name is associated with a specific angel and hierarchy.

[218] e.g., al-Būnī, *Shams al-ma'ārif al-kubrá* (Beirut, 1420/2000), II:259, III:330.

[219] Wensinck, "Mīkāl," *EI*², s.v.; cf. Quran 2:98.

[220] Wensinck, "Isrāfīl," *EI*², s.v.

[221] al-Būnī, *Sharḥ al-Juljulūtīyah* (Beirut, 1421/2000), 224-225 ; cf. lines 60-63 of *al-Ṭarīqah al-kubrá*.

[222] e.g., al-Būnī, *al-Uṣūl wa-al-ḍawābiṭ* (BN Tunis 661), 20v.

[223] Samuel Marinas Zwemer, "The Familiar Spirit or Qarina," *Moslem World* 6 (1916), 360, 365-368; cf. (D. B. MacDonald), "Ḳarīn," *EI*², s.v.; Zwemer, *The Influence of Animism in Islam* (London: Central Board of Missions and Society for Promoting Christian Knowledge, 1920), ch. 6.

[224] al-Būnī, *al-Uṣūl wa-al-ḍawābiṭ* (BN Tunis 661), 16v.

[225] al-Būnī, *Shams al-ma'ārif al-kubrá* (Beirut, 1420/2000), IV:428.

[226] al-Būnī, *Tartīb al-da'wāt* (BN Tunis 9581), 6r.

[227] al-Būnī, *Shams al-ma'ārif al-kubrá* (BN Tunis 4920), p. 160.

[228] H. A. Winkler, *Siegel und Charaktere in der Muhammedanischen Zauberei* (Berlin: Walter de Gruyter & Co., 1930), 97-108.

[229] See below, chapter six, on the uses of letters, including the Balance of Letters, in al-Būnī's corpus.

[230] al-Būnī, *al-Uṣūl wa-al-ḍawābiṭ* (BN Tunis 661), fols. 12r-12v.

[231] al-Būnī, *al-Uṣūl wa-al-ḍawābiṭ* in *Manba' uṣūl al-ḥikmah* (Beirut, 1420/2000), 30, 33; cf.

[232] J. Sesiano, "Wafḳ," *EI*², s.v.

[233] Maddison & Savage-Smith, *Science, Tools, and Magic*, I:107.

[234] Schuyler Cammann, "Islamic and Indian Magic Squares I," *History of Religions* 8 (1969), pp. 190, 193; figs 2a, 2b, 2c, 3a, 3b

[235] al-Būnī, *Baghīyāt al-mishtāq fī ma'rifat waḍ' al-awfāq* in *Manba' uṣūl al-ḥikmah* (Beirut, 1421/2000), 62.

[236] al-Būnī, *Shams al-ma'ārif al-kubrá* (Beirut, 1420/2000), IV:521.

[237] al-Būnī, *Sharḥ al-Juljulūtīyah* in *Manba' uṣūl al-ḥikmah* (Beirut, 1421/2000), 224.

[238] al-Būnī, *al-Uṣūl wa-al-ḍawābiṭ* (BN Tunis 661), 12v.

[239] al-Būnī, *al-Uṣūl wa-al-ḍawābiṭ* (BN Tunis 661), fols. 2v, 4v.

[240] al-Būnī, *Shams al-ma'ārif al-kubrá* (BN Tunis 4920), p. 4; *Shams al-ma'ārif al-wusṭá* (BN Tunis 7901), fol. 5r.

[241] al-Būnī, *Kitāb laṭā'if al-ishārāt* (BN Tunis 9755), fols. 13r, 18r.

[242] al-Būnī, *Sharḥ al-Juljulūtīyah* in *Manba' uṣūl al-ḥikmah* (Beirut, 1421/2000), 224.

[243] al-Būnī, *al-Uṣūl wa-al-ḍawābiṭ* (BN Tunis 661), fol. 4v.

[244] See above, chapter four, for information on the list of al-Būnī's works.

[245] Many of the more complex magic squares in the Tunis MS do not add up properly. It seems likely that this is simply due to scribal error, though the possibility of errors in the original cannot be ruled out.

[246] al-Būnī, *Shams al-ma'ārif al-kubrá*, chapters 1, 9, 13, 17, 31, 34, 38.

[247] al-Būnī, *Shams al-ma'ārif al-kubrá*, chapters 5, 6, 15, 19, 32, 40; cf. Fahd, "Magie comme 'source de la sagesse' dans l'oeuvre d'al-Būnī," 85-104.

[248] A. I. Sabra, "'Ilm al-Ḥisāb," *EI*[2], s.v.

[249] (G. Weil—[G.S. Colin]), "Abdjad," *EI*[2], s.v. In both series here, capital consonants are used to emphasize the Arabic letters (transliterated here), which have actual value, as opposed to short vowels, which have none. For ease of reference, the *abjad* values for Arabic letters according to the eastern system may also be found in Figure 3 and in the transliteration table on pages vi-vii.

[250] al-Būnī, *Kitāb laṭā'if al-ishārāt* (BN Tunis 9755), fols. 7v-7r.

[251] This kind of language is most marked in al-Būnī, *Shams al-ma'ārif al-kubrá*, chapter 31 (Beirut, 1420/2000), III:321-331.

[252] e.g., al-Būnī, *Shams al-ma'ārif al-kubrá* (Cairo, n.d. [1905?]), 8: a magic square and a Latin square for the letter *dal* side by side.

[253] al-Būnī, *al-Uṣūl wa-al-ḍawābiṭ* (BN Tunis 661), fol. 16v.

[254] al-Būnī, *Shams al-ma'ārif al-kubrá* (Beirut, 1420/2000), I:43.

[255] al-Būnī, *Kitāb laṭā'if al-ishārāt* (BN Tunis 9755), fol. 42v.; al-Būnī, *Shams al-ma'ārif al-kubrá* (Beirut, 1420/2000), III:325.

[256] al-Būnī, *Kitāb laṭā'if al-ishārāt* (BN Tunis 9755), fols. 39v-40r.

[257] al-Būnī, *Shams al-maʿārif al-kubrá* (Beirut, 1420/2000), IV:427.

[258] al-Būnī, *Shams al-maʿārif al-kubrá* (Beirut: Dār al-Thaqafah, n.d. [1905?]), IV:416; quoted in Fahd, "Magie comme 'source de la sagesse dans l'oeuvre d' al-Būnī," 103.

[259] al-Būnī, *Shams al-maʿārif al-kubrá* (Beirut, 1420/2000), III:340.

[260] al-Būnī, *Kitāb laṭāʾif al-ishārāt* (BN Tunis 9755), Fol. 35r.

[261] al-Būnī, *Kitāb laṭāʾif al-ishārāt* (BN Tunis 9755), Fol. 35r; al-Būnī, *al-Uṣūl wa-al-ḍawābiṭ* (BN Tunis 661), fol. 20v.

[262] al-Būnī, *al-Uṣūl wa-al-ḍawābiṭ* (BN Tunis 661), fol. 20v.

[263] al-Būnī, *Kitāb laṭāʾif al-ishārāt* (BN Tunis 9755), Fol. 17v.

[264] al-Būnī, *al-Uṣūl wa-al-ḍawābiṭ* (BN Tunis 661), fol. 2v.

[265] al-Būnī, *al-Uṣūl wa-al-ḍawābiṭ* (BN Tunis 661), fol. 14v.

[266] Paul Kraus, *Jābir ibn Ḥayyān: Contribution à l'histoire des idées scientifiques dans l'Islam*, vol. II: *Jābir et la science Grecque*, Memoires de l'Institut de l'Egypt, vol. 45 (Cairo: 1942-43), p. 199; Daniel Martin Varisco, "The Magical Significance of the Lunar Stations in the 13th Century Yemeni *Kitāb al-tabṣira fī ʿilm al-nujūm* of al-Malik al-Ashraf," in "Divination, Magie, Pouvoirs au Yémen," ed. Anne Regourd, special issue, *Quaderni di Studi Arabi* 13 (1995),21.

[267] Varisco, "Magical Significance of the Lunar Stations," 21; cf. *Rasāʾil Ikhwān al-Ṣafāʾ* (Beirut: n.p., 1957), 1, 71; cf. Henry Corbin, *Temple and Contemplation*, tr. Phillip Sherrard (London: KPI in association with Islamic Publications, 1986), 103-114.

[268] al-Būnī, *al-Uṣūl wa-al-ḍawābiṭ* (BN Tunis 661), fols. 2v, 5r.

[269]al-Būnī, *al-Uṣūl wa-al-ḍawābiṭ* (BN Tunis 661), fol. 15r.

[270] al-Būnī, *Shams al-maʿārif al-kubrá* (Beirut, 1420/2000), I:11-14.

[271] al-Būnī, *Shams al-maʿārif al-kubrá* (Beirut, 1420/2000), III:322; cf. 322ff.

[272] Tewfik Canaan, "The Decipherment of Arabic Talismans I," *Berytus* 4(1937), 100; repr. in Emilie Savage-Smith, *Magic and Divination in Early Islam* (Wiltshire, England: Ashgate Variorum, 2004), 156.

[273] Tewfik Canaan, "The Decipherment of Arabic Talismans I," 81-82; repr.,137-138.

[274] al-Būnī, *Kitāb laṭāʾif al-ishārāt* (BN Tunis 9755), fol. 134.

[275] al-Būnī, *al-Uṣūl wa-al-ḍawābiṭ* (BN Tunis 661), fol. 22r.

[276] al-Būnī, *Kitāb laṭāʾif al-ishārāt* (BN Tunis 9755), fols. 13r., 20v.

[277] Kraus, *Jābir ibn Ḥayyān*, II:237-238, 269-270.

[278] While the person and works of Jābir Ibn Ḥayyān remain controversial, for the present it is sufficient to remark that the Jābirian corpus dates from no later than the 3rd/9th century—long before al-Būnī.

[279] Jābir ibn Ḥayyān, *Kitāb al-khamsīn*; quoted in Paul Kraus, *Jābir et la science grecque* (Cairo : Institut d'Égypte, 1942), p. 188, n. 3; quoted in Pierre Lory, "Science des lettres," 93.

[280] Kraus, *Jābir ibn Ḥayyān*, II:234; cf. pp. 95, 98ff., 189, p. 111, n. 5; cf. Kraus, *Jābir ibn Ḥayyān: Essai sur l'histoire des idées scientifiques dans l'Islam*, Vol. 1: *Textes choisis* (Cairo: Libraries El-Khandji and Paris: G.P. Maisonneuve,1935), 129, 134; cf. Jābir ibn Ḥayyān, *Kitāb al-baḥth* (MS Istanbul Jārullāh 1721), fol. 126r; Jābir ibn Ḥayyān, *Kitāb al-taṣrīf* (Paris 5099), fol. 144v;

[281] al-Būnī, *Baghīyat al-mishtāq fī waḍʿ al-awfāq* in *Manbaʿ uṣūl al-ḥikmah* (Beirut, 1421/2000), 66.

[282] al-Būnī, *Shams al-maʿārif al-kubrá* (Beirut, 1420/2000), III:383; ibid. (Cairo, n.d. [1905]), III:88; al-Būnī, *Baghīyat al-mishtāq fī waḍʿ al-awfāq* in *Manbaʿ uṣūl al-ḥikmah* (Beirut, 1421/2000), 66-67.Kraus, *Jābir ibn Ḥayyān*, II:224; cf. Kraus, *Textes choisis*, 93, 214, 237.

[283] al-Būnī, *Shams al-maʿārif al-kubrá* (Beirut, 1420/2000), III:383; cf. *Shams al-maʿārif al-kubrá* (Cairo, n.d. [1905?]), II:88.

[284] Kraus, *Jābir ibn Ḥayyān*, II:224; cf. Kraus, *Textes choisis*, 93, 214, 237,

[285] al-Būnī, *Bughyat al-mushtāq fī waḍʿ al-awfāq* in *Manbaʿ uṣūl al-ḥikmah* (Beirut, 1421/2000), 66; al-Būnī, *al-Uṣūl wa-al-ḍawābiṭ* (BN Tunis 661), fol. 4v.

[286] al-Būnī, *al-Uṣūl wa-al-ḍawābiṭ* (BN Tunis 661), fol. 4v.

[287] al-Būnī, *Kitāb laṭāʾif al-ishārāt* (BN Tunis 9755), fol. 14r.

[288] al-Būnī, *Kitāb laṭāʾif al-ishārāt* (BN Tunis 9755), fol. 21r.

[289] al-Būnī, *Kitāb laṭāʾif al-ishārāt* (BN Tunis 9755), fol. 23r.

[290] al-Būnī, *Shams al-maʿārif al-kubrá* (Beirut, 1420/2000), III:322-323 (ch 31).

[291] al-Būnī, *Shams al-maʿārif al-kubrá* (Beirut, 1420/2000), III:327 (ch. 31)

[292] al-Būnī, *Shams al-maʿārif al-kubrá* (Beirut, 1420/2000), III:324, 327, 331, 332 (ch. 31)

[293] al-Būnī, *Baghīyat al-mishtāq fī waḍʿ al-awfāq* in *Manbaʿ uṣūl al-ḥikmah* (Beirut, 1421/2000), 66-67.

[294] al-Būnī, *Kitāb laṭāʾif al-ishārāt* (BN Tunis 9755), fol. 49v; cf. fols. 28r-49r. (The latter describes each of these in turn, with the exemptions of *alif* and *lām*.)

[295] al-Būnī, *Sharḥ al-Juljulūtīyah al-kubrá* in *Manbaʿ uṣūl al-ḥikmah* (Beirut, 1420/2000), pp. 102-106.

[296] Toufic Fahd, "Magie comme 'source de la sagesse' dans l'oeuvre d'al-Būnī," 68 ; cf. al-Būnī, *Shams al-maʿārif al-kubrá* (Beirut,

1420/2000), II:222. Fahd's list mistakenly leaves out *hā'*, while the Beirut, 1420/2000 edition of *Shams al-ma'ārif* mentions it twice in one list, leaving out *ḥā'*.

[297] Canaan, "The Decipherment of Arabic Talismans I," pp. 94-95, n. 143; repr., pp. 150-151, n. 143.

[298] Canaan, "The Decipherment of Arabic Talismans I," 95; repr., 151.

[299] al-Būnī, *Shams al-ma'ārif al-kubrá* (Beirut, 1420/2000), I : ca. 72.

[300] al-Būnī, *Shams al-ma'ārif* (Cairo: Maṭba'ah Muṣṭafá Muḥammad, n.d.), 59 ; quoted in Pierre Lory, "La magie des lettres dans le Šams al-ma'ârif d'al-Bûnî," *Bulletin d'Études Orientales* XXXIX-XL (1987-88), 101.

[301] al-Būnī, *Shams al-ma'ārif al-kubrá*, ch. 17 (Beirut, 1420/2000), II:219-234.

[302] al-Būnī, *Shams al-ma'ārif al-kubrá* (Beirut, 1420/2000), I :72.

[303] al-Būnī, *Shams al-ma'ārif al-kubrá* (Beirut, 1420/2000), II :253. *Qāf* and *yā'* are luminous letters, so it is unclear why they are in this list, unless through a typographical error.

[304] al-Būnī, *Sharḥ al-Juljulūtīyah al-kubrá* in *Manba' uṣūl al-ḥikmah* (Beirut, 1421/2000), 256ff; cf. Fahd, "Magie comme 'source de la sagesse' dans l'oeuvre d'al-Būnī," 67; al-Būnī, *Shams al-ma'ārif* (Beirut, n.d. [1905?]), I:13, 102sqq.

[305] al-Būnī, *Sharḥ al-Juljulūtīyah al-kubrá* in *Manba' uṣūl al-ḥikmah* (Beirut, 1421/2000), 257; cf. p. 189 (lines 140-148 of the "Long Path"), p. 256.

[306] al-Būnī, *Shams al-ma'ārif al-kubrá* (Beirut, 1420/2000), I:114 (ch. 13); cf. I:116

[307] al-Būnī, *Shams al-ma'ārif al-kubrá* (Beirut, 1420/2000), I:114 (ch. 13).

[308] al-Būnī, *Shams al-ma'ārif al-kubrá* (Beirut, 1420/2000), I:116 (ch. 13).

[309] al-Būnī, *Shams al-ma'ārif* (Beirut, n.d.[1905?]), III:345-350 (ch. 34), quoted in Fahd, "Magie comme 'source de la sagesse dans l'oeuvre d'al-Būnī," 100; cf. Toufic Fahd, "Zā'irdja," *EI*^{2}, s.v.

[310] al-Būnī, *Shams al-ma'ārif al-kubrá* (Beirut, 1420/2000), III:336; cf. al-Būnī, *Shams al-ma'ārif al-kubrá* (Cairo, n.d.[1905?]), III :49.

[311] al-Būnī, *Shams al-ma'ārif al-kubrá* (Beirut, 1420/2000), III:336; cf. al-Būnī, *Shams al-ma'ārif al-kubrá* (Cairo, n.d.[1905?]), III :49. The Beirut edition misprints the *ḍād* as a second *ṣād*.

[312] al-Būnī, *al-Uṣūl wa-al-ḍawābiṭ* (BN Tunis 661), fol. 28r.

[313] The term is translated as "stations" rather than "mansions" here because the former, older meaning better expresses the description: that the moon is traversing the sky through these stations. Cf. Varisco, "Magical Significance of the Lunar Stations," p. 21, n. 4.

[314] al-Būnī, *Kitāb laṭā'if al-ishārāt* (BN Tunis 9755), 184.

[315] Varisco, "Magical Significance of the Lunar Stations,"20.

[316] Varisco, "Magical Significance of the Lunar Stations," 20; cf. Daniel Martin Varisco, "The Origin of the *anwā'* in Arabi Tradition," *Studia Islamica* 74 (1991), 5-28.

[317] Varisco, "Magical Significance of the Lunar Stations," 21.

[318] al-Būnī, *Shams al-ma'ārif al-kubrá* (Beirut, 1420/2000), IV:438.

[319] al-Būnī, *Shams al-ma'ārif al-kubrá* (Beirut, 1420/2000), III: 336; cf. al-Būnī, *Shams al-ma'ārif al-kubrá* (BN Tunis 4921), p. 392.

[320] al-Būnī, *Shams al-ma'ārif al-kubrá* (BN Tunis 4921), p. 392; al-Būnī, *Shams al-ma'ārif al-kubrá* (Cairo, n.d. [1905?]), III:49; (Beirut, 1420/2000), III:336. As with many such figures, the Beirut edition has reproduced the chart from the Cairo edition.

[321] al-Būnī, *Shams al-ma'ārif al-kubrá* (BN Tunis 4920), p. 22; (BN Tunis 4921), p. 392; al-Būnī, *Shams al-ma'ārif al-kubrá* (Cairo, n.d. [1905?]), I:18, III:49; al-Būnī, *Shams al-ma'ārif al-kubrá* (Beirut, 1420/2000), I:24, III:336.

[322] al-Būnī, *Shams al-ma'ārif al-kubrá* (BN Tunis 4921), p. 392; al-Būnī, *Shams al-ma'ārif al-kubrá* (Cairo, n.d. [1905?]), III:49; al-Būnī, *Shams al-ma'ārif al-kubrá* (Beirut, 1420/2000), III:336.

[323] al-Būnī, *Shams al-ma'ārif al-kubrá* (Beirut, 1420/2000), III:322-323(*bā'*), 325 (*ḥā'*), 326 (*dhāl, rā'*); IV: 426 (*ḥā'*).

[324] al-Būnī, *Shams al-ma'ārif al-kubrá* (Beirut, 1420/2000), III:321 (*lām*), 332 (*lām-alif*); IV:426 (*ḥā'*), 428 (*lām*), 436 (*ẓā'*).

[325] al-Būnī, *Shams al-ma'ārif al-kubrá* (Beirut, 1420/2000), III:327 (*sīn*), 329 (*ẓā'*), 330 (*fā'*).

[326] Al-Būnī, *Shams al-ma'ārif al-kubrá* (Beirut, 1420/2000), IV: 426 (*ṭā'*), 430, 431 (*sīn*)

[327] al-Būnī, *Shams al-ma'ārif al-kubrá* (Beirut, 1420/2000), IV:419, 420 (*alif*); 426 (*ḥā'*); 427 (*yā'*); 428 (*kāf*); 431 (*'ayn*); 432 (*fā'*); 434 (*tā'*).

[328] al-Būnī, *Shams al-ma'ārif al-kubrá* (Beirut, 1420/2000), III:321 (*lām*), 325 (*khā'*), 326 (*rā'*), 331 (*hā'*).

[329] al-Būnī, *Shams al-ma'ārif al-kubrá* (Beirut, 1420/2000), IV:549.

[330] Ibn al-Nadīm, I:309; cf. above, chapter 3.

[331] al-Būnī, *Shams al-ma'ārif al-kubrá* (Beirut, 1420/2000), I:104-105.

[332] al-Būnī, *Shams al-ma'ārif al-kubrá* (Beirut, 1420/2000), II :222,223.

[333] al-Būnī, *Kitāb laṭā'if al-ishārāt* (BN Tunis 9755), fols. 41v., 42v.

[334] al-Būnī, *Kitāb laṭā'if al-ishārāt* (BN Tunis 9755), fol. 14v. While the numbers in a magic square are supposed to add up to the same in all columns and rows, that is not true of this magic square.

[335] al-Būnī, *Kitāb laṭā'if al-ishārāt* (BN Tunis 9755), fol. 45v.

[336] al-Būnī, *Kitāb laṭā'if al-ishārāt* (BN Tunis 9755), fols. 21v-22r.

[337] al-Būnī, *Kitāb laṭā'if al-ishārāt* (BN Tunis 9755), fol. 48v.

[338] al-Būnī, *Shams al-ma'ārif al-kubrá* (Beirut, 1420/2000), 75.

[339] See above, chapter four.

[340] al-Būnī, *Manba' uṣūl al-ḥikmah* (Beirut, 1421/2000), 69, 93.

[341] al-Būnī, *al-Barhatīyah* in *Manba' uṣūl al-ḥikmah* (Beirut, 1421/2000), 69-76.

[342] al-Būnī, *Juljulūtīyah* in *Manba' uṣūl al-ḥikmah* (Beirut, 1421/2000), 97-99 ; al-Būnī, *Shams al-ma'ārif al-kubrá* (Beirut, 1420/20000, 99-101.

[343] al-Būnī, *Shams al-ma'ārif al-kubrá* (Cairo, n.d. [1905?]), II:16 (ch. 16)

[344] Louis Massignon, *Origines du lexique technique de la mystique musulmane* (Paris: Libraire Philosophique J. Vrin, 1954), 286, 293.

[345] al-Majrīṭī, *Ghāyat al-ḥakīm* (BN Tunis 9758), fol. 21r.

[346] Ibn Khaldūn, *Muqaddimah*, tr. Franz Rosenthal (New York: Pantheon Books, Inc., 1958), 172.

[347] e.g., al-Būnī, *Shams al-ma'ārif al-kubrá* (BN Tunis 4920), pp. 192, 212.

[348] al-Būnī, *al-Uṣūl wa-al-ḍawābiṭ* (BN Tunis 661), fols. 36r, 44v, etc.

[349] al-Būnī, *Shams al-ma'ārif al-kubrá* (Cairo, n.d. [1905?]), I:82 (chap. 12), II:16 (chap. 16).

[350] al-Būnī, *Shams al-ma'ārif al-kubrá* (Cairo, n.d. [1905?]), II:1.

[351] al-Būnī, *Shams al-ma'ārif al-kubrá* (Cairo, n.d. [1905?]), I:8.

[352] al-Būnī, *Shams al-ma'ārif al-kubrá* (Cairo, n.d. [1905?]), I:11.

[353] See above, chapter six.

[354] al-Būnī, *Shams al-ma'ārif al-kubrá* (Beirut, 1420/2000), 72 (ch. 9).

[355] al-Būnī, *Kitāb Laṭā'if al-ishārāt* (BN Tunis 9755), fol. 27r.

[356] Fahd, "Magie comme 'source de la sagesse' dans l'oeuvre d'al-Būnī," 198 ; cf. Ignaz Goldziher, "Zauberelemente in Islamischen Gebeten," *Orientalischen Studien Th. Nöldeke* I (1906), pp. 30-329.

[357] al-Būnī, *Kitāb laṭā'if al-ishārāt* (BN Tunis 9755), fol. 53r. The text also associates the Greatest Name of God with the letter *qāf* (ق)—probably because its numerical value is 100.

[358] al-Būnī, *Shams al-ma'ārif al-kubrá* (Cairo, n.d. [1905?]), I:84 (ch. 12)

[359] al-Būnī, *Tartīb al-daʿwāt* (BNTunis 9581), fol. 60 recto. It may be significant that these instructions is given in a section devoted to the virtues of the letter *dal* (د).

[360] al-Būnī, *Shams al-maʿārif al-kubrá* (Beirut, 1420/2000), 101 (ch. 12).

[361] al-Būnī, *Shams al-maʿārif al-kubrá* (BN Tunis 4920), pp. 211ff.

[362] al-Būnī, *Shams al-maʿārif al-kubrá* (Beirut, 1405/1985), 268-304 (Chapters 21-30); cf. Fahd, "Magie comme 'source de la sagesse' dans l'oeuvre d'al-Būnī," 94-96.

[363] al-Būnī, *Shams al-maʿārif al-kubrá* (Beirut, 1420/2000), pp. 310, 311 (ch. 27).

[364] al-Būnī, *Tartīb al-daʿwāt* (BN Tunis 9581), fols. 25r-27v (eighth group of Names out of ten); the incomplete large Latin square is on fol. 25v.

[365] al-Būnī, *Shams al-maʿārif al-kubrá* (Beirut, 1405/1985), 53.

[366] al-Būnī, *Shams al-maʿārif al-kubrá* (BN Tunis 4920), pp. 10-11.

[367] al-Būnī, *Shams al-maʿārif al-kubrá* (Cairo, 1905), II:9.

[368] Lory, "La magie des lettres dans le *Šams al-maʿârif* d'al-Bûnî," p. 108, cf. al- Būnī, *Shams al-maʿārif* (Cairo: Maṭbaʿah Muṣṭafá Muḥammad, n.d.), 49, 60,142-143; al-Būnī, *Shams al-maʿārif* (Cairo, 1905), II:11.

[369] Lory, "La magie des lettres dans le *Šams al-maʿârif* d'al-Bûnî," 109; cf. al- Būnī, *Shams al-maʿārif al-kubrá* (n.p., n.d.), 60.

[370] al-Būnī, *Shams al-maʿārif al-kubrá* (Cairo, 1905), II:11; quoting Shaykh Muḥammad al-Khuwāriz, speaking at Mecca in 670 AH [N.B. Since al-Būnī died in 622, this throws into doubt the authenticity of this selection as something written by him.]

[371] It might be interesting to compare all of these mentions of the letters of the Greatest Name, to see if one could come up with a solution for it. However, this is not a strictly rational subject, and probably not liable to completely rational analysis.

[372] al-Būnī, *Shams al-maʿārif al-kubrá* (Cairo, 1905), II:16-17.

[373] al-Būnī, *Tartīb al-daʿwāt* (BNTunis 9581), fol. 29 v.

[374] al-Būnī, *Shams al-maʿārif al-kubrá* (BN Tunis 4920), p. 221.

[375] al-Būnī, *Shams al-maʿārif al-kubrá* (Beirut, n.d. [1905 ?]), pp. 212-218 (ch. 17) ; quoted in Fahd, "Magie comme 'source de la sagesse' dans l'oeuvre d'al-Būnī," 93. See above, chapter six, for more information on the "luminous letters."

[376] al-Būnī, *Shams al-maʿārif al-kubrá* (Beirut, 1420/2000), I:74.

[377] al-Būnī, *Shams al-maʿārif al-kubrá* (BN Tunis 4920), p. 40.

[378] Vadja, "Quelques elements juifs et pseudo-juifs dans l'encyclopédie magique de Bûnî," *Goldziher Memorial Volume* I

(Budapest: n.p., 1948), 388; cf. al-Būnī, *Shams al-maʿārif* (Cairo, 1349 AH), IV:76.

[379] Fahd, "Magie comme 'source de la sagesse' dans l'oeuvre d'al-Būnī," p. 95, n. 112 ; cf. al-Būnī, *Shams al-maʿārif* (Beirut, n.d. [1905 ?]), p. 296 (ch. 28); cf. D. Gimaret, *Les noms divins en Islam*, pp. 240ff.

[380] Francis Maddison and Emilie Savage-Smith, *Science, Tools, and Magic*, (London: The Nour Foundation, 1997), I:60; cf. Doutté, *Magie et religion dans l'Afrique du Nord*, 154-7; Winkler, *Siegel und Charaktere in der Muhammedanischen Zauberei*, 55-149; T. Canaan, "The Decipherment of Arabic Talismans," 144-45 ; Kriss & Kriss-Heinrich, *Volksglaube im Bereich des Islam*, 74-82.

[381] al-Būnī, *Sharḥ al-Juljulūtīyah* in *Manbaʿ uṣūl al-ḥikmah* (Beirut, 1421/2000), 257, 286; cf. "Long Path," lines 143-148 (p. 189),

[382] Doutté, *Magie et religion dans l'Afrique du nord*, 155.

[383] al-Būnī, *Sharḥ al-Juljulūtīyah* in *Manbaʿ uṣūl al-ḥikmah* (Beirut, 1421/2000), 97-99;

[384] al-Būnī, *Shams al-maʿārif al-kubrá* (Beirut, 1420/2000), I:104; cf. al-Būnī, *Shams al-maʿārif al-kubrá* (BN Tunis 4920), p. 116.

[385] H. A. Winkler, *Siegel und Charaktere in der Muhammedanischen Zauberei* (Berlin: Walter de Gruyter & Co., 1930), 55-149.

[386] Winkler, 114-119 (Variants of the 7 signs); those taken from al-Būnī's corpus are nos. 5, 6, 7, 8, 9, 10, 13, 19, 20, and 21.

[387] Josef von Karabacek, Jakob Krall, and Carl Wesseley, *Papyrus erzherzog Rainer: führer durch die Ausstellung* (Vienna: A. Hölder, 1894), pp. 249ff, Nr. 948; quoted in Winkler, p. 56; the 7 symbols are also reproduced in Winkler, p. 114, no. 1, with commentary on p. 116.

[388] al-Būnī, *Shams al-maʿārif al-kubrá* (BN Tunis 4920), p. 110.

[389] al-Būnī, *Shams al-maʿārif al-kubrá* (BN Tunis 4920),p. 110.

[390] al-Būnī, *Shams al-maʿārif al-kubrá* (BN Tunis 4920), p. 111.

[391] Tewfik Canaan, "The Decipherment of Arabic Talismans II," 143.

[392] Cod. Par. 2647, fols. 57a-b.; quoted in Winkler, p. 70.

[393] al-Būnī, *Sharḥ al-Juljulūtīyah* in *Manbaʿ Uṣūl al-ḥikmah* (Beirut, 1421/2000), 257; cf. ibid. p. 189, lines 140-148 of *al-Ṭarīqah al-kubrá*; cf. ibid., pp. 256-258.

[394] Cod. Par. 2647, fols. 57a-b.; Quoted in Winkler, pp. 69-70; cf. p. 96.

[395] Winkler, 96ff.; esp. 99-106.

[396] Doutté, *Magie et religion dans l'Afrique du nord*, 154, 160.

[397] al-Būnī, *Sharḥ al-Juljulūtīyah* in *Manbaʿ uṣūl al-ḥikmah* (Beirut, 1421/2000), 100, 173 ("Short Path"), 198-99 ("Long Path"); cf. p. 99 (lines 54-58 of "The Short Path").

[398] al-Būnī, *Tartīb al-daʿwāt* (BN Tunis 9581), fol. 6 verso; al-Būnī, *Shams al-maʿārif wa-laṭāʾif al-ʿawārif [al-ṣughrá]* (BN Tunis 6711), fols. 65 recto, 66 verso.

[399]al-Būnī, *Shams al-maʿārif al-kubrá* (Beirut, 1420/2000), p. 73 (ch. 9).

[400] Lory, "La magie des lettres dans le *Šams al-maʿârif* d'al-Bûnî," 107.

[401] al-Būnī, *Shams al-maʿārif al-kubrá* (BN Tunis 4920), p. 77.

[402] al-Būnī, *Shams al-maʿārif al-kubrá* (Beirut, n.d. [1905?]), p. 63 (ch. 9); quoted in Fahd, "Magie comme 'source de la sagesse' dans l'oeuvre d'al-Būnī," 87.

[403] al-Būnī, *Shams al-maʿārif al-kubrá* (Beirut, 1420/2000), pp. 61-64 (ch. 7).

[404] al-Būnī, *Shams al-maʿārif al-kubrá* (Beirut, 1420/2000), p. 265 (ch. 19) .

[405] al-Būnī, *Tartīb al-daʿwāt* (BN Tunis 9581), fol. 15 verso.

[406] al-Būnī, *Shams al-maʿārif al-kubrá* (BN Tunis 4920), p. 116; al-Būnī, *Shams al-maʿārif al-kubrá* (Beirut, 1405/1985), p. 97, fig. 25.

[407] al-Būnī, *al-Uṣūl wa-al-ḍawābiṭ* (BN Tunis 661), 34v.

[408] al-Būnī, *al-Uṣūl wa-al-ḍawābiṭ*, in *Manbaʿ Uṣūl al-ḥikmah* (Beirut, 1421/2000), 41.

[409] al-Būnī, *al-Uṣūl wa-al-ḍawābiṭ*, in *Manbaʿ Uṣūl al-ḥikmah* (Beirut, 1421/2000), 40.

[410] al-Būnī, *al-Uṣūl wa-al-ḍawābiṭ* (BN Tunis 661), fol. 36r.

[411] al-Būnī, *al-Uṣūl wa-al-ḍawābiṭ*, in *Manbaʿ Uṣūl al-ḥikmah* (Beirut, 1421/2000), 39-40.

[412] al-Būnī, *al-Uṣūl wa-al-ḍawābiṭ*, in *Manbaʿ Uṣūl al-ḥikmah* (Beirut, 1421/2000), 38-39

[413] al-Būnī, *Shams al-maʿārif al-kubrá* (Beirut, 1405/1985), 510.

[414] al-Būnī, *Shams al-maʿārif al-kubrá* (Beirut, 1405/1985), 418.

[415] cf. al-Būnī, *Shams al-maʿārif al-kubrá* (BN Tunis 4920), pp. 193,194.

[416] al-Būnī, *Shams al-maʿārif al-kubrá* (Beirut, 1405/1985), 269.

[417] al-Būnī, *al-Uṣūl wa-al-ḍawābiṭ* (BN Tunis 661), fol. 36v.

[418] al-Būnī, *Shams al-maʿārif al-kubrá* (BN Tunis 4920), pp. 205-206.

[419] al-Būnī, *Shams al-maʿārif al-kubrá* (BN Tunis 4920), pp. 208-209.

[420] al-Būnī, *Shams al-maʿārif al-kubrá* (Beirut, 1405/1985), 275; al-Būnī,*Tartīb al-daʿwāt* (BN Tunis 9581), fol. 13v.

[421] al-Būnī, *Tartīb al-daʿwāt* (BN Tunis 9581), fols. 7r-v.

[422] al-Būnī, *Tartīb al-daʿwāt* (BN Tunis 9581), fol. 27v.

[423] al-Būnī, *Tartīb al-daʿwāt* (BN Tunis 9581), fol. 9r.

[424] al-Būnī, *Tartīb al-daʿwāt* (BNTunis 9581), fol. 24v.

[425] al-Būnī, *Tartīb al-daʿwāt* (BNTunis 9581), fol. 12r.

[426] al-Būnī, *Tartīb al-daʿwāt* (BNTunis 9581), fol. 27r.
[427] al-Būnī, *Tartīb al-daʿwāt* (BNTunis 9581), fols. 25 verso-26 recto.
[428] al-Būnī, *Tartīb al-daʿwāt* (BNTunis 9581), fol. 12r.
[429] al-Būnī, *Tartīb al-daʿwāt* (BNTunis 9581), fol. 23v.
[430] al-Būnī, *Shams al-maʿārif al-kubrá* (BN Tunis 4920), p. 217.
[431] al-Būnī, *Shams al-maʿārif al-kubrá* (Beirut, 1405/1985), 53.
[432] al-Būnī, *Shams al-maʿārif al-kubrá* (Cairo, 1905), I:80,81,82,86.
[433] al-Būnī, *Shams al-maʿārif al-kubrá* (Beirut, 1420/2000), I:104; cf. al-Būnī, *Shams al-maʿārif al-kubrá* (BN Tunis 4920), p. 116.
[434] al-Būnī, *Shams al-maʿārif al-kubrá* (Beirut, 1420/2000), III:348; cf. al-Būnī, *Shams al-maʿārif al-kubrá* (Cairo, n.d.[1905?]), III:59.
[435] al-Būnī, *Shams al-maʿārif al-kubrá* (BN Tunis 4920), p. 116; al-Būnī, *Shams al-maʿārif al-kubrá* (Beirut, 1405/1985), p.97, fig. 25.
[436] al-Būnī, *Shams al-maʿārif al-kubrá* (n.p, n.d.), 61 ; quoted in Lory, "La magie des lettres dans le *Šams al-maʿârif* d'al-Bûnî," 107.
[437] al-Būnī, *Sharḥ al-Juljulūtīyah* in *Manbaʿ uṣūl al-ḥikmah* (Beirut, 1421/2000), 173, 174, 175, 176, 177, 178-79, 179-80, 180, 181-182, 182, 183.
[438] al-Būnī, *Tartīb al-daʿwāt* (BNTunis 9581), fols. 11r (*al-Wāḥid* ["The One"] and *al-Qawī* [The Strong], 12 recto (*al-Ṣamad* [The Intercessor] and *al-Muqtadar* [The Powerful]), 19r (*al-ʿAlīm* [The All-Knowing] and *al-Ḥakīm* [The Wise]).
[439] al-Būnī, *Tartīb al-daʿwāt* (BN Tunis 9581), fol. 8v.
[440] al-Būnī, *Tartīb al-daʿwāt* (BN Tunis 9581), fol. 7v.
[441] al-Būnī, *Tartīb al-daʿwāt* (BN Tunis 9581), fol. 11r.
[442] al-Būnī, *Tartīb al-daʿwāt* (BN Tunis 9581), fol. 9r.
[443] al-Būnī, *Tartīb al-daʿwāt* (BN Tunis 9581), fol. 33r.
[444] al-Būnī, *Tartīb al-daʿwāt* (BN Tunis 9581), fols. 32v-33r.
[445] al-Būnī, *Shams al-maʿārif al-kubrá* (BN Tunis 4920), p. 12.
[446] al-Būnī, *Shams al-maʿārif wa-laṭā'if al-ʿawārif [al-ṣughrá]* (BN Tunis 6711), fols. 137r-v.
[447] al-Būnī, *al-Uṣūl wa-al-ḍawābiṭ*, in *Manbaʿ Uṣūl al-ḥikmah* (Beirut, 1421/2000), p. 41.
[448] al-Būnī, *Shams al-maʿārif* (Beirut, 1405/1985), 284; *al-Uṣūl wa-al-ḍawābiṭ*, (BN Tunis 661), fol. 36r.
[449] al-Būnī, *Shams al-maʿārif al-kubrá* (Beirut, 1405/1985), 281.
[450] al-Būnī, *Shams al-maʿārif al-kubrá* (BN Tunis 4920), p. 243.
[451] al-Būnī, *al-Uṣūl wa-al-ḍawābiṭ*, in *Manbaʿ Uṣūl al-ḥikmah* (Beirut, 1421/2000), 40.
[452] al-Būnī, *Shams al-maʿārif al-kubrá* (Beirut, 1420/2000), II:252.
[453] al-Būnī, *Shams al-maʿārif al-kubrá* (Beirut, 1420/2000), II:219.
[454] Quran 17:82.

[455] al-Būnī, *Shams al-maʿārif al-kubrá* (Beirut, 1420/2000), I:76. A similar *ḥadīth* in al-Bukhārī's *Ṣaḥīḥ* describes the three things as honey, the cupper's knife, and cautery, and forbids cautery. (al-Bukhārī, *Ṣaḥīḥ*, ed. M. Ludolf Krehl and Th. W. Juynboll [Leiden: E. J. Brill, 1908], vol. IV, p. 50 [*bāb* 4]; quoted in Perho, 105.)

[456] See above, chapter four.

[457] A note regarding transliteration: According to the Library of Congress system, the *tāʾ marbūṭah* (ة) is transliterated *–ah*, except in construct form, where it is transliterated *–at*. Thus, throughout this chapter, the word *sūrah* will be transliterated differently depending on context: e.g., "The second *sūrah* of the Quran" but "*Sūrat Yāʾ-Sīn*." For more information, see the transliteration table on pages vi-vii or Randall K. Barry, *ALA-LC Romanization Tables: Transliteration Schemes for Non-Roman Scripts* (Washington, DC: Library of Congress Cataloging Distribution Service, 1997), pp. 10-19. Available online at <http://www.loc.gov/catdir/ cpso/romanization/arabic.pdf>. Last accessed May 17, 2017.

[458] al-Būnī, *Shams al-maʿārif al-kubrá* (Beirut, 1420/2000), II:268; al-Būnī, *Shams al-maʿārif al-kubrá* (Beirut, n.d. "saffron-paged"), II:259; al-Būnī, *Shams al-maʿārif al-kubrá* (Cairo, n.d. [1905?]), II:97.

[459] al-Būnī, *Shams al-maʿārif al-kubrá* (Beirut, 1420/2000), I:111.

[460] al-Būnī, *Shams al-maʿārif al-kubrá* (Beirut, 1420/2000), II:256

[461] al-Būnī, *Shams al-maʿārif al-kubrá* (Beirut, 1420/2000), II:263).

[462] al-Būnī, *Shams al-maʿārif al-kubrá* (Beirut, 1420/2000), II:239.

[463] al-Būnī, *Shams al-maʿārif* (ed. unknown), II:69; cited in Canaan, "Decipherment of Arabic Talismans I," 75; repr.,131.

[464] al-Būnī, *Shams al-maʿārif al-kubrá* (Beirut, 1420/2000), II:235.

[465] Fahd, "Magie comme 'source de la sagesse' dans l'oeuvre d'al-Būnī," 67.

[466] al-Būnī, *Shams al-maʿārif al-kubrá* (Beirut, 1420/2000), II:249.

[467] Fahd, "Magie comme 'source de la sagesse' dans l'oeuvre d'al-Būnī," 67.

[468] al-Būnī, *Shams al-maʿārif al-kubrá* (Beirut, 1420/2000), I :41; cf. Muḥammad al-Zamakhsharī, *al-Kashshāf ʿan ḥaqāʾiq ghawāmiḍ al-tanzīl wa-ʿuyūn al-aqāwīl fī wujuh al-taʾwīl* (Beirut, 1366/1947), ed. Muḥammad ʿAbd al-Salām Shāhīn (Beirut, 1995), I:31; Muḥammad ibn ʿAlī Abū al-ʿIrfān, *al-Risālat al-kubrâ fī al-Basmalah*, ed. F. al-Zanrī and Ḥ al-Mīr (Beirut, 1995), 21; quoted in William A. Graham, "Basmala," *Encyclopaedia of the Qur'ān*, ed. Jane Damman McAuliffe (Leiden: Brill, 2000), s.v.

[469] al-Būnī, *Shams al-maʿārif al-kubrá* (Beirut, 1420/2000), I:51.

[470] al-Būnī, *Shams al-maʿārif al-kubrá* (Beirut, 1420/2000), I:45.

[471] al-Būnī, *Shams al-maʿārif al-kubrá* (Beirut, 1420/2000), I:41

[472] al-Būnī, *Shams al-maʿārif al-kubrá* (Beirut, 1420/2000), I:48, 49.

[473] al-Būnī, *Sharḥ al-Juljulūtīyah* in *Manbaʿ uṣūl al-ḥikmah* (Beirut, 1421/2000), 103.

[474] al-Būnī, *Shams al-maʿārif al-kubrá* (Beirut, 1420/2000), I:45; al-Būnī, *Sharḥ al-Juljulūtīyah* in *Manbaʿ uṣūl al-ḥikmah* (Beirut, 1421/2000), 101. The text is nearly—but not quite—identical in both sections.

[475] al-Būnī, *Shams al-maʿārif al-kubrá* (Beirut, 1420/2000), I :50.

[476] al-Būnī, *Sharḥ al-Juljulūtīyah* in *Manbaʿ uṣūl al-ḥikmah* (Beirut, 1421/2000), 107.

[477] al-Būnī, *Laṭāʾif al-ishārāt* (BN Tunis 9755), fols. 28r ff., 49v ff.; al-Būnī, *Shams al-maʿārif al-kubrá* (Beirut, 1420/2000), I :41-57 ; al-Būnī, *Sharḥ al-Juljulūtīyah* in *Manbaʿ uṣūl al-ḥikmah* (Beirut, 1421/2000), 115-119.

[478] al-Būnī, *Shams al-maʿārif al-kubrá* (Beirut, 1420/2000), I:41-57; II:219, 200, 221.

[479] al-Būnī, *Shams al-maʿārif al-kubrá* (Beirut, 1420/2000), I:46-47.

[480] al-Būnī, *Shams al-maʿārif al-kubrá* (Beirut, 1420/2000), I:83-87; II:221, 222.

[481] al-Būnī, *Shams al-maʿārif al-kubrá* (Beirut, 1420/2000), I:83.

[482] al-Būnī, *Shams al-maʿārif al-kubrá* (Beirut, 1420/2000), chapter 5: II:234-252.

[483] al-Būnī, *Shams al-maʿārif al-kubrá* (Beirut, 1420/2000), II:241-242.

[484] al-Būnī, *Shams al-maʿārif al-kubrá* (Beirut, 1420/2000), II:232, 235, 237,244-45.

[485] al-Būnī, *Shams al-maʿārif al-kubrá* (Beirut, 1420/2000), II:235.

[486] al-Būnī, *Shams al-maʿārif al-kubrá* (Beirut, 1420/2000), II:237.

[487] al-Būnī, *Shams al-maʿārif al-kubrá* (ed. unknown), II:67; cited in Canaan, "The Decipherment of Arabic Talismans I," 75; repr., 131; cf. Muḥammad Ḥaqqi Nāzilī (d. 1884 CE), *Khazīnat al-asrār* (ed. unknown), 96.

[488] al-Būnī, *Shams al-maʿārif al-kubrá* (Beirut, 1420/2000), I:53-54.

[489] e.g., al-Būnī, *Shams al-maʿārif al-kubrá* (Beirut, 1420/2000), I:47, II:256.

[490] al-Būnī, *Shams al-maʿārif al-kubrá* (Beirut, 1420/2000), II:260.

[491] O'Keefe, 235.

[492] Sezgin, *GAS*, IV :294.

[493] cf. *Rasāʾil Ikhwān al-Ṣafāʾ* (Beirut, 1995), IV: 240ff.

[494] Pierre Lory, "La magie des lettres dans le Šams al-ma`ârif d'al-Bûnî," *Bulletin d'Études Orientales* XXXIX-XL (1987-88), 110.

[495] For a discussion of the issues related to material evidence for the practice of magic in Islam, see Venetia Porter, "Islamic Seals:

Magical or Practical?" in Alan Jones, ed. *University Lectures in Islamic Studies* 2 (London: Altajir World of Islam Trust, 1998), pp. 135-149 and figs. 8.1-8.13; repr. in Savage-Smith, ed. *Magic and Divination in Early Islam*, pp. 179-200.

[496] Fahd, "Siḥr," *EI*², s.v. For a preliminary discussion of Persian sources and their potential for such scholarship, see Francis Richard and Živa Vesel, "Un domaine méconnu: les écrits occultes en persan," *Bulletin des études orientales* XLIV (1992), special issue, *Sciences occultes et Islam*, eds. Annick Regourd and Pierre Lory, 211-215.

L

M

P

Q

R

S

T

U

V

W

CPSIA information can be obtained
at www.ICGtesting.com
Printed in the USA
LVHW111539240721
693536LV00004B/7

9 781567 446159